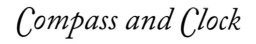

Compass and Clock

1. Thomas Jefferson, Garden Facade at Monticello, Charlottesville, Virginia, 1793–1809.
Thomas Jefferson Memorial Foundation

2. Charles Willson Peale, *The Peale Family*, c. 1770–73 and 1808. Oil on canvas, 56½ x 89½ in. The New-York Historical Society, New York, Gift of Thomas J. Bryan

3. Charles
Willson Peale,
*The Staircase
Group*, 1795.
Oil on canvas,
89½ x 39⅜ in.
Philadelphia
Museum of Art,
The George W.
Elkins Collection

4. Charles Willson Peale, *The Exhumation of the Mastodon*, 1806–8. Oil on canvas, 50 x 62½ in. Museum and Library of Maryland History, Maryland Historical Society, Baltimore

5. Rembrandt Peale, *Rubens Peale with a Geranium*, 1801. Oil on canvas, 28¼ x 24 in. National Gallery of Art, Washington, D.C., Patron's Permanent Fund, © 1998 Board of Trustees

6. Robert S. Duncanson, *Blue Hole, Little Miami River*, 1851. Oil on canvas, 29¼ x 42¼ in. Cincinnati Art Museum, Gift of Norbert Heerman and Arthur Helbig, 1926.18

7. Fitz Hugh Lane, *Bar Island and Mount Desert Mountains from Somes Settlement*, 1850. Oil on canvas, 20⅛ x 30⅛ in. Collection Erving and Joyce Wolf

8. Fitz Hugh Lane, *Boston Harbor, Sunset*, 1850–55. Oil on canvas, 24 x 39¼ in. Collection JoAnn and Julian Ganz, Jr. Partial and promised gift to the Los Angeles County Museum of Art

9. George Caleb Bingham, *Fur Traders Descending the Missouri*, 1845. Oil on canvas, 29 x 36½ in. The Metropolitan Museum of Art, New York, Morris K. Jesup Fund, 1933 (33.61)

10. George Caleb Bingham, *Mississippi Boatman*, 1850. Oil on canvas, 24 x 17½ in. Private collection

11. Frederic Edwin Church, *Mount Ktaadn*, 1853. Oil on canvas, 36¼ x 55¼ in. Yale University Art Gallery, New Haven, Stanley B. Resor, B.A., 1901, Fund

12. Winslow Homer, *Kissing the Moon*, 1904. Oil on canvas, 30¼ x 40⅜ in. Addison Gallery of American Art, Phillips Academy, Andover, Massachusetts, Bequest of Candace C. Stimson

13. Winslow Homer, *The Gulf Stream,* 1899. Oil on canvas, 28⅛ x 49⅛ in. The Metropolitan Museum of Art, New York, Catherine Lorillard Wolfe Collection, Wolfe Fund, 1906 (06.1234)

14. John F. Peto, *Old Companions*, 1904. Oil on canvas, 22 x 30 in.
Collection JoAnn and Julian Ganz, Jr.

15. Thomas Eakins, *The Actress (Portrait of Suzanne Santje),* 1903. Oil on canvas, 79¾ x 59⅞ in. Philadelphia Museum of Art, Gift of Mrs. Thomas Eakins and Miss Mary Adeline Williams

Compass and Clock

Defining Moments in American Culture

1800 · 1850 · 1900

John Wilmerding

HARRY N. ABRAMS, INC., PUBLISHERS

Also by John Wilmerding

Fitz Hugh Lane, American Marine Painter (1964)

A History of American Marine Painting (1968)

Pittura Americana dell'Ottocento (1969)

Robert Salmon, Painter of Ship and Shore (1971)

Fitz Hugh Lane (1971)

Winslow Homer (1972)

Audubon, Homer, Whistler and 19th Century America (1972)

The Genius of American Painting (with others, 1973)

American Art (1976)

American Light (with others, 1980)

American Masterpieces from the National Gallery of Art (1980)

An American Perspective (with others, 1981)

Important Information Inside (1983)

Andrew Wyeth: The Helga Pictures (1987)

American Marine Painting (1987)

Paintings by Fitz Hugh Lane (with others, 1988)

American Views (1991)

Thomas Eakins (with others, 1993)

The Artist's Mount Desert (1994)

For Polly and Joe

A teacher affects eternity;
he can never tell where his influence stops
HENRY ADAMS

Editor: Barbara Burn
Designer: Dirk Luykx
Rights and Reproductions: Janice Ackerman

Wilmerding, John.
Compass and clock : defining moments in American culture : 1800, 1850, 1900 / John Wilmerding.
p. cm.
Includes bibliographical references and index.
ISBN 0-8109-4096-5
1. United States—Civilization—19th century. 2. Space and time. 3. Space and time in literature. 4. Space and time in art. 5. United States—Intellectual life—1783–1865. 6. United States—Intellectual life—1865-1918. 7. American literature—19th century—History and criticism. 8. Art, American—History—19th century. 9. Architecture, American—History—19th century.
I. Title.
E169.1.W528   1999
973.5—dc21   98–54103

Harry N. Abrams, Inc.
100 Fifth Avenue
New York, N.Y. 10011
www.abramsbooks.com

CONTENTS

Introduction:
Clockwise America

BETWEEN 1800 and 1900 American space and time changed as much in idea as in reality. During that span the nation literally became a country, as the narrow linear frontier gradually expanded into the plane of western geography. By mid-century the United States had proclaimed its hemispheric influence with the Monroe Doctrine and Manifest Destiny, and by century's end that influence extended globally from the Caribbean to the Pacific. For a time, looking west and looking forward represented the same vision, from Jefferson's view of the Blue Ridge Mountains at Monticello, or through the gorge of the Shenandoah and Potomac Rivers at Harper's Ferry, to George Caleb Bingham's rendering of Daniel Boone striding through the Cumberland Gap and Frederic Church's panorama across Niagara. As the century neared its end, Frederick Jackson Turner initiated the argument over the fate of the frontier. At the same time nostalgia and modern psychology led to the exploration of internal spaces, while soon after we learned that space itself was relative and fluid.

The rhythms of keeping time also changed considerably during the course of the nineteenth century. In early America the cycle of days and seasons organized life, whereas by the twentieth century, thanks largely to the railroads and telegraph, time became orderly and uniform. Where work in the fields had relied on the circuit of the sun, in the factory it was regulated by the circuitry of clocks. Well into the nineteenth century, travel followed the tempos of nature, but by 1838 the word *timetable* entered our vocabulary, and increasingly thereafter scheduling marked off both labor and leisure. The regulation of American life gradually shifted from the mechanics of nature to the nature of the machine.

The modernization of space and time together accelerated during the last quarter of the nineteenth century, exemplified in various moves toward standardization. When the continental railroad was completed in 1869, signifying the possibility of uninterrupted transport of people and goods from one coast to the other, there were some two hundred different local times kept from east to west. The railroads themselves reduced the number of time demarcations to about eighty and in 1883 introduced modern uniform time zones into their scheduling. A year later negotiators proposed Greenwich, England, as the zero meridian, and during the decade that followed, thanks to growing international cooperation, twenty-four regular time zones were established around the globe. The United States officially adopted its four time zones in 1906, at last subordinating private to public timekeeping.[1] This soon led to a reform of the calendar with agreement on a uniform beginning to the year, four seasons of virtually equal length, and the regular addition of a leap-year day.

In light of these transformations, we can appreciate why the personal journal has been such a revealing and expressive form of American literature. For example, when Meriwether Lewis and William Clark traversed Jefferson's Louisiana Purchase to the Pacific Ocean at the outset of the nineteenth century, their journals maintained a linear narrative through the passage of days, seasons, and climate. By contrast, at mid-century, when Henry David Thoreau recorded his account of two years at Walden, he kept his journey within the circumferences of himself and the pond. Although he heard the sounds of the train and the telegraph wire in the woods, he reshaped his experience through the artifice of imagination. Nature in the book he eventually published was as much metaphor as reality. In turn, at the opening of the twentieth century, Henry James returned to tour America after many years as an expatriate. He wrote about his lengthy visit to the principal cities along the Atlantic seaboard, not as a chronological accounting of facts but as a journey in the pleasures of memory, analysis, and artistic expression. What we will want to consider here, then, is America's mental as well as physical geography.

Correspondingly, the American visualization of time resided in distinctively different images at century's start, midpoint, and ending. From the first voyages of discovery to the creation of the new republic at the end of the eighteenth century, observers perceived America as the New World, a new Eden; this was the dawn of a fresh age, the beginning of an independent social and political order. Sunrise became a favored time, and views to the horizon an appropriate vision, for landscape painters. During the middle years of the nineteenth century artists turned to sun-flooded midday light, in landscapes that seemed expanding and open-ended, to express that moment's beliefs in prosperity and territorial growth. With the waning of the century, it was not so much that culture and society thought America had come to its twilight hours, although anxiety over profound change was widespread, but the period did stimulate a sense of endings, and brooding introspection preoccupied many of the country's foremost artists and writers. Feelings of uncertainty, disruption, and instability permeated the interior life as well as the outer physical world. Such radical concepts as simultaneity and relativity in the early 1900s only confirmed the decisive shifts defining a modern vision.

Beyond what time as duration meant to Americans over this hundred-year period, of equal interest here is time in some of its other definitions, that is, time as occurrence or occasion, a fixed moment when something begins or ends, a specific or significant historical period. One can find much stimulation in attempting to select focal moments or years rich in significance, when there appears to be a confluence of important artistic or cultural landmarks within a momentous, historical turning point. During the nineteenth century in America, for example, just around the year 1836 we can associate Thomas Cole's cycle of paintings *The Course of Empire*, Ralph Waldo Emerson's essays *Nature* and *The American Scholar*, and Alexis de Tocqueville's *Democracy in America*, along with George Catlin's and John James Audubon's comprehensive records of native Indian tribes and the birds of America. Another date of cultural and historical interest is the nation's centennial in 1876, the year of the Philadelphia Exposition, and the display of Alexander Graham Bell's telephone, Thomas Eakins's *Gross Clinic*, Winslow Homer's *Breezing Up*, Henry Hobson Richardson's completion of Trinity Church in Boston, and Mark Twain's publication of *The Adventures of Tom Sawyer*.

However, three dates in particular—1800, 1850, and 1900—and the years immediately surrounding each of them not only provide the pure numerical abstraction of either framing or dividing the century, but they also constitute decisive periods in the nation's history that also proved to be defining moments of extraordinary creative energy and originality across several different spheres of public and private expression, especially challenging in their complex and interlocking achievements.[2] In the broadest sense, these periods were concerned, respectively, with American self-definition at the turn of the nineteenth century, self-confidence at its mid-point, and uncertainty at the opening of the twentieth.

By concentrating on outstanding exemplars of various fields in the decade flanking each of these three dates, we may gain insight into a core shared vision of that moment expressed through different creative intellects. In the juxtaposition of revealing examples from such spheres as political science, history, natural science, architecture, literature, and art, one discovers echoes within and among them that illuminate each other and the age of which they are a part.[3] As if in an octagonal room of some Jefferson building, let us imagine representative individuals or works on adjacent and facing walls to see what they have in common. Examples will vary, from distinctive organizations or institutions established to policies or doctrines pronounced, intellectual theories articulated, and images created in literature and art.

A *New York Times* columnist once asked rhetorically, "Can tranquil times yield great works?"[4] By implication the writer was questioning whether the most potent art emerges in periods of turmoil rather than in peaceful interludes. To engage the argument, it is worth proposing that neither extreme—of uneventful placidity or cataclysmic violence—stimulates great artistic expression. On the one hand, the dullness of stability restrains creative boldness, and on the other, the engagement in war, intense social upheaval, or deprivation can be distracting and all-consuming. What is intriguing about the years surrounding 1800, 1850, and 1900 is their complex tension between tentative order and disequilibrium. Indeed, one explanation of the distinctive richness of ideas and powerful cultural achievements concentrated at these turning points is arguably that context of tension acting as a stimulant. Not only do we find career-defining masterworks by major writers and artists but we also find clusters of work that reflect both culmination of the past and exploration of the future.

Interestingly, all three periods were framed by major conflicts: the century's beginning came between the Revolution and the War of 1812, its midpoint between the Mexican-American and Civil Wars, and its end between the Spanish-American War and World War I. All experienced degrees of uncertainty and a sense of disruptive change. At the same time around each date three of the country's strongest presidents emerged—Thomas Jefferson, Abraham Lincoln, and Theodore Roosevelt. Lincoln, of course, actually reached his greatest influence closer to 1860 than 1850, although he was indelibly associated with America's crisis at mid-century through both his eloquent expression and his resolute character. Before him, Jefferson had come into office after the near-crisis of an election finally decided by Congress, while Roosevelt became the nation's youngest president on the assassination of William McKinley. These presidencies are also associated with important times of territorial expansion: early on the Louisiana Purchase, later the advancing addition of new states and territories in the west, and finally the campaigns to place Cuba, Puerto Rico, the Virgin Islands, and the Philippines under the American flag. Each generation had reasons to feel both anxiety and optimism, to express concern as well as vision for the country's future. So Jefferson in 1801 proclaimed "a rising nation," Lincoln in 1857 warned about "a house divided," and Roosevelt in 1899 asserted that "the American flag is to float unchallenged."[5]

While each of these periods reveals an integrity of its own, there are certain thematic continuities of form and idea that carry throughout the American tradition. For example, nature and landscape were always in the view of Americans, from the early science of Charles Willson Peale, William Bartram, and Alexander Wilson in the federal period through the mid-century visions of Fitz Hugh Lane and Frederic Edwin Church to the late meditations of Winslow Homer and Henry James. Likewise, the sense of self as history regularly preoccupied Americans. Autobiographical expression was often varied, adaptable, inventive, and on occasion of far-reaching originality, as it was with Benjamin Franklin and Peale through Walt Whitman and Thoreau to Mark Twain and Henry Adams.

Yet another leitmotif we shall encounter is the familiar American fascination with newness. The belief has recurred that development of the country, its character, and experience was indigenous and original, although, of course, not everything was de novo.[6] Certainly the geography was special, the political system was inventive, and the arts soon developed a native voice. But, as we know, through the early colonial period the forms of portraiture and architecture, for example, were largely transplanted expressions inherited and transported from abroad. Even Jefferson's personal and idiosyncratic buildings, which we associate with fresh American idealism and rationalism, consciously drew from the precedents of Palladio and ancient Rome. What was important, however, was the adaptability of these models to American materials, circumstances, and ideas. In a similar way the Peale family painted the traditional subjects of art—portraits, landscape, genre, and still life—but subversively transformed these categories with either new amalgams or changed meanings.

Perhaps renewal, revision, and revival are more apt concepts for us. By the middle of the nineteenth century the classical revival dominated architecture, sculpture, and the decorative arts. Literary historians have called the writing of that moment the American Renaissance, while art historians have applied the same term with different associations to American painting at the end of the nineteenth century. Such expressions, in part modes of emulation, were also modes of aspiration and distinction. Revision was another means of creating something different and novel. One of the first Americans to remake himself was Benjamin Franklin, who wrote a different life from the one he had lived and set about correcting the errata in his experience in order to leave us a new model for living. Likewise, Noah Webster continually updated his dictionaries so that definitions and usage would always be alive and current. Just as important, he began calling his compendiums *American* dictionaries of the *English* language to signal the liberation from inheritance. The freethinking minds of his and later generations sought to create an American language not only in speaking and spelling, but also in literature and the arts, science, politics, and society.

After a prologue setting the late-eighteenth-century stage for the drama to follow, we will turn our full attention to the dates of 1800, 1850, and 1900, with Webster's definition of a period or moment in mind: "a time of excellence, one of importance in influence or effect, notable or conspicuous in consequence." Together, these three times were among the high points when America's ideas about and for itself were formed or transformed. Let us metaphorically pick up one of Franklin's inventions, a pair of bifocal spectacles, and consider what close looking and far seeing might reveal.

PROLOGUE

Articulating Independence

IN THE newly created United States a spirit of self-confidence and self-consciousness shaped the imagination of the nation as well as of individuals. Having declared its political independence in 1776, American society turned with released energies to the creation of equally distinct forms of cultural expression. During the vital last quarter of the eighteenth century the country sought through revolution, confederation, and a new constitution to establish an original structure of self-governance and thereby self-identity. At the same time, as the young republic crossed into the nineteenth century, it would face the challenges of a different age, such as unimagined territorial expansion, the tensions of a two-party system, and the coming of industrialization. The years just around 1800 brought to fruition the great ideas initiated by the Declaration of Independence and the Revolution and defined an American originality in almost every sphere of the nation's political, intellectual, and artistic life. The year 1800 was not just the fulcrum between two centuries but a crystallizing moment of passage from the old to the new. Determined and visionary minds did not merely argue for distinctive American forms; they transformed inherited traditions and created bold new models of personal and national self-expression.

Many of these ideas began to ferment over the decade that followed the end of the Revolutionary War. The culminating battle and defeat of Lord Cornwallis occurred in 1781, followed by the treaty negotiations with the British a year later and with Spain and France in 1783. Two of the key figures involved in the diplomacy, John Jay and Benjamin Franklin, were among several intellects whose writings in this period would help to shape, beyond the political, American cultural independence. Ranging from the literary and personal to the civic and historical, their expressions represent the striking newness of American forms and voice. J. Hector St. John de Crèvecoeur's *Letters from an*

American Farmer was published in 1782; Hamilton's, Madison's, and Jay's debates over the Constitution appeared as *The Federalist Papers* later in the decade; and Franklin began publishing his *Autobiography* during the early 1790s at the end of his memorable life. Along with two other authors of influential work that would continue well into the new century, Noah Webster and Thomas Jefferson, all have continually been cited for their originality: for example, "American literature, as the voice of our national consciousness, begins in 1782 . . ." (Crèvecoeur); "America's first entirely developed art was political literature . . ." (Hamilton, Madison, and Jay); and "his greatest invention—the invention of himself, not as fiction, but as a fact both of and in history" (Franklin).[1]

J. Hector St. John de Crèvecoeur

The French-born Crèvecoeur emigrated to North America in the 1750s as a young man and served in the French and Indian War. Later making his way to New York, he anglicized his name, married, and became a British subject. Beginning in the sixties, he went on exploring expeditions across much of the northeast wilderness, settling finally at the end of the decade in upstate New York on farmlands he had purchased.[2] There and in travels to Nantucket, Martha's Vineyard, and Charleston, South Carolina, he wrote down his thoughts on American life and manners. Not merely haphazard or casual notations, these were carefully drawn and organized observations both for his time and for posterity. That he had a higher calling in mind than just preserving a diary of the quotidian was evident in the conscious artifice he brought to his form and narration. His chapters, devoted to different locations or subjects, he called "Letters," ostensibly written by a Pennsylvania farmer named James in response to a request from a Mr. F. B. in London. Within this adapted literary convention, Crèvecoeur succeeded in articulating the first statement of American promise and possibility.

First written in the years before the Revolution, the *Letters* carried a glow of warm optimism, which turned more anxious as the actuality of conflict approached, and historians have noted the brooding "distresses of a frontier man" in the title and outlook of Crèvecoeur's last chapter. Without the heart for divided loyalties, he determined to go back to France but was detained in New York by the British for two years. Suffering some form of nervous breakdown in 1779, he finally departed a year later, and on his way through London he sold his manuscript, which was at last published in 1782. The positive and elegiac message of the body of his *Letters* now perfectly suited the spirit of the emerging independent nation. Crèvecoeur returned to New York to pursue a successful diplomatic career as a consul promoting French trade and agriculture in the mid-eighties. His modest but celebratory writings helped to establish the American literary genre of personal record-keeping carried on later by George Catlin in the 1830s, Henry David Thoreau in the 1850s, and Henry James in the 1900s. But it was Crèvecoeur's early encapsulation of the country's self-perception as Eden that then and thereafter drew primary attention.

One of his recurring images was the expanse of American space, one that would preoccupy writers and thinkers of subsequent generations. For example, early in the first Letter he proclaimed that "here Nature opens her broad lap to receive the perpetual accession of newcomers and to supply them with food. . . . The new and unexpected aspect of our extensive settlements, of our fine rivers; that great field of action everywhere visible. . . ." And in the opening of his third Letter he spoke of "the unknown bounds of North America entirely peopled. Who can tell how far it extends?" Some pages later, the American "stands on a larger portion of the globe. . . . He does not find, as in Europe, a crowded society where every place is overstocked. . . . There is room for everybody in America." Yet further on, Crèvecoeur summarized with a metaphor that would reverberate for generations: "Landing on this great continent is like going to sea."[3] One thinks of Ralph Waldo Emerson's claim in *Nature* (1836) that "the health of the eye seems to demand a horizon. We are never tired, so long as we can see far enough,"[4] or Willa Cather's breathtaking descriptions of sunsets on the great plains in *My Ántonia* (1918), or the national hymn which sings of "amber waves of grain" stretching "from sea to shining sea."

But the theme for which Crèvecoeur would become best known was the question he asked and answered in Letter III, which he titled "What is an American?" Among the essential ingredients were labor, freedom, and newness. As to the first, he wrote, "we are all animated with the spirit of an industry which is unfettered and unrestrained, because each person works for himself." Secondly, quite simply, "Here man is free as he ought to be." Then followed the possibilities of renewal: "Everything has tended to regenerate them: new laws, a new mode of living, a new social system; here they are become men." This led to the famous long paragraph at the heart of this social ode:

> What, then, is the American, this new man? He is either an European or the descendent of an European; hence that strange mixture of blood, which you will find in no other country. . . . *He is an American, who, leaving behind him all his ancient prejudices and manners, receives new ones from the new mode of life he has embraced, the new government he obeys, and the new rank he holds.* He becomes an American by being received in the broad lap of our great Alma Mater. Here individuals of all

nations are melted into a new race of men. . . . The American is
a new man, who acts upon new principles; he must therefore
entertain new ideas and form new opinions. . . . This is an
American.[6]

In this single paragraph Crèvecoeur formulated the so-called American
Dream, by which the citizen might aspire to well-being and fulfillment: "He
thinks of future modes of conduct," an aspiration of Americans ever since. In
the nineteenth century Thoreau thought that "the deepest thinker is the farthest
traveled," and in the twentieth Norman Mailer spoke of the first astronauts
exploring the moon as "a dream of the future's face."[7] For this linking of
American space and possibility we have Crèvecoeur to thank.

The Federalist Papers

Bringing to bear reason, free inquiry, and truth on the mechanics of the new
government was fundamental to an equally unusual set of documents by
Alexander Hamilton, James Madison, and John Jay, known as *The Federalist
Papers*. The documents were notable for many reasons: the brilliant joint
authorship, thoroughness of argument, acuity of insight, balance of pragmatism
and idealism, and not least an intense pace of production that did not sacrifice
quality of thought. In this latter regard, Garry Wills has estimated that under
the name "Publius" the three authors published between October 27, 1787, and
August 16, 1888, eighty-five essays, each of considerable length, on an average
of three a week, or a rate of some one thousand words a day.[8]

Certainly historians are correct in pointing to *The Federalist Papers* as the
first great formulation of American political theory. It is equally true that they
established an unmatched precedent in their elevated, probing, and cogent argu-
mentation. Undertaken in the period following the signing of the Constitution
in Philadelphia, this collaboration of two New Yorkers and a Virginian sought
to make the great pact both worthy of and workable for Americans. The goals
were not just ratification by the states, but also understanding and confirmation
by the public. Like their contemporary Thomas Jefferson, with whom these colleagues shared certain rhetorical flourishes and whose *Notes on the State of
Virginia* they cited twice, they wrote on two levels at once, one continually animated by high moral idealism and the other by the pragmatism needed to make
the new system work.

It is an illuminating coincidence that the *Papers* were the creation of
three authors, although not exactly an equal triangulation since historians
believe Hamilton was responsible for fifty-one numbers, Madison twenty-six,

Jay five, and three were joint productions.[9] At the same time these individuals together were engaged in the central debate of American government, that is, its tripartite organization into the legislative, executive, and judicial branches, and the critical weighing of different needs through moderation, cooperation, and the balance of powers. In addition, they regularly employed a language of juxta-position, what Wills has described as "neo-classical thought patterns," especially in Madison's use of contrasting yet correlated ideas.[10] But we find it also in the Jeffersonian phraseology of nouns or adjectives in trios, as in "the safest course for your liberty, your dignity, and your happiness"; "the genius, manners, and habits of the people"; "such acts of the body as have an immediate, detached, and palpable operation on its constituents"; or "decision, *secrecy*, and dispatch, are incompatible."[11]

Hamilton was the initial driving force in bringing Publius and the *Papers* to life. Author of the first paper, he addressed his fellow citizens directly in the opening sentence: "You are called upon to deliberate on a new Constitution for the United States of America. The subject speaks its own importance; compre-hending in its consequences nothing less than the existence of the UNION, the safety and welfare of the parts of which it is composed."[12] Within these first half dozen lines he struck most of the powerful ideas to receive deliberation over the subsequent months and pages: newness, union, security, and compo-nent parts. The word *union* appears five times in the eight paragraphs of this essay, three times in full capital letters and once as well in italics—an emphasis unused again in the some 175,000 words to follow.

In the next paper Jay picked up the theme of disparate elements linked together in a totality (quite possibly the foundation of the aphorism that the whole is more than the sum of the parts): "Independent America was not com-posed of detached and distant territories, but one connected, fertile, wide-spreading country. . . ." Possessing "a wide variety of soils and productions. . . . Providence has been pleased to give this one connected country to one united people. . . . A strong sense of value and blessings of union." And two papers later he reiterated, "It [one government] can harmonize, assimilate, and protect the several parts and members . . . it will regard the interest of the whole, and the particular interests of the parts as connected with that of the whole."[13]

Madison joined the argument with No. 10, considered by Wills and oth-ers the most cogent and important of the series, and opened by addressing "the numerous advantages promised by a well-constructed Union," among them "a common passion or interest will, in almost every case, be felt by a majority of the whole."[14] What makes these discourses so American in character is the authors' constant stress on adaptability and flexibility to create a structure in which differences may be balanced and resolved. Madison's own phraseology and syntax throughout No. 10 juxtaposed related or opposing concepts, such as the public and private, virtue and wisdom, passion and interest, "distinct parties" and the majority. Perhaps the greatest challenge was the contrast between federal versus state interests, about which he argued that "the federal Constitution forms a happy combination in this respect; the great and aggregate interests being referred to the national, the local and particular to the State legislatures."[15]

Repeatedly in the early papers the authors called for understanding and supporting the virtues of a strong federal union as envisioned by the Constitution. Hamilton concluded No. 11 with the ringing statement: "Let the thirteen States, bound together in a strict and indissoluble Union, concur in erecting one great American system superior to the control of all transatlantic force or influence and able to dictate the terms of the connection between the old and the new world!" and the one following with, "Nothing can be more evident than that the thirteen States will be able to support a national government better than one half, or one third, or any number less than the whole."[16]

Their attention gradually shifted with the middle papers to specific practical benefits of this new American system, for example, "the necessity of the Union as our bulwark against foreign danger, as the conservator of peace among ourselves, as the guardian of our commerce and other common interests." In addition, "the Union will be facilitated by new improvements. Roads will everywhere be shortened and kept in better order; accommodation for travelers will be multiplied and meliorated." For many states with frontier borders there was the prospect of greater "general protection," and ultimately "a government adequate to the national happiness." In tandem, the common security and economy would gain; concerning the former, "to this great national object, a NAVY, union will contribute in various ways," while on the latter, "an unrestrained intercourse between the States themselves will advance the trade of each by an interchange of their respective productions."[17]

Other themes of the central sections were the mechanisms of proportional representation, amendments and alterations to the system, the efficacy and separation of the respective powers, and the subtleties of intermixed or cooperative responsibilities.[18] These last two issues were typical in their statements of ideal principles tempered by the need for practical adaptation. On the one hand, there was the principle that "the preservation of liberty requires that the three great departments of power should be separate and distinct." On this Madison cited "the authority in support of it is Mr. Jefferson," and in further tribute he used Jeffersonian syntax to praise "the author of the *Notes on the State of Virginia* . . . The plan, like everything from the same pen, marks a turn of thinking, original, comprehensive, and accurate."[19]

But having fervently argued that "the members of each department should be as little dependent as possible on those of the others," the federalists

turned in their later papers to the appropriateness of flexibility, and in particular those processes requiring intermixed or cooperative powers. The most
notable were those regarding the making of treaties and diplomatic appoint-
ments, in which both the legislative and executive branches had to be
involved.[20] Here the justification for fusing the defined distinctions was quite
simply "attaching ourselves purely to the dictates of reason and good sense."
What these wise minds realized was that compromise and accommodation
would best serve an imperfect world: "The choice must always be made, if not
of the lesser evil, at least of the GREATER, not the PERFECT, good."[21]

Like Crèvecoeur, Webster, and Jefferson in the same period, Hamilton,
Madison, and Jay equally recognized the driving forces of newness and nationality. They exclaimed, "The form of government recommended for your adop-
tion is a novelty in the political world. . . . the leaders of the Revolution . . .
accomplished a revolution which has no parallel in the annals of human society.
They reared the fabrics of government which have no model on the face of the
globe. They formed the design of a great Confederacy."[22] In the conclusion of
his final paper, No. 85, as if typographically closing a parenthesis around this
grand disputation, Hamilton turned again to capital letters to say: "A NATION,
without a NATIONAL GOVERNMENT, is, in my view, an awful spectacle."[23]

Benjamin Franklin

Benjamin Franklin produced his own form of original expression, his noted
Autobiography, which was begun in 1771, worked on extensively during the late
1780s, and completed not long before his death in April 1790. Parts were published the next year, and fuller versions appeared in French and English in
1793.[24] As James Cox had pointed out regarding this chronology, Franklin and
America were creating and defining their identities at exactly the same time.[25]
Autobiography as understood in its modern definition did not come into use as
a term until after the Revolution, so Franklin's life and his telling of it represented a transformation of the genre as fresh, clever, and powerful as its political counterparts. Before him there existed the confession or memoir, in a
tradition extending from Saint Augustine in the seventh century to Jean-Jacques
Rousseau in the eighteenth. Accounts of one's biography were generally of two
types: the public life of an individual, one's place on the stage of history, and the
private life, intimacies from the spiritual or intellectual interior. Of course, in
colonial New England and elsewhere diaries and journals existed, along with a
well-developed genre of confessional and spiritual writing. Among the better
known examples of the former is the *Secret Diary of William Byrd of Westover,
1709–1712* (not published until 1941), and of the latter the *Personal Narrative* by
Jonathan Edwards (1765). Part of Franklin's inventiveness was the joint manip-

ulation of his public and private personae. He knew he was a significant historical figure in this age of revolution, but he also contemplated personal ambitions, and in his autobiography he played off his past and the present roles as philosopher, sage, and wit.

Just as bold was his startling disjunction between the told chronology of his life, which only goes up to 1747, when he was just over forty years old, and the familiar public statesman, inventor, and civic servant that defined his eminent reputation when he was actually writing the biography in later life. Clearly he was up to something more, and that was the invention of himself, or more properly, a second self. To do this, Franklin was arguably the first to fuse in the writing of autobiography fact and fiction, and ever since, the best American autobiography has blended the narration of history with the imaginative creation of self. The triumphant ingenuity of Franklin's storytelling was that he wrote equally as historian and novelist, and this is at the heart of his achievement in American letters at this time.

Writing and telling stories, anecdotes, or epigrams, along with reading, books, and printing, are common recurring motifs from his opening sentences onward. Nominally, Part One takes the form of a letter written to his son, and by extension to American posterity: "Dear Son, I have ever had a Pleasure in obtaining any little Anecdotes of my Ancestors." For Franklin, we read at the outset, this will be an enjoyable experience, and it will contain narrative tales with a point or purpose. There follows the reasons for "you to know the Circumstances of *my* Life, many of which you are yet acquainted with." Foremost, "having emerg'd from the Poverty and Obscurity in which I was born and bred, to a State of Affluence and some Degree of Reputation in the World . . . my Posterity may like to know, as they may find some of them suitable to their own Situations, and therefore fit to be imitated."[26] This life was to be the original American success story.

Having lived one full life, Franklin now set out to describe another exemplary biography, in which he had, as he said, "the Advantage Authors have in a second Edition to correct some Faults of the First." He frequently used printer's metaphors for his actions, such as correcting the "Errata of my Life . . . By comparing my work afterwards with the original, I discover'd many faults and amended them. . . . Thus I corrected that great *Erratum* as well as I could."[27] The purpose of these amendments was not merely to attain a clean text, as it were, or an accurate record, but also to make improvements and draw up a model life of opportunity, good conduct, and success. "I wish'd to live without committing any Fault at any time."[28] Franklin brought a wry wit to his tales of growing up, travel abroad, apprenticeships, and business ventures, taking Pleasure with a capital P in free embellishments, exaggerations, even distortions and hypocrisies, as much for his own self-interest as that of others.

Figure 1. Charles Willson Peale, *Benjamin Franklin*, 1785. Oil on canvas, 23⅛ x 19⅟₁₆ in. Courtesy of Pennsylvania Academy of the Fine Arts, Philadelphia. Bequest of Mrs. Sarah Harrison, The Joseph Harrison, Jr., Collection

Along with Webster, Franklin believed in the power of reading and learning and that the improvement of self and of country were congruent. In a possible wordplay he spoke of "my early Readiness in learning to read (which must have been very early, as I do not remember when I could not read)." Later he added, "this Bookish Inclination at length determin'd my Father to make me a Printer. . . . In a little time I made great Proficiency in the Business, and became a useful Hand to my Brother. I now had Access to better Books. . . . While I was intent on improving my Language, I met with an English Grammar (I think it was Greenwood's)." He referred to "Lovers of Reading with whom I spent my Evenings very pleasantly and gaining Money by my Industry and Frugality," a statement indicating that one may profit from reading in more ways than one. As a young man in London, "I work'd hard at my Business, and spent but little upon my self except in seeing Plays and in Books. . . . I had pick'd up some very ingenious Acquaintance whose Conversation was of great Advantage to me, and I had read considerably." All of this led to the conclusion of the first part of the *Autobiography* and "my first Project of a public Nature, that for a Subscription Library. I drew up the proposals. . . ."[29] Pride in achievement shines through the final sentence of the paragraph:

> This was the Mother of all the N. American Subscription Libraries now so numerous. It is become a great thing itself, and continually increasing. These Libraries have improv'd the general Conversation of the Americans, made the common Tradesmen and Farmers as intelligent as most Gentlemen from other Countries, and perhaps have contributed in some degree to the Stand so generally made throughout the Colonies in Defence of their Privileges.[30]

There followed between the first and second parts two letters written to Franklin, praising the merits of his biography and obviously included as a conscious part of his general self-promotion. Said one friend, "it almost insensibly leads the Youth into the Resolution of endeavoring to become as good and as eminent as the Journalist," while the second wrote that it will "give a noble rule and example of *self-education*. . . . But your Biography will not merely teach self-education, but the education of *a wise* man; . . . and invite all wise men to become like yourself; and other men to become wise."[31] Franklin might as well have dictated the words himself, but in effect he made them his own by their formal inclusion in his text. The second correspondent, Benjamin Vaughn, spoke also to a theme Franklin and his peers embraced, identification with the country's fortunes: "It will moreover present a table of the internal circumstances of your country. . . . All that has happened to you is also connected with the detail of the manners and situation of *a rising* people."[32]

Part Two Franklin wrote in France in the mid-1780s; it was relatively short, as he was busy with diplomatic affairs. In this section he formulated a series of virtues, platitudes we might call them, but which he rather grandly termed "the bold and arduous Project of arriving at moral Perfection."[33] Back in Philadelphia in August 1788, he commenced Part Three, commenting not about the great constitutional events of the day, but citing with tempered modesty his practical contributions and initiatives achieved through hard work, shrewdness, and ambition. Many are accomplishments we associate his fame with today: "I consider'd my Newspaper also as another Means of Communication"; "I accepted [the Commission of Postmaster] readily, and found it of great Advantage"; "I therefore in 1743, drew up a Proposal for establishing an Academy"; "the next was to write and publish a Pamphlet intitled, Proposals relating to the Education of Youth in Pennsylvania"; "maintain a Free School for the Instruction of poor Children"; "I proceeded in my Electrical Experiments with great Alacrity"; "The Governor put me into the Commission of the Peace; the Corporation of the City chose me of the Common Council, and soon after an Alderman; and the Citizens at large chose me a Burgess to represent them in Assembly"; "The Office of Justice of the Peace I try'd a little"; "the Revd. Gilbert Tennent, came to me, with a Request that I would assist him in procuring a Subscription for creating a new Meeting-house"; "After some time I drew a Bill for Paving the City, and . . . an additional Provision for lighting." (He couldn't help punning about his "Idea of enlightening all the City.")[34]

All this culminated when "the College of Cambridge of their own Motion, presented me with the Degree of Master of Arts. Yale College in Connecticut had before made me a similar Compliment. Thus without Studying in any College I came to partake of their Honours." Shortly thereafter, Franklin offers one hint of his participation in the overriding challenge of the future: "I projected and drew up a Plan for the Union of all the Colonies, under one Government so far as might be necessary."[35] But to the end Franklin concerned himself as much with practical ideas as with ideals, and his final pages contain observations about efficient hull and sail designs for vessels and the "Utility of Lighthouses, and made me resolve to encourage the building of more of them in America."[36] With his enlightened associates of this time Franklin took his place as thinker and doer, committed to liberty for one and for all.

As most literary historians have noted, Franklin matched his style to his message. One acknowledged "the crisp, factual authority, its cheerful worldliness, and its sensible egotism"; another noted that "his detached vision objectifies ideas, equalizes all concerns, and frees him to experiment with and concentrate upon a whole variety of probabilities. Similarly, he is free in his form"; and a third described the self-assured printer's prose as "cool as type itself."[37] All told, his autobiography was as inventive as his life. Although Franklin may be faulted (despite his corrections) for periodic excesses of ego, he set an example for Americans to make themselves, just as he had fashioned his life, and in the process made autobiography American.

Washington's Farewell Address

Washington's celebrated Farewell Address, delivered September 17, 1796, will serve as a summary index of this complex period of transition and triumph. What has been most remembered about the piece, especially in a late-twentieth-century America concerned with its military institutions and overseas commitments, is the first president's exhortation to "avoid the necessity of those overgrown military establishments which . . . are to be regarded as particularly hostile to republican liberty." Just as familiar are the lines "the great rule of conduct for us in regard to foreign nations is, in extending our commercial relations, to have with them as little *political* connection as possible. . . . It is our true policy to steer clear of permanent alliances with any portion of the foreign world."[38] But the larger aim of these concerns was "the continuance of the union as a primary object of desire," and "our detached and distinct situation invites and enables us to pursue a different course."[39] The Revolution had made possible the creation not just of a new nation but of a new national identity as well, and both required protection and cultivation.

Indeed, Washington opened his remarks by asserting that "it is of infinite moment that you should properly estimate the immense value of your national union to your collective and individual happiness. . . . The name of American, which belongs to you in your national capacity, must always exalt the just pride of patriotism."[40] He then dwelt upon the significant achievement and promise of the federal system, which had a decade before been so ardently debated by Alexander Hamilton, James Madison, and John Jay in *The Federalist Papers,* and which bound the separate states together in relation to the national government. Speaking of "the sacred ties which now link together the various parts," he felt "every portion of our country finds the most commanding motives for carefully guarding and preserving the union of the whole."[41] He acknowledged the regional attributes of the country's different quadrants, but returned to the central strength America had attained for itself: "While, then every part of our country thus feels an immediate and particular interest in union, all the parts combined can not fail to find in the united mass of means and efforts greater strength, greater resources, proportionately greater security from external danger, a less frequent interruption of their peace by foreign nations. . . ."[42]

This aspiration for balancing the parts with the whole is just as much a defining element in the federal style of architecture, painting, and rhetoric, as a closer look at Jefferson, Peale, and Noah Webster will later amplify. Repeatedly in the body of his message Washington stressed the significance of interrelationships: "To the efficacy and permanency of your union a government for the whole is indispensable." He urged "those intrusted with its administration to confine themselves within their respective constitutional spheres," and noted "the necessity of reciprocal checks in the exercise of political power, by dividing and distributing it into different depositories."[43]

Toward the end of his speech Washington turned to other related concerns, one of which Benjamin Rush and Noah Webster shared with him as crucial for empowering the new American democrat, and that was the public's education. "Promote, then, as an object of primary importance, institutions for the general diffusion of knowledge. In proportion as the structure of a government gives force to public opinion, it is essential that public opinion should be enlightened."[44] Washington's death at the end of the century was perhaps the most visible reminder of an age ending, but the active, hortatory voice he used throughout this address spoke as firmly of the present and the future.

PART ONE

Circa 1800:
Expanding
Horizons

Ideas,
Individuals,
and Issues

DURING the ten-year period astride the turn of the century, 1795 to 1805, America's political world was in the process of both consolidation and transition. As the first president, George Washington completed eight years in office and refused a third term; his Farewell Address in 1796, which cautioned against United States involvement in foreign alliances, has gone down in history as perhaps his most celebrated statement. With Philadelphia having served as the temporary national capital for ten years during the 1790s, the permanent capital was established in 1800 in a newly planned site in Washington, D.C., laid out in the French classical manner as proposed by Thomas Jefferson and designed by Pierre L'Enfant.[1] That year Jefferson was elected president, succeeding John Adams in a contentious vote settled finally by the House of Representatives. This was a momentous turning point, as the Federalist party, led by Hamilton and Adams, yielded for the first time to the Virginian's new Democratic-Republican alliance, marking the first transfer of power among the nation's emerging political factions. Many in the country were uncertain the system would work, especially with Washington himself so recently departed. The death of the foremost founding father in the last days of the old century was an omen of loss and a source of far-reaching nostalgia and anxiety. But events of equally monumental significance followed in the early years of Jefferson's presidency, most notably the negotiation of the Louisiana Purchase in 1803 and, shortly thereafter, the beginning of the Lewis and Clark Expedition across the continent to the Pacific coast and back. As historians point out, this acquisition of territory doubled the young country's size in one stroke, while Jefferson's charge to his colleagues to explore and document its physical nature was an equally dramatic claim of intellect and imagination.[2]

Significant artistic and scientific advances were also occurring abroad and at home in this same period. The year 1798 marks the invention of lithography by the German Aloys Senefelder, whose new method of printmaking by using a polished stone plate, instead of the digging into metal surfaces in engraving and etching, revolutionized the graphic arts. The greater ease of execution and the possibility of printing many more impressions without wearing down the plate were advantages that would perfectly suit American needs and sensibilities. Soon after the turn of the nineteenth century, American artists took up the technique, whose economical production and accessibility well served a democratic society and the call for printed views, pamphlets, and popular illustrations. To serve as a repository for American documents, the Library of Congress was founded in 1800. A year later the discovery of mastodon bones in upstate New York led to the pioneering scientific and museological enterprises of Charles Willson Peale. At the same time the great German naturalist Baron Alexander von Humboldt was undertaking a five-year exploration of the New World wilderness in the equatorial mountains of northern South America. Concluding his tour in 1804, he visited Peale in Philadelphia, after which both men went to the White House, where they were entertained by a deeply interested and sympathetic Jefferson.[3] For his part, Peale bracketed this crucial time with two landmark activities: In 1795 he organized the Columbianum in Philadelphia, the first academy for training artists and exhibiting their art, followed ten years later by his founding of the Pennsylvania Academy of the Fine Arts, America's first art museum. In the interim he energetically pursued the exhumation of mammoth skeletons and the promotion of his natural-science museum, all held up as evidence of national distinction and achievement.

This period also saw the emergence of a consciously national literature with the publication in the later 1790s of what can be called the first American novels. The most notable figure in this regard usually cited by literary historians is Charles Brockden Brown, whose novel *Wieland* appeared in 1798 and *Edgar Huntly* and *Arthur Mervyn* the year after. In addition, there was the highly imaginative narrative *Memoirs of the Notorious Stephen Burroughs of New Hampshire*, whose first of many editions appeared in 1798, and the fiction of Susanna Rowson, who continued writing actively through the period following her immigration from England in 1794.[4] One of the more notable and popular literary achievements of the time was Joel Barlow's *Vision of Columbus*, first published in 1787, later revised as *The Columbiad*, and expanded over the next two decades.[5] Along with Noah Webster, Barlow was a member of the so-called Hartford Wits, an informal group of Connecticut writers involved in American politics and education. His epic poem in the manner of Milton consisted of thousands of lines celebrating the patriotic history of the New World's discovery, settlement, struggle and triumph through revolution, culminating with the establishment of the new American nation.

Optimism and self-confidence permeate the narrative as the classic seventeenth-century form is turned to a New World vision:

> There lies the path thy future sons shall trace,
> Plant here their arts and rear their vigorous race:
> A race predestined, in these choice abodes,
> To teach mankind to tame their fluvial floods.

An expansive landscape would be the natural setting for realizing the possibilities of an original democratic society:

> Based on its rock of right your empire lies,
> On walls of wisdom let the fabric rise;
> Preserve your principles, their force unfold,
> Let nations prove them and let kings behold.
> EQUALITY your first firm-grounded stand;
> Then FREE ELECTION; then your FEDERAL BAND;
> This holy Triad should for ever shine
> The great compendium of all rights divine. [6]

Notable here are the use of the Latinate word *compendium* and the spiritual overtones to the tripartite structure of social governance, which was to have a direct parallel in the balanced harmonies of contemporary federal architecture.

A National Architecture

This would also be a new architecture in style and form, based on past English precedents but crystallizing a fresh American practicality and adaptability. Indeed, a major transformation was under way at this point in American architecture and the decorative arts. Jules Prown has given the most succinct summary of stylistic change that culminated around the turn of the century: "In general terms, the transition in style was from rococo in the third quarter of the eighteenth century, the end of the colonial period, to neoclassical during the years of the establishment of the Federal Republic in the last quarter of the century." It was, he further asserts, "the most complete and dramatic stylistic change in the entire history of American art."[7] The earlier style, inherited from eighteenth-century England, celebrated undulating curves, whether surface or linear, with detailed motifs of natural organic forms.[8] Lightness, delicacy, and animation were pervasive as much in building plans and elevations as in the shimmering surfaces of silver, wood, and fabric. This elegance well suited the

aspirations of both Georgian England and America, but with the Revolution the liberated colonies needed a new imagery of expression appropriate to nationhood. Increasingly, they turned specifically to the ancient world of Greece and Rome for forms, such as the temple, and iconography, such as the eagle, as emblems of rational republican order and governance.

Replacing the spirals and curlicues of the rococo were now the clear abstractions of pure geometries and proportional relationships, the "artifacts of reason." Circles and squares foremost, and their variations—ovals and rectangles—gave clarity and dignity to America's public structures and domestic furnishings alike. Their bold abstractions and intellectually rigorous designs were the physical counterparts of the strong cadences, coherent vision, and grand ideals stated in Jefferson's Declaration of Independence, the Constitution, the Bill of Rights, and *The Federalist Papers*. The so-called federal period associated with the decades on either side of 1800 referred at once to a balanced political, as well as artistic, organization. This proved to be a moment of flourishing

Figure 2. Samuel McIntire, Pingree House, Salem, Massachusetts, 1804

Figure 3. Charles Bulfinch, Massachusetts State House, Boston, 1795–98

architectural originality along much of the Atlantic seaboard, from Charleston to Boston.

Representative of the refined harmonies of federal architectural expression were Samuel McIntire, Charles Bulfinch, and Benjamin Latrobe, some of whose finest work flourished around 1800 in Salem (Massachusetts), Boston, and Philadelphia, respectively. The first was a native-born woodcarver who rose to the opportunities of patronage by Salem's most sophisticated and prosperous merchants and ship owners. From the late 1780s into the first decade of the new century, McIntire built houses first in wood and later in brick for the prominent Derby, Nichols, and Pingree families of this thriving North Shore seaport. A practical and accomplished woodworker, McIntire made notable ensembles of furniture, as well as suites of panel moldings, railings, cornices, and overmantels for his interiors; and he embellished his simple but elegant exteriors with strong accents of window frames, porticos, balustrades, and fencing. William Pierson has analyzed these buildings with unmatched sensitivity, but it is worth noting here that the exemplary Pingree House of 1805 (fig. 2) summarizes the Salem architect's attention to carefully calibrated proportions of plane and integration of individual parts.[9]

His more worldly counterpart in Boston, Charles Bulfinch, also designed some of the most important and memorable buildings of this period, for both private and public clients. However, Bulfinch's early distinction was

Figure 4. Charles Bulfinch, First Harrison Gray Otis House, 1795–96. Society for the Preservation of New England Antiquities, Boston

his youthful trip abroad in the mid-1780s and direct exposure to civic architecture in England and on the Continent. On his return, he immersed himself in multiple aspects of Boston public life, serving as selectman, superintendent of police, town planner, and, for over two decades, designer of government and school buildings, wharves and warehouses, markets and theaters, town row housing, and individual dwellings. Two parallel achievements, in the public and private spheres, respectively, stand out among his greatest works at the turn of the century. First, in Hartford, Connecticut, in the mid-nineties he completed its Old State House, and then at the end of the decade he built the serene and dignified Massachusetts State House at the head of Boston Common (fig. 3). Drawing on his recollections of William Chambers's Somerset House in London for the facade (as he had the great crescent row housing in Bath for his Tontine Crescent building in Boston), Bulfinch created a crisper and more restrained American interpretation. We are struck by its integrated balancing throughout of horizontals and verticals, of linear elements and broad planarities, of brick and painted or gilded wood. Above all, the symbolic formal associations of the classical tradition here acquire a practical American fusion of democratic order and idealism.

Concurrently, Bulfinch was at work designing, for the prominent Boston Federalist Harrison Gray Otis, no fewer than three town houses in the emerging fashionable residential sections of Boston. Almost symmetrically five

Figure 5. Benjamin Henry Latrobe, *View of the Bank of Pennsylvania, Philadelphia,* 1798–1800. Watercolor on paper. Museum and Library of Maryland History, Maryland Historical Society, Baltimore

years apart (1795, 1800, and 1806), the houses were located near the waterfront east of Beacon Hill, near Louisburg Square on the hill itself, and on the developing Beacon Street facing the Common. From the heavier and more derivative cubic block of the earliest dwelling (fig. 4) Bulfinch moved decisively to more subtle and refined proportional relationships in the later commissions. Inventive variations in detailing, and idiosyncratic handling of the decorative vocabulary on the exterior of the second and the interior of the third, mark the perfection of his architectural maturity. Especially in the ground plan of the third house, Bulfinch attained a remarkable flexibility and the ability to function within the exterior constraints of a symmetrical facade and a narrow, semidetached plot. In contrast to the relative heaviness of earlier Georgian architectural forms on the one hand and to their visual diversions of sumptuous surface textures on the other, the Otis houses made creative use of interior asymmetries fluently bound together by spiral and oval spaces.[10] Matched only by Jefferson's, Bulfinch's originality around 1800 was not least the marshaling of his aesthetic sensibility in the service of convenience.

Philadelphia, Cultural Capital

Like Boston, Philadelphia experienced a burst of creative energy at this time, even after the federal capital moved to Washington in 1800. It was there that Benjamin Latrobe, the country's first professionally trained architect, created the earliest fully conceived neoclassical buildings and where William Rush,

arguably the country's first professional sculptor, reached his maturity as a carver of independent figural pieces.

Born in England, Latrobe arrived in the United States in 1796 as a highly trained and practicing professional, bringing with him knowledge of John Soane's austere geometric classicism, which he adapted to his first American commissions. The essence of that manner appeared in his Bank of Pennsylvania in Philadelphia (1798–1800; fig. 5), acknowledged to be "the first monument of the Greek Revival in America."[11] Instead of the linear and planar delicacy of New England forms, Latrobe's buildings articulated in stone powerful cubic concentrations of mass and space, inaugurating a national architectural style that would reach its peak half a century later.

Simplicity, rationality, clarity of organization, and functional massing were hallmarks of his several early masterpieces, such as the Center Square Pump House for the Philadelphia Waterworks of 1801 (see fig. 7) and his monumental Baltimore Cathedral of 1804 (fig. 6). The basic geometric massings of these buildings—cubes, cylinders, domes—clearly contained as well as expressed the interior functions: in the case of one, the separation of an elevated water tank, pumping machinery below, and surrounding operating offices; and in the other, the sequence of entrance portico, vestibule, central worship space, and principal altar area. Of the latter's interior especially historians have consistently remarked on the similar clarity of interlocking parts and the clean demarcation of spatial volumes.[12] With such works as these Latrobe pioneered visible physical expressions of both America's functional and its intellectual needs.

Figure 6. Benjamin Henry Latrobe, *Baltimore Cathedral*, 1804–21. Watercolor on paper. Museum and Library of Maryland History, Maryland Historical Society, Baltimore

Figure 7. John Lewis Krimmel, *Fourth of July in Center Square, Philadelphia*, 1810–12. Pennsylvania Academy of the Fine Arts, Philadelphia, Purchase from the estate of Paul Beck, Jr.

The son of a local ship carver, William Rush, who likewise contributed a great deal to Philadelphia's burgeoning cultural eminence, began his own career carving ship figureheads in the mid-1790s and soon after turned to portrait busts. Latrobe placed Rush "at the head of a branch of the arts which he himself has created. His figures, forming the head or prow of the vessel, place him in the excellence of his *attitudes* and *action*, among the best sculptors that have existed."[13] If slightly hyperbolic regarding the history of sculpture, the assessment correctly called attention to Rush's role at the close of the eighteenth century as the first major figure in America's sculptural arts. In addition, he was active at this time in the founding of the Columbianum with Charles Willson Peale.

Gradually, Rush evolved from a carver to a modeler who later worked in terra cotta, though not in the marble favored by the pure neoclassicists. His most noteworthy pieces spanned this critical period of cultural growth, from portraits of Franklin (1787), Washington (1790), and John Adams (1799), to the allegorical figures of *Comedy* and *Tragedy* (1808; fig. 8), *Allegory of the Schuylkill*

River (1809), *Wisdom* and *Justice* (1812), and later portrait busts of prominent Philadelphians, including Samuel Morris, William Bartram, and Caspar Wistar (1812).[14] Rush's fine graphic surfaces and his preference for the relatively light mediums of pine and terra cotta, instead of the solidity, weight, and sense of permanence in stone, allies his production with the federal spirit of McIntire and Bulfinch to the north.

Of course, Philadelphia itself in these years had been a hospitable and stimulating environment as the country's temporary center of government in the 1790s. Benjamin Franklin's inventive presence presided over the city, and George Washington was in residence. Early in the decade the Bill of Rights was ratified as part of the Constitution, and the national government learned how to function. Along with the concentration of political intellects was a constellation of scientific and artistic luminaries who joined Latrobe and Rush with energetic accomplishments in various realms. William Strickland was another

Figure 8. William Rush, *Tragedy* and *Comedy*, 1808. Pine, originally painted, H. (*Tragedy*) 90 in; (*Comedy*) 90½ in. Philadelphia Museum of Art, purchased with funds contributed by the Mary Anderson Trust

architect who made a prominent mark locally in the new neoclassical mode. The early landscape painters Francis Guy, William Groombridge, and William and Thomas Birch were active around the city, while one of the country's foremost portraitists, Gilbert Stuart, dominated that genre, executing in the late 1790s his definitive likenesses of the first president (fig. 9). Yet other painters came from abroad to work there, among them Adolph-Ulrich Wertmuller and Robert Edge Pine. The prolific Thomas Sully would later emerge to consolidate and carry on the city's portrait tradition established by Stuart. The silver and furniture making in Philadelphia were among the finest being created in the republic at that time.[15]

The world of the natural sciences in Philadelphia had no less-esteemed or influential personalities in Alexander Wilson, William Bartram, and Caspar Wistar, with their contributions to ornithology and botany. Charles Willson Peale embraced the worlds of art and science in his multiple devotions that included painting, archaeology, and museology, and Benjamin Rush, the sculptor's second cousin, represented Philadelphia's commanding leadership in medicine and public education.[16] Having studied medicine in Philadelphia and Edinburgh, Rush taught at the College of Philadelphia (now the University of Pennsylvania) and served on the staff of the Pennsylvania Hospital. A towering figure in American medical history for more than three decades, from the 1780s into the second decade of the nineteenth century, Rush was also a signer of the Declaration of Independence and ratifier of the Constitution from Pennsylvania. In 1786 he promoted "A Plan for the Establishment of Public Schools and the Diffusion of Knowledge in Pennsylvania," and in 1787 "Thoughts upon Female Education," as extensions of the ideals and challenges of the Revolution.

Rush was the model of service to country, believing that making medicine understandable and education broadly available to the citizenry would truly "republicanize" the professions.[17] Clarity and accessibility could only enhance the enlightened well-being of all. Concluding "An Inquiry into the Comparative State of Medicine, in Philadelphia, Between the Years 1760 and 1766, and the Year 1805," he exhorted: "Dear cradle of liberty of conscience in the western world! nurse of industry and arts! . . . May Heaven dispel the errors and prejudices of thy citizens upon the cause and means of preventing their pestilential calamities! and may prosperity and happiness be revived, extended, and perpetuated for ages yet to come!"[18]

These individual enterprises were but a part of America's larger mission of self-definition, one in which the political and social sense of nationhood received sweeping tangible confirmation in President Jefferson's announcement of the Louisiana Purchase on the Fourth of July 1803. At last, after the regional squab-

Figure 9. Gilbert
Stuart, *George
Washington (The
Landsdowne
Portrait)*, 1796.
Oil on canvas,
96¼ x 60¼ in.
Pennsylvania
Academy of
the Fine Arts,
Philadelphia,
Bequest of
William Bingham

bles during the periods of the Revolution and confederation, a new vision of national geography and growth seemed possible to imagine. Not only was territorial expansion under way, so also was the population of the former colonies, with the most rapid growth rate in the western world at that time.[19] From the end of the Revolution to the turn of the century the republic's inhabitants went from two to four million, continuing to double with every generation. People were on the move from New England to the south and to the west, and the shifting of the national border dramatically westward enlarged American horizons mentally as much as physically. All this literally provided room for the transformation and prosperity of what one historian has described as a "free society belonging to obscure people with their workday concerns," which swiftly "made America into the most liberal, democratic, and modern nation in the world."[20]

What, then, are some of the recurring themes or characteristics of this first defining moment in American self-consciousness? Arguably, they include the preoccupation with national identity, new forms, federalism, practicality, democratic education, autobiography, and nature. Three individuals especially—Thomas Jefferson, Charles Willson Peale, and Noah Webster—and their inventive forms of expression around 1800 highlight this early American vision.

Jefferson's Visions

THROUGH his sentences, Thomas Jefferson authored the fundamental ideas of America. (Was there ever written or spoken a more potent phrase than "All men are created equal"?[21]) His texts gave shape to America's fundamental structures of government, religious freedom, and university education. Beyond his far-ranging inquisitiveness, agility of intellect, and diversity of interests, Jefferson as author wrote extensively in many formats, from the public Declaration of Independence to state papers and formal addresses to personal accounts and memoranda, and thousands of private letters of memorable substance and eloquence. Consistently, his style suited his subjects: He sought the dignity, clarity, and balances of classical form to articulate the great moral issues of the day that were on his mind. For instance, consider the tangential but characteristic example of Jeffersonian phrasing in the lines he asked to stand as his memorial: "Author of the Declaration of American Independence, and of the Statute of Virginia for religious freedom & Father of the University of Virginia."[22] Here as elsewhere he constructed sentences with repeated solid nouns, like so many rhythmic columns, holding up the lintel of his linear narrative and the gentle swags of prepositional modifiers. He was especially drawn to a few alliterative words often structured within the equilibrium of a three-part sequence: in these lines note the recurring sounds of A's, D's, S's, R's, F's, and V's. From the Declaration to his private letters, we can all recall similarly memorable phrases. Just as important was Jefferson's self-identification as author and father, one who created through writing, ideas, and architecture the framework of his country.

No doubt forever to be associated with the Declaration for his creation of the idea of the new nation, Jefferson possessed a creative vision that produced works of comparable greatness as well in the subsequent decades of his life, most notably Monticello and the First Inaugural Address at the turn of the century and the University of Virginia in the 1820s. But for all the quantity of writings, he produced only one book, *Notes on the State of Virginia*, first printed privately in Paris in 1785 and distributed more widely in English two years later. As a document of its time, it is as fresh and innovative as its companion utterances by Crèvecoeur and Webster. Written in the aftermath of the Revolution and of his wife's death in 1782, and before his diplomatic mission to France in mid-decade, the *Notes* began as a set of answers to questions about America put to him by the French legation, but Jefferson expanded them to wider meditations, on both his immediate countryside and the country as a whole.

His principal title as well as the chapter headings, which he called "Queries" after the original questions, reveal his subtle, interlocking concerns with the real and the ideal, the factual and the philosophic. *Notes* grounds us in the specifics of measurements and records, "memoranda" Jefferson called them in his Garden and Farm Books. The second noun, *State*, at the center of the title acts as a fulcrum between the specifics of his initial notations and the generalizations about geography to which they lead. The word also has double meanings balanced together, references at once to a particular state in the republic and to its condition, as in a state of mind or place. The word *Virginia*, it follows, suggests several general associations: its naming in honor of the virgin queen Elizabeth, an original colony on the virgin continent, and a symbolic embodiment of America itself. Jefferson's close friend in the Continental Congress and associate in the American Philosophical Society, Charles Thompson, understood this last point when he wrote that the history was "not merely of Virginia but of No. America."[23]

His beloved state was not just at the heart of the nation; from some of his observations we can assume Virginia was its apogee. Moreover, Monticello on his mountaintop at Charlottesville was the epicenter of this "more perfect union," from which both measurements and views extended equally in all directions. For example, in describing Virginia's mountains in Query IV, Jefferson claimed that they "are not solitary and scattered confusedly over the face of the country" but are "disposed in ridges one behind another, running nearly parallel with the sea-coast."[24] Flawed irregularities might appear elsewhere, but here there is only order. Later, on climate in Query VII he observed that "the hill of Monticello" is a "position being nearly central between our northern and southern boundaries, and between the bay and Alleghaney [sic], may be considered as furnishing the best average of the temperature of our climate." To him, the rejected colonial capital of "Williamsburgh is much too near the South-eastern corner to give a fair idea of our general temperature."[25]

By the same token, in his familiar dismissal of Williamsburg's architec-

Figure 10. Gilbert Stuart, *Thomas Jefferson,* 1805. Oil on canvas, 26½ x 21 in. National Portrait Gallery, Smithsonian Institution; jointly owned by Monticello, The Thomas Jefferson Memorial Foundation, Inc., and the National Portrait Gallery, Smithsonian Institution, Washington, D.C.

ture, his political and aesthetic motivations were inseparable: "The Palace is not handsome without. . . . The College and Hospital are rude, mis-shapen piles, which, but that they have roofs, would be taken for brick-kilns. . . . The genius of architecture seems to have shed its maledictions over this land." It was the job of architecture to elevate, instruct, and embody ideals, as Jefferson himself would undertake in his adaption of Roman forms for the new state capitol at Richmond and later for the University of Virginia. "Architecture being one of the fine arts . . . perhaps a spark may fall on some young subjects of natural taste, kindle up their genius, and produce a reformation in this elegant and useful art."[26]

In another very different yet related realm he took issue with a French accusation that "America has not yet produced one good poet, one able mathematician, one man of genius in a single art or a single science." Rising to the occasion, Jefferson responded: "Having given a sketch of our minerals, vegetables, and quadrupeds, and being led by a proud theory to make a comparison of the latter with those of Europe, and to extend it to the Man of America, both aboriginal and emigrant, I will proceed to the remaining articles comprehended under the present query." He notes that "between ninety and an hundred of our birds have been described by Catesby," and that "in war we have produced a Washington. . . . In physics we have produced a Franklin, than whom no one of the present age has made more important discoveries. . . . We have supposed Mr. Rittenhouse second to no astronomer living."[27] Although elsewhere he made problematic observations about the black in contrast to the native Indian populations, his literary and intellectual achievement as a whole was to provide the best early exemplum of American history. It was a precedent for others soon to follow, such as James Sullivan's *History of the District of Maine* (1795) and Jeremy Belknap's *History of New-Hampshire* (1812).[28] But none has surpassed Jefferson's in its ingenuity, breadth, and, ultimately, wisdom. For all his note taking in response to a professional inquiry, his loftier goals and manner of speaking always shines through, as near the end of his history he could include such sentences as: "Reason and free inquiry are the only effectual agents against error" and "Truth can stand by itself."[29]

Inaugural Views

The formal beginnings of a national government followed ratification of the Constitution in 1788 with the first elections for Congress held early the next year and Washington's inauguration in April 1789. The political tension between the Federalists and anti-Federalists dominated much of the decade of the nineties, and in particular the next three elections, as Americans sought to make constitutional government work. The decade and the century concluded with Jefferson's election to the presidency in 1800, an even more pivotal occasion, signaling not just the rise of a new political vision but also the influence of a broad intellectual visionary.

It is stating the obvious that Jefferson was an architect of the new nation in more ways than one, through his critical texts as well as his buildings. In both, he designed clarity of structure, harmony among the parts, and flexibility of purpose and function for all components. If one of the foundations of the 1780s was the establishment of an American voice in words, syntax, imagery, and aspiration, Jefferson certainly refined and strengthened that voice in the first years of his presidency. We might see the towering achievements of the

Declaration in 1776 and the University of Virginia in the 1820s, respectively early and late in his life, as elegant parentheses framing the versatile products of his genius centered around 1800. These include his First Inaugural Address, his building of the second Monticello, and the Louisiana Purchase, soon after explored by Lewis and Clark.

The First Inaugural Address was more than the opening statement of a new administration; coming at the start of the new century, it inaugurated as well the broader sense of fresh horizons for all the country's endeavors. It is a relatively short speech, well known for its call for reconciliation in the preservation of the larger union: "We are all Republicans, we are all Federalists." But within its economical form Jefferson also drew on themes preoccupying colleagues in the preceding years, he reaffirmed the present independence and newness of the country, and he crafted an uplifting imagery of progress and promise for the future.

Some of these ideas were clearly on his mind in the years leading up to this moment, as may be seen in both his private correspondence and public writings of the late 1790s. For example, he echoed *The Federalist Papers* in a letter of 1795 to an associate: "We have chanced to live in an age which will probably be distinguished in history, for its experiments in government on a larger scale than has yet taken place." More particularly, three years later in his *Draft of the Kentucky Resolutions* he stressed the constitutional separation of powers, resolving that the several states "constituted a General Government for special purposes—delegated to that government certain powers, reserving each State to itself, the residuary mass of right to their own self-government." Beginning his presidency, he was especially mindful of stabilizing the counterpulls of opposing political ideologies, and the third paragraph of his Inaugural Address opens with a masterfully crafted sentence of paired nouns and balanced concepts: "Let us, then, with courage and confidence pursue our own Federal and Republican principles, our attachment to union and representative government."[30]

But taking primacy even over soothing of political discord was Jefferson's soaring vision, stated in the second sentence of his Address, of "a rising nation, spread over a wide and fruitful land . . . advancing rapidly to destinies beyond the reach of mortal eye . . . I contemplate these transcendent objects, and see the honor, the happiness, and the hopes of this beloved country." The notion of spatial plenitude was one Jefferson had earlier begun to define in his *Notes on the State of Virginia*, when he described the significance of experiencing the views outward from his Virginia mountains. He himself had such prospects from Monticello, but also at Harpers Ferry he observed, "the passage of the Potowmac through the Blue Ridge is perhaps one of the most stupendous scenes in nature. You stand on a very high point of land. . . . In the moment of their [the rivers] junction they rush together against the mountain, rend it asunder, and pass off to the sea. The first glance of this scene hurries our sense into the opinion, that this earth has been created in time. . . . But the distant finishing which nature has given to the picture is of a very different character. It is a true contrast to the foreground. . . . This scene is worth a voyage across the Atlantic."[31] The Inaugural Address recasts the meaning of that distance from Europe as one of the blessings of America's separateness, physically as well as politically, and its consequent possibilities for future advance: "Kindly separated by nature and a wide ocean from the exterminating havoc of one quarter of the globe . . . possessing a chosen country, with room enough for our descendants to the thousandth and thousandth generation."[32]

Again we are struck by Jefferson's consciously modulated sentence structure, especially his harmonies of alliteration and triadic groupings of words or phrases, beginning with "the honor, the happiness, and the hopes of this beloved country." Of course, we are most familiar with this stylistic device of his from the Declaration of Independence a quarter century before, where at the outset he referred to "life, liberty, & the pursuit of happiness," and at the close to "our lives, our fortunes, & our sacred honor." It was a rhetorical rhythm he continued to employ, as in his letter to Elbridge Gerry of January 26, 1799: "The first object of my heart is my own country. In that is embarked my family, my fortune, & my own existence."[33] The Inaugural Address repeated these cadences in its stately progress to the end with such phrases as "freedom of religion, freedom of the press, and freedom of person under the protection of habeas corpus"; "the creed of our political faith, the text of civic instruction, the touchstone by which to try the services of those we trust"; and "regain the road which alone leads to peace, liberty, and safety."[34]

Three weeks after the inauguration Jefferson wrote another letter to a correspondent, in which he expanded his spatial metaphors of American nature and nationality to one of clearing light: "As the storm is now subsiding, and the horizon become serene, it is pleasant to consider the phenomenon with attention. We can no longer say there is nothing new under the sun. For this whole chapter in the history of man is new. The great extent of our Republic is new."[35] With such language Jefferson gave intellectual shape to the new age. Concurrently, he was giving it shape physically and concretely in the designing and building of his own dwelling at Charlottesville.

Monticello

As a young man in the late 1760s Jefferson determined to plant a cherry orchard and build a house on the hilltop he named Monticello, and there began forty years of construction, demolition, and rebuilding of one of the most personal yet timeless structures in the history of architecture. He worked on the first

Monticello throughout the seventies and early eighties until his departure in 1785, when he succeeded Franklin as minister to France. Abroad he gained first-hand familiarity with Andrea Palladio's Renaissance villas around Venice, which helped Jefferson transform the largely book-derived house he had started into something more three-dimensionally substantial, complex, and coherent. In contrast to the derivativeness he associated (aesthetically and politically) with eighteenth-century English architecture, he sought out Palladio's purer forms and in turn their precedents in the Roman originals. Back home, and taking up government service, beginning as Secretary of State in the early nineties, he started to tear down the first Monticello in 1796 and designed its rebuilding over the next few years. By the time of his election as president, it was still unfinished, although its new, enlarged shape had reached fruition.[36] For all the forward-looking refinements and flexibility of McIntire's and Bulfinch's contemporary buildings in New England, Jefferson's second Monticello took life around 1800 with an originality unsurpassed then or since.

If Franklin wrote an inventive form of autobiography, Jefferson was equally creative in his self-expression. As is already evident, his life was in his texts and his architecture. It is significant that the autobiography he did write in his last years centered around his original text of the Declaration and his identity as author. But it is just as true to see Monticello as his autobiography, one that extended also into his later years with the University of Virginia, the former, we might say, an embodiment primarily of his private life, the latter of his public life. Monticello was a deeply personal statement of his views on nature, politics, and history. It occupied his intimate attention for much of his maturity, it was the central locus of his scientific, literary, and cultural activities, and its design directly reflected his diverse needs and pursuits. Today still his living presence is felt not only in all the quirky and practical inventions around the house, but also in the idiosyncratic handling of scale, space, and surface. We sense the individual purpose and rightness of each room, all organically held together in a unified and lucid whole.

At Monticello designer and client were one, the architect was his own patron, and the entire project was an extension of the person. But it was also in harmony with its setting and nature at large. Jefferson's initial selection of the site was bold and unprecedented. Contrary to the tradition of English colonial and Georgian houses in America up to that time, this dwelling was to sit upon a mountaintop, despite such attendant problems as bringing water to the summit. In addition to that structure, the complex in time would come to include a working farm, planned forests, cultivated flower and vegetable gardens (with some 250 plant varieties), an orchard with over 150 varieties of fruit, vineyards, nurseries, and a greenhouse.[37] The house itself rose in tiers, becoming more compact in the upper levels and culminating in a low dome. Thus its very shape was both a repetition and metaphor of the hillside it crowned. At the same time the windows around the octagonal dome room above afforded views in all directions, literally a world view, while its hemispherical shape also alluded to the dome of the sky and the cosmos above. In this regard it is not far-fetched to see the architecture of Monticello as an analogy to Jefferson's thinking about the federal structure of government, with their interrelated parts bound in union and both working with the mutual dependency of the solar system. Indeed, in a 1798 letter Jefferson clarified this very imagery: "I dare say that in time all [the state governments] as well as their central government, like the planets revolving around their common sun, acting and acted upon according to their respective weights and distances, will produce that beautiful equilibrium on which our constitution is founded, and which I believe it will exhibit to the world in a degree of perfection, unexampled but in the planetary system itself."[38]

Monticello's first design employed a simple, compacted cruciform plan (fig. 11) and an equally straightforward two-story elevation with shallow porticos on opposite sides. The second Monticello, which Jefferson began rebuilding in the 1790s, doubled the mass into a fuller cruciform and three stories within, all so subtly integrated on the exterior as to suggest a single grand spatial entity. Consolidating the whole without rigidity or obviousness, the dome does not rise over the building's center but rests over the largest interior space of the main entrance hall above the west portico (fig. 12). Balance and flexibility are now the supreme governing elements of his achievement. As William Pierson, Howard Adams, and other historians have pointed out, Jefferson at once separated and joined the private versus public rooms in the house, expressing their individual character and usage through their different shape or scale. Both within and without, horizontal massings or details contrast with vertical counterparts. Surfaces of brick and painted wood balance one another as the principal materials, while slate and glass act as integrated subordinate elements.[39]

Just as Bulfinch and McIntire had made effective use of the oval, ellipse, and spiral as planning devices to make interior spaces more adaptable and functional, so Jefferson introduced the octagonal form to temper his basic rectangular block, the octagon being the perfect intermediary between the circle and the square. Where Monticello's original exterior displayed linear and planar severity in the triangular pedimented porticos of its facades, the "second edition" acquired greater liveliness and volumetric integration through the faceted surfaces of the octagonal dome and the cropped corners of walls below. The results suggest an overriding symmetry throughout, yet no spaces or facades are the same, and the dominant decorative scheme for each room differs one from another. What holds all this together? At least two critical forces we might expect of Jefferson: his concept of equilibrium relies on axiality and balance everywhere, instead of pure symmetry, and his intuitive feelings for nature led to the active

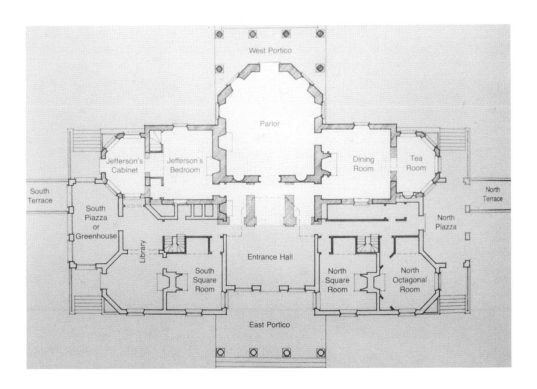

Above: Figure 11. Thomas Jefferson, Ground plan of Monticello. Thomas Jefferson Memorial Foundation, Monticello, Charlottesville, Virginia

Left: Figure 12. Thomas Jefferson, Dome Room interior at Monticello. Thomas Jefferson Memorial Foundation, Monticello, Charlottesville, Virginia

use of light flowing throughout the passages of space. This unifying flow extends by means of the several porches, triple-hung windows, and the surrounding terraces out into the landscape itself. From either side of the house these terraces reach out like arms to embrace the gardens and all of variegated nature beyond. A powerful assertion of human individuality, Monticello grew organically into its own maturity, integrated on one side with nature and on the other with its creator.

The University and Nature Beyond

Interested like many of his generation in public education for Americans, Jefferson in 1803 offered a proposition to the Virginia legislature for a university. When the idea finally came to fruition, and his grand design led to actual construction in the 1820s, the university was in part an expansion of his plan of Monticello. In terms of American campus planning, there was an even more emphatic rejection of English precedents here, as Jefferson turned away from the monastic quadrangle (used by Princeton, Harvard, and Yale) and the dominance of religion evidenced in the central placement of the chapel in earlier campuses. Instead, he placed at the head and heart of his design the Rotunda (fig. 13), a half-scale translation in wood of the Roman Pantheon, which held a library and the country's first planetarium. Here was his dome room on a public scale, a center of knowledge and a symbol of the cosmos, flanked by two ranges of classical pavilions and columned arcades extending again out into nature. Housed within were separate departments, representing the modern disciplines of learning, yet unified in an architectural and curricular whole. Even more than Monticello, the great lawn contained by these architectural arms became an active space of nature (the beginning of landscape architecture in America), reaffirming for a final time Jefferson's belief in the freedom of the human mind, so perfectly distilled earlier at Monticello.[40]

Given the dramatic siting of both his house and the university, their views out to the larger landscape, and by implication the sweep of America itself, were integral to Jefferson's thinking. Quite intentionally, his telescope and surveying instruments stood in front of the window and doorway of his cabinet-study room, emblems of his constant examination of the world around him. As we have seen, the American horizon was on his mind from the time of his *Notes on Virginia* on. His prophetic phrases there describing the "distant finishing" of nature, or the "wide and fruitful land . . . advancing rapidly to destinies" in the First Inaugural, and his wonderful query at Monticello, "where has Nature spread so rich a mantle under the eye?"—all come to personal and national resolution in Jefferson's negotiations for the Louisiana Purchase and his subsequent sponsorship of the Lewis and Clark expedition.[41]

Barely twenty years after America's formal independence, its president dramatically enlarged the national domain in one gesture, making the United States one of the world's largest countries at the beginning of the nineteenth century.[42] The recognized pressures behind the negotiations were the settlements growing westward, notably in the Ohio valley, and the related increase in commercial traffic on the Mississippi River. Jefferson focused his concern on New Orleans and the outlet to the Gulf of Mexico, crucial territory recently

Figure 13. Thomas Jefferson, The Rotunda at the University of Virginia, 1823–27

purchased by the French but still governed by the Spanish. With Napoleon's diversion to renewed war in Europe finally came a willingness to sell the lands. The symbolic potency of Jefferson's deal was obvious in its announcement on Independence Day 1803. Now America's western boundaries as well as its exploring impulses moved hundreds of miles to the unknown interior, inaugurating a new sense of continent, empire, and destiny.

Jefferson had already conceived of an exploratory expedition across the country to the Pacific, one that would have both scientific and commercial purposes. To lead the project he selected his fellow Virginian and private secretary, Meriwether Lewis, who was then thirty-two years old and who in turn asked the young (twenty-eight-year-old) frontiersman William Clark to join him. In a charge of instructions, made final in June 1803, the president spelled out goals and details of the undertaking: "The object of your mission is to explore the Missouri river, and such principal streams of it, by its course and communication with the waters of the Pacific ocean, . . . whether the Columbia, Oregan [sic], Colorado, or any other river, may offer the most direct and practicable water-communication across the continent, for the purposes of commerce."[43]

Being scientifically inclined, Jefferson then became quite specific in his instructions: "You will take observations of latitude and longitude, all remarkable points on the river . . . and other places and objects distinguished by such natural marks and characters, of a durable kind, as that they may with certainty be recognized hereafter. . . . Your observations are to be taken with great pains and accuracy." He characteristically followed with a list of categories he hoped would be documented, such as knowledge of the people; their possessions and relations with others; their languages, traditions, monuments, and occupations; their food, clothing, and "domestic accommodations"; their diseases and "moral and physical circumstances which distinguish them," and their laws, customs, and articles of commerce. From the inhabitants he turned to aspects of natural history, including "the soil and face of the country . . . the animals of the country generally; their remains . . . the mineral productions of every kind . . . volcanic appearances; Climate, as characterized by the thermometer."[44]

With preparations well under way, Lewis acknowledged that the announcement meanwhile of the Louisiana Purchase "increased infinitely the interest we felt in the Expedition." Thus with some formality he and Clark began their official account of the trip by noting that "the attention of the Government of the United States was earnestly directed toward exploring and improving the new territory." Now the mission had expanded to one of national self-definition that would proceed by a measuring that was mathematical as well as moral. Paragraphs in their journal accordingly alternate being filled with numbers and symbolic associations. Typical of the former is the following: "All preparations being completed, we left our camp on Monday, May 14th, 1804.

This spot is at the mouth of the Wood river, a small stream which empties into the Mississippi, opposite the entrance of the Missouri. It is in latitude 38° 55' 19.6" north, and longitude from Greenwich 89° 57' 45" west." And typical of the latter is: "The morning of the 4th of July was announced by the discharge of our gun. . . . At 10¼ miles we reached a creek on the south, about 12 yards wide, coming from an extensive prairie which approached the borders of the river. To this creek, which had no name, we gave that of Fourth of July creek."[45] Such language of scientific and intellectual measurement here was the foundation of an American tradition of personal and geographical exploration that came to life repeatedly thereafter in the nineteenth century, from George Catlin and Henry David Thoreau to the railroad survey expeditions of the 1870s and 1880s. That Independence Day periodically proved to be a fateful mark in America's affairs never seemed more so than when John Adams and Jefferson both died on that day in July 1826, the fiftieth anniversary of the Declaration of Independence.

The Peales:
Painting and Science

Figure 14. Charles Willson Peale, *The Artist in His Museum*, 1822. Oil on canvas, 103³/₄ x 79⁷/₈ in. The Pennsylvania Academy of the Fine Arts, Philadelphia, Gift of Mrs. Sarah Harrison, The Joseph Harrison, Jr., Collection

SHARING Jefferson's vision of culture and science deeply intertwined, as well as many common professional associations, such as the American Philosophical Society, was his almost exact contemporary and friend Charles Willson Peale. Born in 1741, Peale also lived an active career well into the next century, and like Jefferson he produced a major work of personal and artistic power at the end of his life, the painting he called *The Artist in His Museum* (1822; fig. 14). Further, much of Peale's art was intentionally autobiographical, and several of his major paintings were as ingeniously fresh and unconventional for the visual arts as their literary or political parallels were in their spheres. In the years around 1800 he made something new of American art, transforming especially the traditions of portrait painting with a new informality and unpretentiousness as well as a consciously nationalist sense of optimism and independent achievement.

Art and Family

Growing up in Maryland, Peale had some early art training, which he augmented in the mid-1760s with a visit to John Singleton Copley in Boston and two years of study thereafter in London with Benjamin West. Back in America at the end of the decade, Peale began painting in Maryland and Philadelphia, where he moved his family at the beginning of the Revolution. He enrolled in the army and served under Washington, whom he painted in the battles at Trenton and Princeton. During the same years the first of Peale's many offspring were born, many of whom, in an American sense of aspiration and ambition, were given the names of famous painters (Raphaelle, Rembrandt, Rubens, Titian, and Angelica Kaufman) or scientists (Benjamin Franklin and Linnaeus).[46]

Figure 15. Charles Willson Peale, *The Peale Family*, c. 1770–73 and 1808. Oil on canvas, 56½ x 89½ in. The New-York Historical Society, New York, Gift of Thomas J. Bryan (see color-plate 2)

Indeed, a number of them did become highly accomplished artists or naturalists in their own right.

Almost from the outset Peale painted himself, not out of unusual vanity or ego but to know himself and the surrounding world. He painted self-portraits alone or in family groups nearly a dozen times, and members of his family sat for more than a dozen canvases in every period of his career.[47] The first major example, *The Peale Family* (colorplate 2; fig. 15) was analogous to Jefferson's Monticello in that it grew organically over many years of its creator's life, beginning in the early 1770s. Peale kept placing new figures in the composition as grandchildren were added to his family, with the last additions including the family dog Argus, painted in during 1808. Nominally the subject was a family gathering around a table, not in the artist's studio but surrounded by references to art on all sides. On an easel at the back left rests a painting of the three Graces and a mantel bearing sculpted busts recedes into the upper right, while at the table Charles's brother St. George works on a drawing of their mother seated across from him. Charles himself at the upper left looks on, his head significantly placed at the juncture between the figures and the painted canvas, as his outstretched painting arm holds his palette. Thus an otherwise conventional family group takes on enhanced significance as an image of art in the making: past, present, and future; of art in different media: painting, sculpture, and drawing; of the spectrum of subjects: portraiture, history, genre, and still life; and of three generations of sitters, with present and future artists among them. In this way Peale put his life and profession into his art. In fact, he projected himself into this image in multiple ways: by his actual figure, by his palette as an emblem of the artist, by his inscription and signature at the bottom of the picture, and by the visual double entendre of the still life on the table. The curling peel of a peach was a pun on his name, while the nearby knife was also a stand-in for the artist's palette knife. The whole speaks to domestic harmony and the importance of family to Peale, who married three times and fathered nine children. But the knife extending off the table's front edge, by implication into viewer's space, along with the central glance of his wife, engages us with a disarming directness and intimacy.

This sense of immediacy and informality Peale carried to a remarkable level of refinement and subtlety in his first great masterpiece, *The Staircase Group* (1795; colorplate 3; fig. 16). This moment marks the beginning of perhaps the most productive and influential period of his artistic and scientific endeavors. Painted at the apogee of Philadelphia's cultural and political eminence, the picture was to be the centerpiece for the Columbianum, an "American Academy of Painting, Sculpture, Architecture and Engraving" organized by Peale for the upper floors of the State House. This was in effect the first organization in America dedicated to the training and exhibition of artists, the antecedent of the Pennsylvania Academy of the Fine Arts also founded by Peale in Philadelphia ten years later. At the Columbianum he assembled some sixty

Figure 16. Charles Willson Peale, *The Staircase Group*, 1795. Oil on canvas, 89½ x 39⅜ in. Philadelphia Museum of Art, The George W. Elkins Collection (see colorplate 3)

artists and amateurs and sponsored life classes for students,[48] efforts that represent an important foundation for the visual arts in federal America, coming, as they did, right after Crèvecoeur's invocation on "what is an American." But Peale's painting was in itself a tour de force of pictorial ingenuity and a moment of revelation in a new national expression.

Although the picture is repeatedly cited and reproduced in the literature, art historians have not devoted the extensive and probing attention to it that they have to his two other large and important works, *The Exhumation of the Mastodon* (1806–8; colorplate 4; see fig. 17) and *The Artist in His Museum.* Perhaps *The Staircase Group* is so easy in its charm of representation and beguiling in its simplicity that, as George Washington did, according to a Peale son, we bow to its felicity and pass on by. Certainly, the relaxed openness of the two boys, Titian Ramsay I above and Raphaelle below, who turn to glance at us, seems so directly engaging that we smile but do not think further about their presence. Because the painting is life-size and the finish of details so polished, we first respond to Peale's precedent-setting illusionism. But the gaze of the youths as they regard us looking in, along with the centrally placed emblems of art—palette, brushes, and maulstick—suggest that this work, more than portraiture, is about seeing, painting, artifice, and art.

We can easily imagine Peale in his study, asking his sons to pause for a moment as they start up this simple federal stairway, perhaps to try some sketching themselves in a room above. Clearly, they have turned in response to the artist, Titian in a casual pivot around an unseen bannister or wall edge, his head leaning down into the space and effectively stabilizing the upper left corner, as Raphaelle shifts his left leg around to stop his upward movement to hold a pose for his father. But the focus of the boys' attention away from the interior of the house, and from their immediate preoccupations, reaches across the picture plane both into Peale's imaginary painting space and into our own viewing space. The artist has further blurred illusion and reality by mounting the picture within a door frame and adding a real wooden step at the bottom.

The paradox of complexity within simplicity, a device exploited to architectural perfection by Jefferson at Monticello, is also evident in Peale's distilled compositional structure. What seems to make these poses and this moment so expressive derives partly from the contrast between the informal stances and the architectural austerity, the animate and the inanimate. Peale deftly holds in equilibrium the various planar and linear geometries of the staircase with the more organic and fluid forms of the figures. What may strike us first is the rather narrow vertical rectangle of the canvas, which obviously frames the two standing full-length forms. Peale's use of this format for his two boys is something new in American art. Generally, the full-length pose had traditional associations with portraits of European royalty and was therefore not especially compatible with American democratic ideas. During the years before the Revolution John Singleton Copley employed it appropriately for his wealthier merchant patrons, such as Mr. and Mrs. Jeremiah Lee of Marblehead, Massachusetts, whom he painted in elaborate standing formats in 1769 (Wadsworth Atheneum, Hartford). Copley had also painted successfully the direct, relaxed portraits of his fellow silver artisans, Paul Revere and Nathaniel Hurd (Museum of Fine Arts, Boston, and Cleveland Museum of Art), both dressed in their work clothes and facing straight out to the viewer. But both of these portraits were modest, bust-length compositions and are restrained in comparison to the psychological and pictorial complexity of Peale's work. What Peale achieved was the fusion of a large, ambitious design with the casual, intimate character of a head-and-shoulders close-up in one of the first full-length American portraits of a truly democratic subject.

The vertical rectangle also reinforces the rising staircase it contains, with interior subdivisions in the two wall planes and smaller contrasting notes in the horizontal step risers. Within these planes several linear diagonals cross on the picture's surface as well as within in shallow space: the step edges and molding, axes of the legs, cast leg shadows, maulstick, and clutched brushes in Raphaelle's hand. Balanced in these intricate visual rhythms are the major oval planes or volumes: Titian's and Raphaelle's faces and the angled wood palette, further echoed in the paint daubs, coat buttons, and wallpaper designs. The rising maulstick ties the two youths together as thoughtful individuals, just as the repeated shapes of Raphaelle's head and palette, one directly above the other, affirm the making of art as requiring the mutual dependency of head and hand.

Finally, there is the minor but telling detail of a calling card at the bottom edge of the lower painted step. This bears Charles Willson Peale's signature on, or more properly within, the painting. Although he does not include his literal self portrait here, and virtually effaces his presence as painter in the tight, illusionist stroke throughout, this card accidentally dropped at the very juncture between real and painted space anchors his professional and conceptual presence in his work. His name on the small oblique rectangle is but a microcosm of the larger canvas whole and its magical testimony to the youth of art in America. In its graceful spiral and elliptical lines we recognize at last the affinities to the best architecture of McIntire, Bulfinch, and Jefferson. In its balances, clarities, and economy we find the equal to the finest Franklin aphorism, federalist paper, or Jefferson letter.

Art and Science

Shortly after, Peale largely set aside his art to devote time to his scientific enterprise and his museum work, saying he "should bid adieu to Portrait Painting."[49]

In 1791, even before organizing the Columbianum, he had established the Philadelphia Museum, which contained a portrait gallery and collections of natural-history specimens. In words reminiscent of Webster and Jefferson, Peale argued to the Pennsylvania legislature: "In a country where institutions all depend upon the virtue of the people, which in turn is secured only as they are well informed, the promotion of knowledge is the First of duties."[50] With the transfer of the capital in 1799 from Philadelphia to Washington, D.C., the old State House became vacant, and Pennsylvania granted its use a couple of years later to Peale for his museum. In this period he delivered several dozen lectures on natural history and published a *Scientific and Descriptive Catalogue* of the museum's collections, which by then included over a thousand varieties of birds, animals, insects, and fish. Peale announced, in capital letters reminiscent of Hamilton's in his final Federalist Paper: "Natural history is not only interesting to the individual, it ought to become a NATIONAL CONCERN, since it is a NATIONAL GOOD."[51] He promoted his museum as "a world in miniature," with the goal of providing broad and popular, that is democratic, education.

Just about the time that Jefferson ascended to the presidency, and also the leadership of the American Philosophical Society, an important discovery in the fields of upstate New York gave dramatic new focus to the scientific interests he shared with Peale. In 1801 a Dr. Graham of Newburgh reported finding an enormous assemblage of mammoth bones, and with the Philosophical Association's sponsorship, Peale immediately set forth on what would be the first organized scientific expedition in the country. That June he traveled by diligence to New York City, where he caught a boat up the Hudson River to West Point. En route he constantly sketched the scenery in watercolor, one of the first commitments by an American artist to landscape subject matter and one that would be a prominent element in his next major picture inspired by this enterprise. From West Point Peale was driven out to the farm of John Masten near Newburgh, and there he first saw and drew the incomplete skeleton laid out on Masten's granary floor. Over the coming months he would call it the "Great Incognitum," "Behemoth," "Carniverous Elephant of the North," "an Antique Wonder of North America," "American Miracle," and ultimately a key link in understanding God's "great chain of being."[52] This was proof that along with a national literature, art, and government, there was now American natural science and archaeology. Peale determined to undertake further excavations with a combination of zealous pride and consciousness of purpose, envisioning possibilities both as a centerpiece for his museum and as a worthy subject for his art.

He negotiated the purchase of the discovered bones, which he took back to New York and on to Philadelphia, and a month later he returned with his son Rembrandt to continue the digging at the original site as well as at another nearby. Between the two excavations Peale was able to assemble a full skeleton and

part of a second. Rembrandt had the task of carving the missing pieces to complete the second mammoth for a tour of Europe. Meanwhile, Peale installed and presented the first in the Mammoth Room of his museum, which opened to the public in December 1801. Then he engaged the architect Benjamin Latrobe to draw up designs for a new museum adjacent to the Philadelphia State House. Hoping for government support in the creation of a national institution, Peale wrote his friend Jefferson: "I have long contemplated that by Industry such a variety of Interesting subjects might be collected in one view as would enlighten the minds of my countrymen and demonstrate the importance of diffusing a knowledge of the wonderful and various beauties of Nature more powerful to humanize the mind, promote harmony, and aid virtue, than any other School yet imagined. . . . in the end these labours would be crowned in a National

Figure 17. Charles Willson Peale, *The Exhumation of the Mastodon*, 1806–8. Oil on canvas, 50 x 62½ in. Museum and Library of Maryland History, Maryland Historical Society, Baltimore (see colorplate 4)

imagined. . . . in the end these labours would be crowned in a National Establishment of my museum."[53]

The president was sympathetic but felt restrained by the powers of Congress, and Peale had to proceed on his own. Yet his ideas subsequently took hold in the creation of the Smithsonian Institution, which took for its motto the "diffusion of knowledge." In any case, Peale soon had the full use of the State House, where he actively added to his ornithological and other natural-science specimens, along with his growing series of portraits of prominent Americans. All these would appear together in ordered rows in his final large-scale self-portrait, *The Artist in His Museum*. More immediately, he began to conceive of another ambitious painting depicting the work of the excavation in active progress, with his guiding presence at center stage. It merits discussion here because its initial conception dates to 1804, when he talked of producing "a large historical, emblematic Picture."[54] Those two adjectives are significant, for he foremost thought of his painting *The Exhumation of the Mastodon* (fig. 17) as a historical piece, which for Peale meant both personal and national history combined. In addition, he wrote that the "subject [was] grand, nay awful," as an heroic drama of sublime character and dimensions, emblematic of larger themes.[55] To this end he included numbers of family and professional colleagues who were not actually present, overlaying the documentary elements with higher symbolic power.

In the composition Peale stands at the right center, the largest and most strongly illuminated figure, in the pose of the Apollo Belvedere, as Lillian Miller has pointed out.[56] The artist would have known the image through casts and reinterpretations of the image, for example, in the work of his London teacher Benjamin West, who so admired the original on his own first trip to the continent a generation earlier. With his gaze and outstretched right arm, Peale directs our attention to the active excavation below, while his other hand in a balancing gesture holds a full-scale drawing of the skeleton's leg. The artist-scientist literally stands between the two disciplines and mediates between the raw elements of nature and the orderly reconstruction on paper, canvas, and in the museum. Miller has also shown how Peale also drew on the memory of his teacher's major history paintings, *Agrippina with the Ashes of Germanicus* (1768; Yale University Art Gallery) and *Penn's Treaty with the Indians* (1772; Pennsylvania Academy of the Fine Arts) for the grouping of the Peale family on the right. As with his earlier family portrait, Peale continued to work on the painting over several years, actively adding figures until 1808 and making the image itself a dynamic work in progress.

Although only Rembrandt accompanied him to the site, Peale presents his current wife and several children at his side, while an earlier, deceased wife appears with another child on the bank framed by the great wooden tripod.

Appropriately in the center foreground he shows the farm owner John Masten climbing the ladder from the pit and looking back over to the artist-director of the operation. The other key identifiable individual was Peale's neighbor and colleague, Alexander Wilson, a leading ornithologist of the day, who stands alone with arms folded, observing the scene at the back left. Thus Peale assembles a large and complex gathering of people in balanced, interrelated poses of action and contemplation, active discovery and thoughtful interpretation.

When Peale first visited Masten's farm in 1801 to view the discovered bones, he not only made early drawings of the fragments, but he also made a sketch in his journal of the wooden tripod and giant wheel that he envisioned to drain the marsh.[57] Here was the artist at his most inventive and practical: the great contraption with its series of buckets on a continuously turning pulley and chain, descending into pit to remove the water, was exactly what he eventually constructed at the site and depicted in the final painting. To keep the wheel moving and the heavy buckets rising, Peale had colleagues and visitors constantly walking on steps inside the wheel, thus involving his countrymen in this shared national enterprise. The final element of his presentation was, of course, the landscape itself; besides water and rock, Peale also juxtaposes forest and open field, and, in the distance, bright skies at the left and the storm at the right. Where his tranquil watercolor sketches of Hudson River scenery on the trip up were in a picturesque mode, here he intentionally chose, as he said the "grand, nay awful" aspects of sublime drama suitable to his subject of courageous and heroic action.

For its time the subject was one that celebrated a venerable science now practiced anew in America. But its pictorial treatment by Peale was equally inventive in its fusion of the traditionally distinct categories of subject matter practiced by European art. For the *Exhumation* combines history painting, even an incipient American mythology, with the everyday life of genre, portraiture, and landscape. At the heart of it all was the Jeffersonian fusion of scientific and artistic pursuits. It was no accident in the design of Monticello that the president situated his greenhouse next to his library and cabinet, so that he might investigate the world of nature as one, by books as by plants as by instruments. Peale's art was similarly an autobiographical expression of his dual professional callings. Furthermore, in both content and form he did not hesitate to harness the joint powers of the practical and the ideal in the new American vision.

Art and Nature

Charles Willson Peale's legacy and influence extended to his professional associates in Philadelphia and to his many family members, who followed in careers as both artists and scientists. Among the most accomplished of his sons was

Figure 18. Charles Willson
Peale, *William Bartram,*
c. 1808. Watercolor on paper.
Independence National
Historic Park, Philadelphia

career did not emerge until the second decade of the nineteenth century and is
therefore just beyond the period under consideration here. Nevertheless, his
delicate, polished compositions exude all the balanced geometries, usually pyramidal arrangements, and clear separation of parts, yet unity of the whole, so that
we can readily see how they are indebted to the foundations of the federal style,
whether seen in the writings of Jefferson and Madison, the architecture of
Bulfinch and Latrobe, or his own image captured by his father in *The Staircase
Group.*

The other talented son who assisted Peale in the organization of his
museum, Rembrandt, likewise pursued work as a naturalist as well as portraiture. After starting the Pennsylvania Academy of the Fine Arts in 1805,
Peale senior's attention turned back to renewed activity in painting; by 1811
he removed himself from the daily administration of his museum, leaving
Rembrandt and his younger brother Rubens in charge, along with another muse-

um they operated for Peale in Baltimore. Just before Rembrandt and Rubens left for Europe in 1802, the younger boy sat for his brother in one of the most memorable portraits created by an American. *Rubens Peale with a Geranium* (1801; colorplate 5) recalls the deceptive simplicity and openness of character of their father's 1795 double portrait of Titian and Raphaelle. This, too, was an affectionate tribute of one family member to another, and of one artist to another.[58] In its own way the picture also reconfigured the conventional format of portrait painting up to that time, by giving such prominence to the potted plant that occupies a full half of the picture space, equal in the artist's and our attention to the figure of Rubens. With the traditional portrait on one side balanced by a creation of nature on the other, Rembrandt pays his own tribute to the intertwined professions of the family; at the same time he now adds the new subject of still life to the center stage of American painting. As a microcosm of nature, this geranium possesses the same power and importance as the landscape in the *Exhumation* and forecasts the wide bounty of nature that would so engage American artists in the half-century to follow.

Meanwhile, the fields of zoology and ornithology were undergoing comparable changes, especially in the hands of Peale's friend Alexander Wilson, who is depicted so noticeably in the background of the *Exhumation* picture. With his investigations of American birds, Wilson became the pivotal figure between the early pioneering watercolor illustrations of Mark Catesby in the mid-eighteenth century and the consummate artistry of John James Audubon in the nineteenth. Wilson arrived in Philadelphia from Scotland in 1797, a propitious moment in the area's artistic and scientific life. Peale had become a member of the American Philosophical Society the year before, when Jefferson was elected its president. That organization, as well as Peale's museum in Philadelphia, became the locus for an active community of scientific intellects who dramatically advanced the natural sciences in America at this time.

The sciences of botany and ornithology were already well established, first by Catesby's work and then by John Bartram and his son, William. William had trained with his father and during the mid-1770s traveled extensively, making observations throughout eastern Florida and other southern colonies. These resulted in a comprehensive publication in 1791 of his travels, amply illustrated with his first-hand illustrations. After the opening of Peale's museum, William Bartram collaborated with his friend by adding specimens to the collection, and the artist honored the professional association when he added his portrait of Bartram to the museum in 1808 (fig. 18).[59] Two other prominent naturalists joined this group in subsequent years: the French-born Charles-Alexandre Lesueur, who was active in the Philosophical Society and close to the Peale family after his arrival in 1816, and Thomas Say, who worked at the museum with the Peale sons and helped to establish the disciplines of entomology and conthe Peale sons and helped to establish the disciplines of entomology and conchology in America.[60]

Wilson was a schoolmaster whose school was on land owned by Bartram. He met Peale in 1802, just as the artist was engaged in his excavations of the mastodon and conceiving his large picture of the subject. Primarily trained as a botanist, Wilson began collecting and documenting birds under Peale's enthusiastic influence. He assisted with the classification of the museum's collections, adding classical names to the vernacular terms used by Peale. Wilson's great achievement was his nine-volume publication, between 1808 and 1814, of *American Ornithology*, rightly called the first comprehensive treatment of American birds and of American natural history generally.[61] Although the volumes appeared more than a decade after the turn of the century, they embodied the work of a new vision being forged by Peale, Jefferson, and others around 1800. As we have seen, that vision arose in the years after independence, when American culture sought to distinguish itself from European traditions.

Wilson, Peale, and their associates in the natural sciences likewise believed in the creation of a new identity and practice of these disciplines in the new world. This nationalism took several forms, among them a conscious effort to correct mistakes of European colleagues, to promote parity in the recognition of American achievements, to publish expressly for a national rather than foreign audience, to link research endeavors to indigenous political and cultural goals, and to assert the primacy of native talent at the center of pragmatic, immediate experience.[62] Like Peale, who prominently directed the course of his archaeological investigations and made his own first-hand observations and recordings, Wilson believed in field experience. Moreover, he sought its rendering with both the precision of scientific accuracy and the visual coherence of an artistic eye. This meant the direct sketching of living creatures seen in their natural habitats and the implicit primacy of the artist in the field. In this active, even celebratory, approach to nature, Wilson added his contribution to the ascendancy of an intellectual democracy.

His shared goal with others was to assert an American role for the sciences, but also to educate as wide an audience as possible. As he wrote, in the lyric spirit of Jefferson's First Inaugural: "When the population of this immense western Republic will have diffused itself over every acre of ground fit for the comfortable habitation of man—when farms, villages, towns and glittering cities . . . overspread the face of our beloved country . . . then, not a warbler shall flit through our thickets but its name, its notes and habits will be familiar to all."[63] Like his contemporaries, Wilson made his down-to-earth practice serve an uplifting ideal.

Noah Webster
and
American Language

IF JEFFERSON largely created a life in architecture, as Peale did in portraiture, Noah Webster lived in his words. Like theirs, his role was critical in the rise of a national spirit during the federal era. Born in Hartford, Connecticut, in 1758, he studied at Yale during the Revolution in the same class as the poet Joel Barlow. The class instruction of the day—study of ancient languages, the Bible, oratory, and disputation—proved important formative elements in Webster's later passion for American words. Of comparable impact was his study of law, after college, with Oliver Ellsworth (a future Chief Justice of the United States); his teaching school in the late 1770s; and his publishing and writing for a magazine in the 1780s. As Webster wrote to George Washington in 1785, "I wish to enjoy life, but books and business will ever be my principal pleasure. I must write."[64]

Partly out of his teaching experience and partly out of his emerging belief that the fortunes of education and government were intertwined, Webster began work on improving English textbooks and compiling American spellings for national use. Paralleling the ideas being concurrently promoted by Washington, Jefferson, and Benjamin Rush, these efforts sought a widespread, practical application. For Webster the first major result was the publication in 1783 of his *Elementary Spelling Book*, Part I of the three-part *Grammatical Institute of the English Language*. On the one hand, he sought to bring order, clarity, and consistency to word use, and on another to nationalize language by basing it on American reality and needs. Toward the end of his life he asserted, "The spelling-book does more to form the language of a nation than all other books."[65]

To promote this nationalist sensibility in education, Webster argued that students should be educated in America, their teachers should be citizens, and the students should complete their learning by travel throughout the country, indeed, "twelve or eighteen months in examining the local situation of the different states; the rivers, soil, the population, the improvements and the commercial advantages of the whole." Equally important was the priority of a native tongue over dead languages: "Every man should be able to speak and write his native tongue with correctness."[66] Webster's stress was as much on accuracy as on patriotism, and his first spelling book offered both as one, a declaration of cultural independence no less far reaching than its political counterpart. "The author wishes to promote the honour and prosperity of the confederated republics of America and cheerfully throws his mite into the common treasure of patriotic exertion. . . . This country must in some future time be as distinguished by the superiority of her literary improvements as she is already by the liberality of her civil and ecclesiastical constitutions." His most pithy and often quoted remark was that "America must be as independent in *literature* as she is in *politics*, as famous for *arts* as for *arms*."[67] Like Crèvecoeur, Webster at the same moment was laying the foundation for the American tradition, and their call for a national speech would continue in later incarnations. Certainly one of the most famous was Walt Whitman's *Leaves of Grass* (1855), whose introduction declared, "The United States themselves are essentially the greatest poem."[68]

Along with Jefferson and Peale, Webster shared an interest in a national language and education. For all of them orderly classification was mere necessity. Throughout his life Jefferson demonstrated his love of books and well-crafted language, once admitting, "I cannot live without books," and his library both as a room and as a collection of volumes was central to his life's work.[69] In 1798 he wrote an "Essay on the Anglo-Saxon Language," calling for the simplified spelling and writing of words, more phonetic pronunciation, and literary composition based on natural rhythms and harmonies. This would make American language at once more practical and uniform, and therefore more democratic and national. He later wrote to John Waldo about reforming grammar and to an English correspondent about clarifying national spelling and pronunciation. The teaching of modern languages received special attention in his design for the curriculum proposed for the University of Virginia in 1818.[70]

For his part, Peale in 1800 delivered his "Discourse Introductory to a Course of Lectures on the Science of Nature," in which he might as well have spoken for Webster in claiming that "education is essential for obtaining happiness." Peale's classification of scientific specimens was analogous to the ordering of language, and he joined the two with his own literary metaphor: "It is by this kind of order, we may with ease and pleasure, acquire knowledge from the great book of nature."[71] Only a few years earlier, Webster had exhorted his countrymen, "Americans . . . you have now an interest of your own to augment and defend: You have an empire to raise and support by your exertions, and a national character to establish and extend by your wisdom and virtues." He

ardently felt the country should have universal education and publically supported schools. As he said, "every child in America should be acquainted with
his own country," and the nation requires "a system of education that should
embrace every part of the community."[72] In turn, the foundation of democratic
education ought to be a national language.

Evolution of the Dictionary

Having published Part I of his *Grammatical Institute* in 1783, Webster began
actively adding to it over succeeding years, with Part II devoted to grammar
appearing in 1784 and Part III, *An American Selection of Lessons in Reading and
Speaking*, the year after. Significantly, he nationalized the whole project, as it
were, by renaming it in 1788 *The American Spelling Book*, and, as if with the constitutional debates that same year in mind, specifically referred to "the elements
of a *federal* language."[73] All the sections underwent constant revisions, and new
editions were published from the mid-eighties well into the new century. Like
Monticello or a Peale group portrait, the project was one of organic and living
growth, updated according to practical need and discovery of new material. For
example, Part III became the *New England Primer* in 1789 and in 1801 was
"improved and adapted to the use of schools."[74]

Other themes within Webster's publications strike a familiar note. One
important purpose of his grammars was to remove "the improprieties, introduced by settlers from various parts of Europe; to reform the abuses & corrup-
tions. . . ." In 1805 he rather startled an English publisher to whom he had
submitted his manuscript for *A Philosophical and Practical Grammar of the English
Language*, in which he announced his intention to correct "some of the More
Prominent Errors of the English Grammars" and the many British phrases
"which are not brought within the rules."[75] A second guiding principle was
practicality, such as learning the elements of language one step at a time, by
studying first one and then two letters, next whole words alone, followed by
those of similar formation or sound. In the 1795 edition of the *Grammatical
Institute* Webster arranged like-sounding words across the page "to make children attentive to the different ways of expressing the same sound." He append-
ed pronunciations to the letters of the alphabet and diagrammed the natural
division of syllables. By 1798 he was stressing "*the spoken language*, which is the
only true foundation of grammar."[76]

A third distinguishing aspect of these volumes was their nationalism.
Gradually, between the earlier editions of the 1780s and the later variants of the
1820s, the religious content markedly declined, and Webster's readings concentrated on moral or patriotic aphorisms relating to the founding fathers and revolutionary history. With the cult of the first president at its peak in 1787,

Webster advised: "Begin with the Infant in his cradle; let the first word he lisps be Washington." The subtitle of that year's *Grammatical Institute* stated that it was "Calculated to Improve the Minds and Refine the Taste of Youth and Also to Instruct Them in Geography, History, and Politics of the United States." To this end, Webster replaced British with American narratives, and recommended for study the examples of revolutionary oratory, believing that "a love of our country and an acquaintance with its true state are indispensable and should be acquired early in life."[77]

Once the *Grammatical Institute* was in wide circulation, Webster began working on a dictionary. Others following his example also undertook compilations in the late 1790s: one was Sam Johnson, Jr., son of the first president of Columbia University and author of *A School Dictionary*. Webster's own *Compendious Dictionary* appeared a few years later and included a chronology of major events in American history. By now he had refined the principal functions of his efforts: to give spellings, indicate pronunciations, define words, provide etymologies, and include appropriate illustrations. Jefferson found his New England colleague too pedagogical but admitted, "the new circumstances under which we are placed, call for new words, new phrases, and for the transfer of old words to new objects. An American dialect will therefore be formed."[78] And indeed, in their time such new words as congressional, departmental, and presidential did enter democratic discourse. Webster like Franklin was also instrumental in the passage of the country's first state and federal copyright laws. The very notion of copyright went to the heart of protecting the uniqueness of language and individual expression.

Webster further shared with Franklin the values of self-reliance and pursuing opportunity, of adaptability and flexibility, of hard work and human improvement. In addition, Webster wrote out of his own life in several forms, not with the cleverness and singularity of Franklin's *Autobiography*, but with a similar commitment to writing as a means of shaping one's identity and goals. Webster's personal reflections appeared respectively in his letters, an autobiographical memoir he wrote at the end of his life (1832), much like Jefferson, and his diary, which underwent a substantial change in 1798. On April first that year he recorded: "Removed with my family to New Haven. My attachment to the State of Connecticut, my acquaintances, my habits, which are literary & do not correspond with the bustle of commerce & the taste of people perpetually inquiring for news & making bargains . . . are among my motives for this change of Residence."[79] For the next decade he largely devoted himself to his personal writing, and the diary shifts from factual one-line notations to fuller, more reflective narrative paragraphs, often centered around detailed descriptions of the changing climate, daily weather, and the growth of plants or crops.

Thus, just around the turn of the century Webster made a major mark in the beginnings of dictionary publishing in America, in articulating the role of national education as the catalyst for making the country's future different from its colonial past, and in causing language to be responsive to current needs. As one biographer summarized, he "taught the masses to spell and read."[80] Beyond the practical, however, he stimulated a generation and more of colleagues who took up the cause of promoting "the diffusion of knowledge." One of the more prominent figures to emerge was Samuel Harrison Smith, who was born during the Revolution. Though twelve years Webster's junior, Smith was concurrently writing his own "Remarks on Education," which he published in 1798, and thus joined the common cause: "An enlightened nation is always most tenacious of its rights." In outlining his system to give American youth "the advantages of a liberal and just education," Smith enumerated its virtues in three parts, for the individual citizen, for the United States, and for the world. As to the first, "the citizen, enlightened, will be a free man in its truest sense." For the second part, "viewing the efforts of such a system on the United States, the first results would be the giving perpetuity to those political principles so closely connected with the present happiness." And in the third, "more important, still, will be the example of the most powerful nation on earth, if that example exhibit dignity, humility, and intelligence."[81]

In reviewing this industrious and optimistic age of active thinkers and thoughtful doers, we are constantly aware of their abiding devotion to America's youth, both as a country and as a people. If we could satisfactorily conclude with an apposite credo for them, it might be their belief in the present and hope for the future.

PART TWO

Circa 1850:
Apex
and
Apogee

Paradoxes of Tension and Calm

BY THE MIDDLE of the nineteenth century America's future was well under way. It was at once promising and problematic, optimistic and uncertain, self-confident and contentious, fulfilling yet incomplete. This paradox of fruition and frustration well serves the dramatic, complex, and expressive years surrounding the mid-century mark. Inextricably woven together were the equally powerful forces of slavery, union, and frontier. Fueled by the ideology of Manifest Destiny and the waves of western migrations, the country experienced during the 1840s its greatest growth in territory since the Louisiana Purchase.[1] Symbolizing the psychological and physical lure of the West was the 1848 discovery of gold in California and the subsequent gold rush. Meanwhile, the troublesome Wilmot Proviso of 1846, proposed but never fully passed by both houses of Congress, sought to keep slavery out of any territories acquired from Mexico. With Texas admitted to statehood at the end of 1845, tensions with Mexico were inflamed and led to war with that country the next year. The conflict was settled in 1848, but the political arguments over new free and slave states roiled on, reaching their next threshold with the fateful Compromise of 1850, including its provocative Fugitive Slave Act. For a brief interim the competing forces suppressed sectional concerns, but they flared up once again in the Kansas-Nebraska Act of 1854, which overturned the antislavery provisions of the original 1820 Missouri Compromise agreed to in the last years of Jefferson's life. Now legislation permitted the creation of two new territories formerly in Mexican hands, one as a potential slave state, and the violent border warfare that ensued in the region gave rise to the apt phrase of "Bleeding Kansas."[2] In attempting to balance existing free and slave states, with new territories in each category and with others allowed to make local decisions, the government and the country as a whole became only more fractious.

Thus, as political metaphor, the term *compromise* came to embody perfectly the profound ironies and contradictions at the heart of this period. On one level, an implied sense of agreement between differing forces had provided the country until now with a certain settled stability; on another, the compromise crafted at mid-century led to its own undoing and to that of its predecessors. Part of the charged energy of the day was due to a surface equilibrium that contained within a powerful volatility. The collective dreams of order, balance, and wholeness were to hold for a golden moment of extraordinary creativity in American life before fragmenting into disarray by the 1860s. In one of the most succinct overviews of events during the decade of the fifties, James McPherson reminds us that the period had clear brackets of violence on either side: the Mexican-American War at the end of the forties and the Civil War at the beginning of the sixties, with the crisis largely suspended and smouldering in between.[3] For all the uncertainty and periodic outbursts of violence, this was a time of unprecedented economic and technological progress, as well as cultural ambition and achievement.

Capturing Space and Time

We may seek related metaphors, geographical and chronological, respectively, in the compass and the clock. The former is an apposite image of the country's accelerated growth in territory and population. The major crossing axes of all four quadrants were of equal significance for the national destiny. In the direction of east to west, of course, was the addition of new states and territories, on an average of three or more each decade, along with a shift of the center of population inexorably pushing toward the Midwest and the geographic heart of the country. From emigrants on foot and horseback coming through the Cumberland Gap, to pioneers driving prairie "schooners" across the Plains, to laborers building the transcontinental railroads for the iron "horse," people and commerce constituted strong moving energies along the country's central latitudes. Other signs of a parallel movement in symbolic power were the birth states of the nation's presidents, which before mid-century had been Virginia and elsewhere along the East Coast, but now yielded to Kentucky, Tennessee, Ohio, and Illinois.

At the same time, an equal contrasting force of travel and transportation existed in the crossing north-south axis of the Mississippi River, the country's geographical spine at the junction of east and west. In both directions flatboat and steamer traffic plied these strategic waters. But more than a broad current supporting trade and settlement, the great river was also the potent imaginative landscape for two of America's greatest novels addressing slavery and issues of black-white relationships. Written just after the mid-century mark, Harriet

Figure 19. Asher B. Durand, *Progress*, 1853. Oil on canvas, 48 x 71$^{15}/_{16}$ in. The Warner Collection of Gulf States Paper Corporation, Tuscaloosa, Alabama

Beecher Stowe's *Uncle Tom's Cabin* calls attention to the northward flow of fugitive slaves and the aspirations for black freedom in the northern free states and Canada. Its memorable later counterpart, *The Adventures of Huckleberry Finn* (1884) by Stowe's Hartford neighbor Mark Twain, is a narrative that by contrast unfolds going down river.

Like the compass, the clock (well before digitized time) was a full circle in conception and form. We think of the twenty-four-hour day as a complete cycle, as well as its two halves, day and night, as rounding the clock face to its apogee at number twelve. This image also serves as a way of thinking about the moment of 1850. For at this time America very much saw itself in the fullness of the noon hour, in its sense of expansiveness and self-confidence and in the actualities of flourishing prosperity and productivity. It is no accident that pervasive in many American landscape paintings of these years was the radiant and suffusive glow of midday light. Like Thomas Cole's central allegorical image of *Consummation* in the Course of Empire series (New-York Historical Society), created several years earlier, the fortunes of the country now seemed to stand at high noon. Some of the most indelible and canonical landscape views painted at mid-century exude a stillness, clarity, and intensity of light that seem to reflect a spiritual as much as meteorological condition. Consider such familiar examples as William Sidney Mount's *Eel Spearing at Setauket* (1845; fig. 30), George Caleb Bingham's *Jolly Flatboatmen* (1846; fig. 40), Fitz Hugh Lane's *Entrance of*

Somes Sound (1851; fig. 36), Asher B. Durand's *Progress* (1853; fig. 19), and George Inness's *Lackawanna Valley* (1855; fig. 20).

But the fullness of time cannot be frozen, and the pinnacle of the noon hour has yet to yield to time's necessary passage; thus, both aspects of our clock imagery have bearing on the 1850 mark. And a second look at these period landscapes reminds us that within the poised balances of individuals and their surroundings, of black and white Americans, and of nature and technology, there are the perhaps still unconscious discordances and contests between these forces soon to erupt. We know that a decade later they did, and American painters at least signaled those disruptions with their extensive concern in the early 1860s for subjects of violent sunsets, thunderstorms, and shipwrecks.

But for a few years around mid-century itself America's cultural achievements and sense of self reached a special pinnacle worthy of the hour. As McPherson has summarized, the period witnessed important new developments in the technologies of mass production, communication, and transportation. Balloon-frame construction in architecture revolutionized building practices, especially on the frontier. Now the tensions of interlocking wood members replaced a reliance on post-and-beam construction and thus lightened the whole physical mass, increasing speed and efficiency in construction itself. A comparable transformation in manufacturing also took place with the pro-

Figure 20. George Inness: *Lackawanna Valley*, 1855. Oil on canvas, 33⅞ x 50³⁄₁₆ in. National Gallery of Art, Washington, D.C., Gift of Mrs. Huttleston Rogers, 1945

Figure 21. Fitz Hugh Lane, *Yacht "America,"* 1851. Oil on canvas, 24½ x 38¼ in. Peabody Essex Museum, Salem, Massachusetts

Figure 22. Currier & Ives, *Clipper Ship "Flying Cloud,"* 1852. Lithograph. Shelburne Museum, Shelburne, Vermont

duction of interchangeable parts for machinery, tools, and the like, notably exploited a decade earlier by Samuel Colt in Hartford, Connecticut, in the firearms industry and his famous revolver.

Meanwhile, the invention of the telegraph by Samuel F. B. Morse in 1839, along with rapid advances in production of newspapers, now dramatically accelerated the accessibility and proliferation of information throughout urban and rural areas alike. Finally, the pace and nature of transportation were also undergoing radical change during the decade of the 1850s, as the steam engine greatly increased its presence and role on both land and sea. The active construction of rail lines and the expansion of railroad companies across the Midwest and reaching for the Far West had obvious direct effects on the movement of goods as well as people. On both the major inland river ways and the waters of the East Coast steamboats now appeared in the same landscapes with canoes, rowboats, and sailing craft, most memorably captured in the paintings of the time by George Caleb Bingham on the Missouri and Mississippi Rivers and by Fitz Hugh Lane in Boston Harbor. Like their landbound counterparts, for example, Durand's *Progress* (fig. 19), Inness's *Lackawanna Valley* (fig. 20), and Thomas P. Rossiter's *Opening of the Wilderness* (1858; Museum of Fine Arts, Boston), these images depicted the steam engine in glorious and productive harmony with nature. Just for this brief period of the later 1840s and 1850s were civilization and wilderness, the forces of steam and sail, in mutual balance. Significantly, the energies expressed in Inness's Pennsylvania landscape were the white puffs of steam rising from the engine moving into center foreground, the roundhouse, and mills behind, all blending smoothly with the silvery haze suffusing the atmosphere above (and diverting our attention, with the boy's, from the field of tree stumps cut down before us). By the next decade the steam engine was an agent of warfare in its first use by the ironclads during the Civil War, and its presence more frequently appeared in plumes of black smoke, as in their stark intrusion into the pristine white Arctic landscapes of William Bradford.

While the age of steam was in its ascendancy, America's achievements with sailing vessels were also triumphant at this time. Participating in its first international competition off the coast of England, an American yacht won in 1851 the sailing race whose cup would thereafter carry the country's name and remain in American hands continuously for another century and a quarter (fig. 21). A similar symbol of the nation's dominant presence on the world's oceans was its production of the largest and swiftest sailing vessels of the age, the great and graceful clipper ships, epitomized in Donald McKay's *Flying Cloud*, designed in 1851, and holder of the record eighty-nine-day sail from New York to San Francisco in 1854. (This voyage's time would also stand unmatched until modern times, beaten finally by a trimaran in 1989.[4]) Central to the clipper's

Figure 23. Mathew Brady, *Thomas Cole,* 1846. Daguerreotype. National Portrait Gallery, Smithsonian Institution, Washington, D.C., Gift of Edith Cole Silberstein

appeal was its supreme elegance of conception combined with comparable practicality. The *Flying Cloud* and her sister ships from McKay's Boston yards, such as the *Great Republic* and *Sovereign of the Seas,* were able to carry cargo faster than previous vessels of such size and repeatedly raced from the Atlantic to Pacific around South America and back throughout the 1850s. Their naval architecture, finely coordinating the physics of mass and volume with wind and water, were marvels of design, and made widely popular images disseminated in the color lithographs of Currier and Ives after mid-century (fig. 22).

Another development that came to be central to the American vision was the camera, partly because it too was a combination of the technological and scientific on the one hand and the aesthetic on the other. It served both practical needs and artistic aspirations. The first phase of the new medium came with the daguerreotype, invented in France in 1839 by Louis Daguerre, whom

Samuel F. B. Morse visited that same year. Morse returned to the United States with an outline of Daguerre's procedures and set up one of the first operations of the new technique. Within a decade it had taken hold and become more popular in America than anywhere else in the world. The process involved sensitizing a silver-plated sheet of copper with iodine vapor. Placed in a camera obscura, the plate was exposed to light, and the image before it was gradually revealed by contact with heated mercury vapor.

By the 1850s the medium was at the height of production and appeal. Because of the lengthy exposure time required, its principal subjects were stiffly posed portraits and fixed architectural landscapes. Among the most famous and accomplished studios flourishing at mid-century were those of Mathew Brady in New York and Albert Sands Southworth and Josiah Hawes in Boston. Brady went to New York in 1839 to meet Morse and to learn about the new process. Within five years he had perfected the technique and successfully opened his Daguerrean Miniature Gallery of Broadway and Fulton Street in lower Manhattan. Unsurpassed as a manager and self-promoter, Brady traveled to Washington, D.C., in 1849 to capture likenesses of prominent politicians such as Henry Clay, Zachary Taylor, Daniel Webster, and John C. Calhoun, whose images would be lithographed in an ambitious book, *The Gallery of Illustrious Americans,* published the following year. But Brady's sitters equally included the most prominent artistic and cultural figures of the day, among them Thomas Cole (1846; fig. 23), Horace Greeley (1851), Henry James Sr. and Jr. (1854), and later the sculptor Harriet Hosmer (1857) and Walt Whitman (1867). Brady's figures tend to sit in simple, relaxed poses, slightly at an angle with their eyes turned toward the camera in a confident but comfortable manner. He lit their faces clearly, with a range of shadow across the rest of the body (in contrast to the strong Rembrandtesque lighting associated with his Boston counterparts Southworth and Hawes) and an often dark, enveloping space behind. Almost paradoxically, Brady captured at once the precise facts of surface details and a sharp sense of individual personality.

Southworth and Hawes also posed their figures carefully; their attention to detail and tonalities resulted in a comparable technical and expressive power. Surely one reason why the daguerreotype had such wide acceptance in America, even after the more enduring process of negative and positive had been invented and become available, was its unsurpassed clarity of image. This aspect served the wish to record city and landscape views. Even more important, each plate was unique and must have perfectly suited one's psychological sense of individuality, let alone the more general populist notions of a democratic society. Everyone could afford a daguerrean image, the famous and anonymous alike, and estimates suggest that up to twenty million pictures were taken during the two decades leading up to the Civil War. Southworth and Hawes

Figure 24. Albert Sands Southworth and Josiah Hawes, *McKay's Shipyard, East Boston*, 1855. Daguerreotype. Courtesy, Museum of Fine Arts, Boston. Gift of Richard Parker in memory of Herman Parker

also captured some of the strongest views of the day in their pictorial records of the Boston streets and waterfront, then alive with its shipbuilding industry.

Form and Function

One individual who memorably celebrated this conjunction of the aesthetic and the practical in the clipper ship was the so-called Yankee stonecutter, Horatio Greenough. It was he—observing the leanness of design in which all parts served their purpose and worked as an organic whole, with nothing extraneous or ornamental, no unnecessary sail or rigging line apparent—who first articulated the concept of form following function that would be so centrally embraced in the American tradition from Louis Sullivan to Frank Lloyd Wright. Born in Boston, Greenough moved from his native Boston to Florence in 1825 at the age of twenty to pursue his career as a neoclassical carver. He was one of the first recipients of a major artistic commission from the United States government in 1832, when Congress authorized him to execute a full-scale marble statue of George Washington for the Capitol (too heavy for the floor, it was later moved to the Smithsonian Institution), which he worked on for the remainder of the decade. A key figure in the flourishing of Greek-revival sculpture just before mid-century, Greenough also turned to formulating his theories of design in a revealing series of essays published at the end of his short life as *Travels,*

Observations, and Experiences of a Yankee Stonecutter.[5] Appearing in 1852, as the grandest of the clippers were setting sail from Boston harbor, his essays captured the exuberant spirit of native ingenuity and lofty but concrete aspirations.

In one of his most famous assertions, regarding the tensile elegance shared by a trotting horse and a sailing vessel, Greenough wrote: "The men who have reduced locomotion to its simplest elements, in the trotting wagon and the yacht *America*, are nearer to Athens at this moment than they who would bend the Greek temple to every use. I contend for Greek principles, not Greek things. If a flat sail goes nearest wind, a bellying sail, though picturesque, must be given up. The slender harness and tall gaunt wheels are not only effective, they are beautiful—for they respect the beauty of a horse, and do not uselessly task him."[6]

This passage contains a number of the artist's essential beliefs, noteworthy among them the necessity of integrated design for any structure. Elsewhere, he returned to American shipbuilding as a model of economy, efficiency, and graceful form: "Observe a ship at sea! Mark the majestic form of her hull as she rushes through the water. . . . Behold an organization second only to that of an animal. . . . What academy of design, what research of connoisseurship, what imitation of the Greeks produced this marvel of construction?" He then speculated, "Could we carry into our civil architecture the responsibilities that weigh upon our shipbuilding, we should ere long have edifices as superior to the Parthenon. . . ."[7]

Greenough's themes center around such repeated nouns as organization, integration, simplicity, and function. In commenting on the teaching of art, he desired "to see working normal schools of structure and ornament, organized simply but effectively," and elsewhere he summarized, "organization is the primal law of structure." He saw the "principle of structure . . . plainly inculcated in the works of the Creator" and viewed "the human frame, the most beautiful organization on earth."[8] Not only the human figure was an exemplum for Greenough; he also argued more broadly: "Let us consult nature, and in the assurance that she will disclose a mine richer than was ever dreamed of by the Greeks." Thus, "as the first step in our search after the great principle of construction, we [should] observe the skeletons and skins of animals," which might reveal an organic wholeness like that of the best-designed clipper ship.[9]

Part of this outlook was the concentration on essentials, in which ornamentation should be subordinate to the whole and carry relevant expressive meaning. Quite simply, Greenough called for "the subordination of details to masses, and of masses to the whole," and this meant that "sculpture, when it adorns buildings, is subordinate to them." He concluded: "The aim of the artist, therefore, should be first to seek the essential; when the essential hath been found, then, if ever, will be the time to commence embellishment. I will venture to predict that the essential, when found, will be complete. I will venture to predict that completeness will instantly throw off all that is not itself. . . ." In another paragraph Greenough's voice shifts marvelously from practical declaration to poignant eloquence: "The redundant must be pared down, the superfluous dropped, the necessary itself reduced to its simplest expression, and then we shall find, whatever the organization may be, that beauty was waiting for us. . . ."[10]

Beauty was waiting, finally, because it was a natural expression of pure function. "The connection and order of parts, juxtaposed for convenience, cannot fail to speak of their relation and uses." Whether in seeing the trotter or the driver, the sailing vessel or its driving hand, Greenough distilled his thoughts in sentences as lean and compact as the forms he celebrated: "I define Beauty as the promise of Function; Action as the presence of Function; Character as the record of Function."[11] No wonder that in both thought and action he was at the center of Greek-revival expression in mid-century America. On the one hand, his carving of marble figures at once alluded to the perfection of ancient forms and to the organic unities of nature; on the other, his ideas about "inner distribution" and the "connection and order of parts" surely also captures the organizing spirit of paintings such as those by George Caleb Bingham and Fitz Hugh Lane. These are pictures with all the solidity of structure, harmony, and balancing of integrated components and the grandeur of expression we associate with neoclassical idealism. Their reductive geometries and equipoise of plane and line embody not only some of the basic elements of luminist painting but also some of the larger currents of a proud national self-assurance at the time.

The pure Greek-revival style flourished in architecture and design at this time, but it also dominated America's first substantial school of sculptors, significantly many of them women, who successfully pursued expatriate careers in Florence and Rome. A number of the best-known works from this group were appropriately associated with native themes, projects, or monuments. In addition to his *Washington*, Greenough himself also executed a major figural composition, *The Rescue* (fig. 25), for a pedestal adjacent to the east front door to the Capitol Building in Washington. His colleague Thomas Crawford meanwhile was at work carving an ensemble of figures entitled *Progress of American Civilization* (1850–56) for one of the central Capitol pediments. In turn, having completed his first marble of *The Greek Slave* in 1843, Hiram Powers executed several additional versions over the next decade, the most famous of which gained its celebrity at London's Crystal Palace exhibition in 1851 and at its successor in New York two years later. Although inspired by classical models, the figure ultimately exudes a contemporary romanticism concerned with such immediate issues as slavery at home and the recent Greek War of Independence abroad. But it also raises subtle matters of nudity, sexuality, and morality in Victorian eyes, evident in Greenough's defense of the unclothed female figure as

Figure 25. Horatio Greenough, *The Rescue*, 1838–51. United States Capitol, Washington, D.C.

"one too deeply concerned to be aware of her nakedness. . . . It is not her person but her spirit that stands exposed." A contemporary minister sermonized: "The *Greek Slave* is clothed all over with sentiment, sheltered, protected by it from every profane eye."[12]

In the simplified volumes of these figures, their balanced verticals rising from stable platforms, and the often pyramidal massings of group compositions, we again can find analogous structures in the obelisk and in the architectural temple-form portico, as well as in Bingham's assembled flatboatmen and Lane's

Figure 26. Severin Roesen,
*Flower Still-Life with Bird's
Nest*, 1853. Oil on canvas,
40 x 32 in. Collection
JoAnn and Julian Ganz, Jr.

harbor-bound vessels. Indeed, similar arrangements also recur in the foremost
still-life subjects of these years, another artistic category that gained one of its
heights of development in the nineteenth century. Massed fruits or flowers in
solid volumes dominated sturdy tabletops in a profusion of colors and rich, sensuous textures. Representing corners of the garden, kitchen, or dining room,
these overflowing vases of blossoms and baskets of fruit exuded a larger belief
in the plenitude and well-being of American nature.

  The two most representative and accomplished still-life painters in this
period were John F. Francis and Severin Roesen, who were both closely associated with the Philadelphia tradition of tabletop still lifes that extended back to
the Peale family at the beginning of the nineteenth century. Francis was actually born there in 1808 and after some early travel exhibited regularly at the
Pennsylvania Academy from the 1840s on. Roesen, who was several years
younger, moved from his native Germany to New York in 1848. For the next few
years he showed his still lifes, frequently titled *Nature's Bounty*, at the American
Art-Union in New York and soon after at the Academy in Philadelphia (fig. 26).
In differing degrees both painters drew on direct or indirect knowledge of sev-

enteenth-century Dutch and German examples, whose crisp realism and exu-
berance well suited American materialist and mercantile sensibilities. This age
of expansionist impulses and spreading prosperity found appropriate expression
in the ripe produce of field and garden.

Much like Walt Whitman's contemporary language of all-embracing
and celebratory enumeration of place names and typologies, Roesen and Francis
depicted flowers and fruits in full profusion. In fact, the former's dense massings
of blossoms and petals bring together a diverse variety of flowers, all in full
bloom at once, despite their different growth cycles in the season. For his part,
Francis appropriately indulged in compositions of rich cheeses, cakes, and
desserts, amply piled up in compotes and dishes; another favorite type consisted of fully ripe apples along with chestnuts spilling out of baskets overturned
toward the viewer, often accompanied by sturdy jugs and glasses filled with
cider (fig. 27). Both the amplitude and the lack of restraint in these images make
a striking contrast with the refined elegance and wiry delicacy of still lifes in the
federal period half a century earlier,[13] in which we generally find a reliance on
thin planarities and exquisite balances. The containers tend to be graceful
blown-glass decanters and oriental export porcelains, fragile yet costly, and rested in quiet isolation on highly polished wood surfaces supporting well-crafted
tea or side tables. The later, mid-century pieces are significantly larger and seem
more aggressive in scale, as the ample volumes of fruits no longer remain with-

Figure 27. John F. Francis, *Still Life: Yellow Apples and Chestnuts Spilling from a Basket*, 1856. Oil on canvas, 25 x 30 in. Collection JoAnn and Julian Ganz, Jr.

in their containers. Now heavier, native-cut glass, common market baskets, and rougher woven cloths allude to a more popular middle-class world.

The essential elements of these still lifes suggest provocative affinities with a number of contemporaneous artistic expressions. We have already noted that the prevalence of such geometries as the sphere and pyramid creates a structure of forms akin to Bingham's genre subjects. But we may also consider these reductive shapes, especially the circle, in relation to Thoreau's meditations on nature's essentials in *Walden* and particularly the enclosing circumference of the pond, making it a symbolic eye reflecting the sky above. In content, the bursting abundance of flowers and fruits appears to have its counterpart in Walt Whitman's *Leaves of Grass,* (1855), in which "Sprouts take and accumulate. . . . stand by the curb prolific and vital / Landscapes projected masculine full-sized and golden."[14] Repetitions of words, sounds, or phrases breathlessly propel the verse onward, as Whitman gathers his diverse inventories of Indian names and nicknames, animals and birds, minerals and flowers, professions and callings, continents and countries, states and cities—in sum, "The melodious character of the earth!"[15] A parallel citation of typologies appears in Herman Melville's *Moby-Dick* (1851), where Chapter 32, "Cetology," enumerates the many species of whales, in a celebration of language as much as of natural science.

Minority Voices and Views

A comparable largeness of vision is evident in many of the arts in mid-century America, a moment that also saw the emergence of important women and black artists, who added their own fresh accomplishments to the period's ferment of creativity. A sign of the times was the first Women's Rights Convention, held in Seneca Falls, New York, in 1848, as part of the movement for equal rights then led by Lucretia Mott and Elizabeth Cady Stanton. During the decade or so afterward, women's literary voices began to declare their independence with such figures as Louisa May Alcott and Lydia Signourney and, by the end of the 1850s, the first highly original poetic work of Emily Dickinson. These developments have led one modern historian to call them a "rich literary movement . . . when American women's culture came of age," constituting the "American Women's Renaissance."[16] The most prominent and productive painter in this context was Lilly Martin Spencer, whose best-known genre works date from the decade of the fifties. In 1848 she moved from Cincinnati to New York and later lived in New Jersey, where she reared thirteen children. Not surprisingly, she made the mother's domestic sphere the primary subject of her art for about ten years, with pictures of young families at home and mothers preparing meals in the kitchen (fig. 28).[17] Prominent in these scenes are either glowing, plump

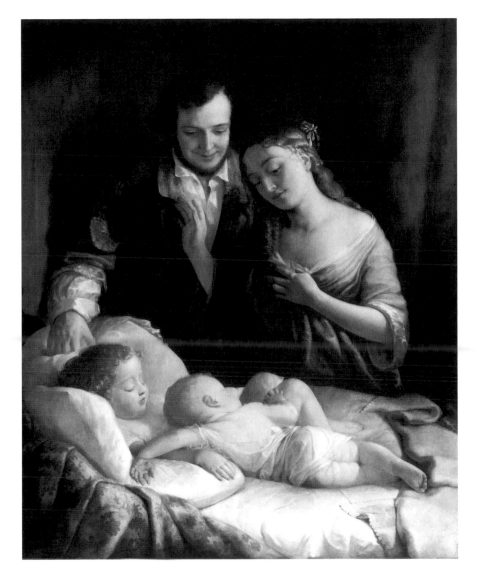

Figure 28. Lilly Martin Spencer, *Domestic Happiness*, 1849. Oil on canvas, 55½ x 45¼ in. The Detroit Institute of Arts, Bequest of Dr. and Mrs. James Cleland, Jr.

infants or piles of ripened fruits and vegetables, repeated assertions of nature's fertility in all spheres.

We can find a slightly different yet related attention to geometries in the foremost African-American artist of this generation, Robert Duncanson. Along with the daguerreotypist James Pressley Ball and sculptor Edmonia Lewis a little later, Duncanson brought black creativity into the center of American art, just as Harriet Beecher Stowe's *Uncle Tom's Cabin* was forcing attention to the most powerful social and moral issues of race in national life at mid-century. Born in New York State in 1821, Duncanson grew up in Canada and in 1841

Figure 29. Robert S. Duncanson, *Blue Hole, Little Miami River*, 1851. Oil on canvas, 29¼ x 42¼ in. Cincinnati Art Museum, Gift of Norbert Heerman and Arthur Helbig (see colorplate 6)

moved to Cincinnati, where his career came to maturity during the next two decades, a reminder again of the Midwest's growing claim on national attention in this period. Understandably impelled to exile himself from America during the Civil War, Duncanson produced what many propose as his finest pictures during the years before the outbreak of conflict, including the work generally cited as his masterpiece, *Blue Hole, Little Miami River* (1851; colorplate 6; fig. 29).[18] Like many landscapes of this period, it coalesces around stable geometries and balances: trees framing each side, the foreground figures echoed by the protruding tree stumps in the middle and again in the center distance, the mirroring of sky and water, and above all the unifying circle of the pool itself. Implied as well is the dual sense of reflection, as repeated imagery and as mental reverie. We may readily call to mind similarly distilled compositions from the later 1840s through the 1850s by such contemporaries as Thomas Cole, Fitz Hugh Lane, William Sidney Mount, John F. Kensett, Sanford Gifford, and Frederic Edwin Church.

Mount, for example, completed his classic early masterpiece, *Eel Spearing at Setauket* (fig. 30) in 1845, distinguished by its soberly balanced triangular design and carefully echoed forms. Commissioned by George Washington Strong, a New York lawyer, it was intended to commemorate the Long Island estate of Strong's father. We see the family house centered on the distant hillside and the property stretching across the middle background of the picture. The painting is all about reflection in its several senses. The subtitle, *Recollections of Early Days—"Fishing Along Shore,"* suggests a scene of nostalgia shared by both artist and patron recalling golden moments of early morning fishing in their youth. Further, there are the literal reflections of the boat in the foreground and on the shoreline beyond, which fill much of the canvas, and the dominant pair of figures is repeated in the forms of the second couple rowing in the exact center of the composition behind them. Not least, within all this ordered clarity and stillness, we are mindful of the powerful concentration of glance and pose held by the boy, dog, and black woman. We do not know Mount's political views on the charged racial issues of the time such as abolitionism, but part of the undeniable power of this work by a white artist is the almost heroic dignity he brings here to figures socially marginalized by age, race, and gender. In a period of increasing racial turmoil, Mount's remarkable image strives to suspend the tension in a vision of intense tranquility.

Another celebrated example of compositional clarity is Asher B.

Figure 30. William Sidney Mount, *Eel Spearing at Setauket*, 1845. Oil on canvas, 28½ x 36 in. New York State Historical Association, Cooperstown, New York

Figure 31. Asher B. Durand, *Kindred Spirits*, 1849. Oil on canvas, 44 x 66 in. New York Public Library

Durand's *Kindred Spirits* (fig. 31), the well-known memorial tribute occasioned by Cole's early death in 1848. Historians have noted its several fusions: especially of the real and the ideal, that is, the literal American landscape and nature's transcendent spirit, as well as the sister arts in the persons of Cole the painter and William Cullen Bryan the nature poet standing beside him, and the union of man with nature. Of particular interest is the central tunnel of light in the woods, an almost perfect circle, which suggests a metaphoric eye opening not just out to the physical distance but to the spirit beyond.[19] Thus we engage

simultaneously in the acts of seeing and of imagining. Along with Duncanson's *Blue Hole* and Thoreau's *Walden,* or Emerson's famous "transparent eyeball" even before them, these are places that invite voyages of thought and perception. David Lubin has made a case for the central bodies of water in many of Duncanson's early compositions standing as metaphoric barriers between foreground and distance, and thus as passages across which one longingly looks. Subliminally, he proposes, these are expressions of escapism for an alienated black artist during years of growing racial tension and ultimate conflict.[20] Certainly the mirrored surfaces and often circumscribed pools or lakes in the landscapes of Duncanson and his contemporaries do invoke meditation, or, in Bryan Wolf's words, "perceptual pilgrimage."[21] For most of them the serenity of spirit and harmony of design convey a sense of spacious optimism and possibility. To appreciate how much they belong to the early 1850s, we need only compare these bright circles of light to the opaque black pool and threatened calm dominating the center of Martin Johnson Heade's *Approaching Thunder Storm* (1859; fig. 32). Now on the threshold of war with itself, America was moving from daydream to nightmare.

For a relatively brief golden hour, however, her painters and writers stood together with visionary prospects before them. During those few years at the center of the century they enlarged and enriched the language of their arts to a degree rarely matched at any other time in American history.

Figure 32. Martin Johnson Heade, *Approaching Thunder Storm,* 1859. Oil on canvas, 28 x 44 in. The Metropolitan Museum of Art, New York, Gift of Erving Wolf Foundation and Mr. and Mrs. Erving Wolf, 1975 (1975.160)

The Painters' Illuminations: Lane, Bingham, and Church

UNTIL relatively recently, the special flowering of American painting in the middle years of the nineteenth century seldom received the concentration of critical attention and praise given to the extraordinary achievements of American literature at the same time. There are probably several reasons for this, among them the general primacy of literature over the visual arts for a long while in academic disciplines and, in addition, the traditional view of eigh-teenth- and early-nineteenth-century American art as largely derivative from Europe. Also, in the history of American art itself the figure of Thomas Cole has long dominated perceptions about national landscape painting. Considered the earliest major painter of this subject in America, he fundamentally shaped its conventions of both imagery and composition from the time of his first crucial sales in the mid-1820s to his death in 1848. Many of the principal artists who followed Cole in the third quarter of the century were his students or admirers, including Frederic Edwin Church, Sanford Gifford, and Jasper Cropsey. Accordingly, a good many accounts have seen this younger generation as one of continuities more than of variations. But historians have increasingly illuminat-ed the original and national character of American art around mid-century, and it is possible now to argue Cole's death as not just a point of transition, but as one of pivotal change.

By 1850 many of the artists born in the first quarter of the century either reached a turning point in their stylistic development or, coming to their maturity, now sought their own artistic vision in Cole's wake. Some, such as Asher B. Durand (b. 1796) and Fitz Hugh Lane (b. 1801), were near contempo-raries of Cole and were well-established painters by the time of his death. In New York and Boston, respectively, they began to change their landscape com-

positions subtly but decisively, generally away from Cole's dense and closed pictorial structures and his idealized narratives; instead, they gradually embraced more spacious designs, with an emphasis on distance rather than foreground and on radiant expanses of light and air, with poetic meditation replacing anecdotal detail and moralizing storytelling. Subjects full of action and movement now yielded to images of silence and stillness. Several factors doubtless contributed to these changes, among them the heightened consciousness of the physical sciences and the rising influence of John Ruskin's thinking and writings, both of which prompted a more naturalistic vision and precise rendering of a landscape's tangible, particular elements. Additionally, the contemplation of place by contemporary writers such as Thoreau surely also offered influential precedents for experiencing the expansive, transcendental qualities of nature.

Other artists, including George Caleb Bingham (b. 1811), John F. Kensett (b. 1816), and Martin Johnson Heade (b. 1819), represented a middle generation of painters who grew up familiar with the early conventions of genre and landscape painting and were ready to fashion their own special imagery around midcentury. First, in his boatmen pictures of the late 1840s Bingham created refined compositions of geometric harmonies and balances, while in the election series of the early fifties he visually distilled his essentially national subject matter. Both Kensett and Heade began their early landscapes in the manner of Cole's

Figure 33. Thomas Cole, *Catskill Creek*, 1845. Oil on canvas, 26 x 36 in. The New-York Historical Society

interior woodland views, but by the early fifties Kensett was turning to expansive horizontal designs for his vistas near Newport and Narragansett Bay.
Likewise, Heade by the end of that decade also embraced panoramic formats for
his familiar depictions of the marshes at Ipswich and Newburyport and the
beaches of Rhode Island. A third, slightly younger trio of painters, all born
around the quarter-century mark, were among Cole's closest followers: Cropsey
and Gifford (both b. 1823) and Church (b. 1826). Their early work understandably emulated the older master's formulas of lakes or streams framed by mountains, occasional architectural ruins seen at melancholy twilight, and allegorical
themes set in nature. In their mid-twenties at the time of Cole's death, each continued for a few years to pay homage to his style, with crosses or castles in their
landscapes. But increasingly after 1850 each moved away from overtly narrative
imagery and turbulent landscape compositions toward more poetic, light-filled
vistas in differing degrees associated with the luminist sensibility. A more sustained look at three of these figures—Lane, Bingham, and Church—will illustrate
the strength of this artistic transformation taking place, all the more interesting
given the different artists' ages, backgrounds, and images.

Fitz Hugh Lane

In Fitz Hugh Lane's work at mid-century we may identify three loose groupings
of subject and compositional type. The first group dates from the late 1840s and
represents his first mature efforts in painting after his training and work in
Boston as a lithographer earlier in the decade.[22] That graphic experience firmly
grounded his technique in two essential ways: the role of line and outline in
delineating forms and the understanding of mass and space in terms of tonal
modulation or contrast. Thereafter, Lane always relied on drawing and shading
in the conception and execution of his oil paintings, where color and light were
often later additions in the studio process.

Much like the paintings by his Hudson River School contemporaries
based in New York, Lane's initial oils from about 1847 to 1849 tend to be busy
in design as well as narrative activity. Usually carefully framed on either side by
trees or masts and focused on a centrally positioned form, such as a small
schooner or island, these works depict a range of figures and incidents dispersed
across the foreground. Although in most of these the air is calm and the light is
clear, people are engaged in the daily discourse of business, gesturing or moving
in a sequence of small actions on the shoreline stage before us. For example,
Gloucester Harbor (1847; fig. 34) gives us a view of the inner-harbor waterfront,
with Five Pound Island in the middle ground and Ten Pound Island in the distance behind it. The arms of the harbor stretch out on each side, punctuated by
houses, wharves, and sheds, and a rocky beach at low tide arcs gently across the

foreground. Along the beach several men are engaged in activities related to small-boat building: cutting, trimming, and splitting logs and tarring the bottom of a skiff. The results of such efforts are visible in the variety of rowboats and small schooners in the harbor. There is a similar juxtaposition in the stonework: at the lower left sits a massive boulder that forms a contrast with the pile of cut granite blocks in the right-hand corner, another local resource in a stage of preparation for the stone piers around the harbor.

Lane continued this type of descriptive pictorial narrative through the following year with related views of industry around Gloucester's inner harbor. On the beach of another picture titled *Gloucester Harbor* (1848; Virginia Museum of Fine Arts, Richmond), several individuals are engaged in different stages of cleaning, transporting, and selling fish, once more set in natural relationship to sailing vessels just offshore. In turn, occupying the foreground of *The Fort and Ten Pound Island, Gloucester* (1848; Newark Museum) is a wooden frame holding the curved beams of a ship's hull in the process of construction. Men nearby attend to the details of shipbuilding, long an important industry in this port, as reflected in the different-sized vessels poised across the middle and far distance. Concluding this series in 1849 was *Lanesville, The Mill* (private collection), where a lumber mill on a stream emptying into the Annisquam River north of Gloucester illustrates the various elements of this central enterprise in the area's livelihood.[23] Appropriately, Lane situates the mill building at the near

Figure 34. Fitz Hugh Lane, *Gloucester Harbor*, 1847. Oil on canvas, 25 x 35½ in. Cape Ann Historical Association, Gloucester, Massachusetts, Gift of Samuel H. Mansfield

Figure 35. Fitz Hugh Lane, *Twilight on the Kennebec*, 1849. Oil on canvas, 20 x 30 in. Private collection, courtesy Peabody Essex Museum, Salem, Massachusetts

center of his composition, at the crossing of two axes. On one, the placid dammed-up pond in the right foreground balances the open water of the river in the far left distance, while the other contrasts raw, dense nature with cultivated land, orderly stone fences, and images of transportation in the opposing corner. A railroad bridge only recently had brought steam transport across the Annisquam directly into the heart of Gloucester, and Lane here makes a point of noting the changes taking place in contemporary travel, as the eye in turn picks out the distant sailboat, horse and wagon, and arriving steam engine. Together, this sequence of paintings essentially consists of landscapes dominated by genre subject matter in their foregrounds. Shortly the content and style of his art were to change decisively.

The next major grouping of Lane's pictures dates largely from the early 1850s, after he had settled permanently in Gloucester in an imposing stone house he built on the waterfront and begun a series of summer excursions to the Maine coast.[24] Having achieved a new level of professional self-confidence and independence, he also demonstrated a new adventurousness in his observation and treatment of the northern New England coastline. One critical painting, *Twilight on the Kennebec* (1849; fig. 35), marks the turning point from his previous work. One of his first works to be sent to the National Academy in New York for exhibition, it was listed in the catalogue with a caption that read: "The western sky is still glowing in the rays of the setting sun. In the foreground is a vessel lying in the shadow. The river stretches across the picture."[25] Lane and his close friend, Joseph L. Stevens, Jr., had actually made the trip the previous summer to the Maine coast, staying with the Stevens family in Castine, but the vision of a summer sunset must have burned deeply in the artist's memory, for its intense colors of reds, pinks, orange, yellow, and lavender came to life on his canvas painted in his Gloucester studio the following winter, when he dated and sent it off to New York for exhibition. Like his *Lanesville, The Mill* of the same year, this painting also subtly depicted the intersection between sail and steam, as a beached schooner at low tide fills the left foreground, counterpointed by a distant steamboat plying its way upstream on the far-right horizon. But it was Lane's palette of hot cadmium colors, recently available to artists premixed in tubes, that was new and startling. A significant technical advance, this color range permitted a fresh, intense response to the dramatic northern twilights he experienced down east and provided both him and his colleague Frederic Edwin Church with an expanded pictorial vocabulary for their landscape paintings of the next few years. Indeed, their Maine sunset paintings were to define some of the most original images of the 1850s.

Lane returned to Maine with Stevens for the next three summers, venturing even farther to the east on these occasions. They chartered a small sailboat in Castine and, sometimes accompanied by a couple of friends, cruised across Penobscot Bay to the Mount Desert Island area. An 1850 canvas of *Bar Island and Mount Desert Mountains from Somes Settlement* (colorplate 7) bears a number of the stylistic hallmarks of Lane's recent Gloucester work: the palette is a similar mix of greens and blues, figural activity dominates the foreground, and the composition appears carefully balanced. Three small schooners line up along a flattened diagonal, leading the eye smoothly into the middle ground; behind them are Bar Island and two framing points of land to either side, and in the distance an echoing trio of shoulders of Sargent and Brown Mountains. Although the fishermen on the beach, two men (probably Stevens and Lane) rowing ashore, and the red long johns prominently drying on a forestay all call attention to the narrative content, there is a new spaciousness and light airiness to this picture not present in the preceding Gloucester scenes.

This shift of emphasis toward a more open design and brighter coloring culminates in 1852 with the glassy sun-flooded image of *Entrance of Somes Sound from Southwest Harbor* (fig. 36), often considered Lane's first classic luminist painting. Now a much broader expanse of near empty sky and mirror-still water has replaced his earlier fair-weather clouds and breeze-rippled surfaces. Two low mountain profiles occupy the two far sides of the composition, but they are cropped and do not interrupt the strongly horizontal organization of forms. Two conversing figures stand quietly off to the left, as most of the elements lead

our attention into the distance and even out of the scene to either side and upward to the serene blue sky. Lane still employs his favored device of echoes and balances throughout: the foreground rocks and mountain profile above, the red-shirted figures in foreground and middle ground, the contrasting verticals and horizontals of masts and sails, and most strikingly, the rhythmic sequence of mirrored reflections stretching across the entire middle distance of the scene. On one level the painting was certainly about the actualities of local commerce, with its hillsides cleared of timber and lumber being loaded aboard the large schooner, but on another level its pervasive harmonies and brilliant clarity also convey an optimistic, self-confident world at one with itself.

Perhaps Lane's best-known sequence of pictures illustrating his stylistic evolution from the 1840s to the mid-1850s is his Boston Harbor group.[26] Here, as in other subjects, he moved from a congestion in both design and content to even greater serenity in composition and mood. Characteristic of his late forties work was *The Britannia Entering Boston Harbor* (1848; Collection Mr. and Mrs. Roger A. Saunders), where the arrival of the ocean steamer is at the center of a celebrating crowd of ships and local observers in nearby rowboats. Filling the sky is a mix of white clouds and black smoke as well as colorful fluttering flags. The water surface is a vibrant pattern of small white caps adding to the overall visual animation of the scene. All of these aspects are transformed in his views

of the next few years: *Boston Harbor at Sunset* (1853; private collection) and *Boston Harbor* (1854; White House Collection) both move our attention to the distant shore, and the central focus is on the silhouetted dome of the Boston State House. A brilliant sunset dominates the skies of the former, while a soft, late-afternoon palette colors the other, as light now becomes a commanding theme for Lane. He pushes himself even further in two of his most radiant canvases, both also known as *Boston Harbor, Sunset* (colorplate 8 and Museum of Fine Arts, Boston) and probably dating to about 1855. Light and color radiate in a sequence of cadmiums to all corners of these canvases; appropriately, the most intense coloration fills a central corridor of space, with a myriad of grand vessels held in place to either side by the motionless air and water. The eye is aware of pure geometries in near (but not symmetrical) balances. We sense that the activities of this world pause in awe of nature's grander, transcendent powers. Even Lane's pigments and their application have changed, from his earlier impastos and textures to thin stains and transparencies, the latter as much metaphoric as literal. In both his understanding of landscape and his distillation of its forms Lane had, through these critical years, achieved not only a perfection of his own style, but also an original and vivid revelation of America in this transient moment of glory.

That transience is evident in a third grouping of his pictures from the

Figure 37. Fitz Hugh Lane, *Off Mount Desert Island*, 1856. Oil on canvas, 23³/₁₆ x 36⁷/₁₆ in. The Brooklyn Museum of Art, Museum Collection Fund (47.114)

mid-fifties, as the larger mood of the country as well began to intensify. For example, on the surface his Maine paintings continued their expression of tranquillity and spaciousness, but at the same time that a subtle abstraction and sense of detachment has begun to modify his observations. Derived from a drawing made on his visit in 1851, Lane's painting of *Blue Hill, Maine* (private collection) dates from a few years later, when he had clearly shifted his visual emphasis from foreground details and activities to the still landscape in the distance. What is notable about this oil is that, when compared to the actual view from his vantage point, the contours of the hill have been intentionally adjusted. Lane appears to have smoothed out the irregular profile of the left side of Blue Hill in order to have it more evenly balance its opposite shoulder and thus give the entire design a fuller serenity and sense of perfection. The soft and rounded curve of the hillside has the additional effect of inviting our eyes to sweep easily over and around Blue Hill into the vaporous ether beyond. In a slightly later work, *Off Mount Desert Island* (1856; fig. 37), for the first time we recognize the general area but no longer the specific site of his view. Although the rolling mountainsides of the island are familiar, Lane has generalized the setting and, with its greater intensity of pinks in the sunset, made it seem universalized and even lonely.

Clearly, his mood was evolving again in the middle of the decade, and his paintings of the later 1850s and early 1860s constitute a late style much more noted for their melancholy, anxiety, and feelings of loss. To be sure, Lane's late paintings are among his most admired and constitute some of his finest achievements in terms of conception and technical execution. But we may argue that he first shaped a purely personal style around 1850 and, moreover, one perfectly expressive of the self-assured, prosperous temperament of their time. A decade later, the nation was on the brink of self-destruction, and Lane himself experienced increasing ill health during his last years. Unsurprisingly, his images of the early 1860s include his first storm subject, beach scenes of vast emptiness, skies that seem pumped dry of moisture, twilights that seem to stress light draining away, tides at their lowest ebb, and vessels that are either wrecked, abandoned, or deteriorating like skeletons.[27] Frequently, his late style conveyed moods of austerity, tension, and distress. Powerful for their own day, they also starkly illustrated the changes in time and fortune from a decade earlier, when the fullness of tide and day had been both facts and metaphors.

George Caleb Bingham

In another region of the country the foremost genre painter of the day, George Caleb Bingham, was also producing his strongest work during a similarly concentrated period. The circumstances of his early life reflected the country's larg-

er population shifts, as the new western states and territories increasingly became the locus of commercial and political attention. Born in Virginia in 1811, Bingham migrated west with his family in 1818, a personal move he would later fuse with regional mythology in his image of *Daniel Boone Escorting Settlers* (1851–52; fig. 38). For the rest of his life, both he and posterity would associate his career with the life and landscape of the Midwest. Though he would return to the East Coast in 1838 to advance his artistic awareness and would remain over the next decade closely involved in the marketing of his paintings through their replication as engravings by the American Art-Union in New York, Bingham's greatest work celebrated and scrutinized the great national vision of expansion as it edged toward tension and conflict.

Bingham evidently learned to sketch early and first made his livelihood as an artist by painting portraits. On his trip east he saw in Philadelphia historical and genre works by Emanuel Leutze and William Sidney Mount, respectively, portraits by Thomas Sully, and landscapes by Joshua Shaw. He rapidly absorbed the examples of their styles and in the early 1840s began producing more smoothly modeled figures in the manner of Sully and picturesque rural landscapes reminiscent of Shaw. Then in an almost startling leap of stylistic

Figure 38. George Caleb Bingham, *Daniel Boone Escorting Settlers Through the Cumberland Gap*, 1851–52. Oil on canvas, 36½ x 50¼ in. Washington University Gallery of Art, St. Louis, Gift of Nathaniel Phillips, 1890

Figure 39. George Caleb Bingham, *Fur Traders Descending the Missouri*, 1845. Oil on canvas, 29 x 36½ in. The Metropolitan Museum of Art, New York, Morris K. Jesup Fund, 1933 (see colorplate 9)

maturity during the year 1845, he directly embraced his Missouri subject matter with a bold new clarity of organization and illumination. Painted that year—coincidentally the same date as its eastern counterpart, Mount's *Eel Spearing at Setauket*—was Bingham's first masterwork, *Fur Traders Descending the Missouri* (colorplate 9; fig. 39), along with its apparent pendant, *The Concealed Enemy* (Stark Museum of Art, Orange, Texas).[28]

Missouri, of course, in these years was at the center of rising tensions over geography and slavery, and the course of Bingham's art was a subtle indicator of the increasing intrusion of political and social forces into a region that was being settled physically and unsettled emotionally. Over a remarkable decade balanced around the mid-century mark the artist painted the finest core of his mature art, a period that concluded with his decision in the mid-1850s to leave for a new phase of work in Dusseldorf, Germany, as conflict at home reached a point of irreversible momentum. During this period his pictures of frontier life seemed to coalesce in four general sequences—the first inaugurated by the *Fur Traders*—each with its own distinct compositional and thematic typologies. Generally, these moved from centrally balanced geometries and images of boatmen in passages of calm, open water to clearly asymmetrical designs and traders or politicians at work ashore, and finally to more complicated, even agitated, spatial arrangements with denser accumulations of landscape elements or figures.

The first cluster of works follows quickly on the *Fur Traders* in the next two years, and includes *The Jolly Flatboatmen* (fig. 40) and *Boatmen on the Missouri* (fig. 41), both 1846; *Lighter Relieving a Steamboat Aground* (1846-47; White House Collection), and *Raftsmen Playing Cards* (1847; The Saint Louis Art Museum).[29] As several historians have noted, these early pictures have an aura of nostalgia in their arcadian simplicity, benevolent lighting, and, despite their evident recording of contemporary life, a sense of an earlier history and purer time gone by. For example, *Fur Traders'* original exhibition listing as *French Trader and His Half-Breed Son* alludes to the opening of river trading by Canadian voyageurs as early as the Revolutionary period, while its companion image, *The Concealed Enemy*, presents an Osage Indian awaiting the white man in Missouri during the first quarter of the nineteenth century, before his native tribes were subject to fighting and removal in the early 1830s.[30] The dugout canoe of *Fur Traders* is followed in the other boatmen canvases by simple flat boats with only hints of keelboats and steamers in the distance. Initially at least, the American pioneer (who, contemporary sensibilities remind us, is white and male) inhabits a pristine world, and Bingham frames his figures at ease or at leisure, in structural as well as spiritual harmony with the surrounding landscape.

Although most recent discussion of these paintings has focused on penetrating the revealing layers of cultural, social, and political meanings embedded in them, we should look again at Bingham's formal devices as perfect envelopes of his literal contents. Part of the expressive power of the *Fur Traders* is its conscious balancing of masses, seemingly at the center of a serene and orderly universe. With the stability and rhythm of a Greek-revival temple facade, the horizontal of the dugout canoe serves as a firm plinth for the columnlike forms of bear cub, boy, and man. This clear tripartite disposition has a major reinforcement in the three receding planes of figures, dark expanse of foliage behind, and lighter cloud formations above and beyond. A minor echo appears in the triangular repetition of logs snagged in the river, one in front and two just behind the bow and stern. In addition, the mirror imagery reflected in the water surface suggests a further stasis between ground and sky, the worldly and otherworldly.

We know there are other balances of subject held in equipoise here: perhaps foremost the half-breed son at center, who represents the transition in the American frontier experience from native to white man and from wilderness to civilization. More subtle is the sense of time poignantly caught at a moment of

Figure 40. George Caleb Bingham, *The Jolly Flatboatmen*, 1846. Oil on canvas, 38⅛ x 48½ in. The Manoogian Collection, on loan to the National Gallery of Art, Washington, D.C.

perfection, not unlike a photograph. This only reminds us of the pervasive rise and popularity of that new medium in these very years. Both in the stillness of this scene and, more obviously, in the posed figures looking out directly at us does Bingham seem to embrace this modern aesthetic. Yet for all the fixing of time we subtly become aware of its inexorable motion: in the traders descending the river with their catch, in the young cub who tells us it is early spring, and in the cool light that marks the beginning of day, an hour and a season that will move on, in the touches of foam around the wood snags and bow indicating the canoe's silent movement downstream, and in the puff of pipe smoke just as gently drifting in the morning air.

With his next boatmen pictures Bingham turned to more emphatically pyramidal arrangements for figures who relax or enjoy themselves as their flatboats imperceptibly move on the broad riverway. Whether playing cards, having a smoke or drink, or dancing to a couple of fellow music makers, these are already larger social groupings than the family pair in *Fur Traders*. Moreover, these gatherings interact among themselves, paradoxically at once excluding and including the viewer. The flatboats still establish solid, horizontal bases in the foreground, one anchored to the framing edges by oars that extend outward to each side, and another where the boat platform recedes orthogonally from in front of the foreground edge. The combinations of seated and standing men assemble above in the manner of an architectural pediment. Both the human and structural elements have the clear massings of contemporary neoclassical sculpture. Bingham masterfully integrates all these planar and solid geometries into a harmonious whole, yet avoids the deadness of static symmetry.

The Jolly Flatboatmen (fig. 40) is the perfect example of inertia and motion held in balance, as the eye moves from the mute abstract forms below up through three tiers of figures, the first reclining or seated, the next seated but active with musical instruments, and the lone dancing figure at the apex. Natural as his form may be, it is also a marvel of opposites. His two outstretched arms balance one another, visual rhythms repeated in the extended outside fingers of each hand, while below at the very center of this composition is the contrasting instability of one foot raised in stopped action, the literal animating core of both the design and the subject.

Like high noon, Bingham could not hold this classic poise for long, but at its apogee his work, along with Lane's at the same time, joined a down-to-earth sensibility and attention to the details of the everyday world to an abstracted, even symbolic allusiveness and the paradox of time versus timeless-

Figure 41. George Caleb Bingham, *Boatmen on the Missouri*, 1846. Oil on canvas, 25 x 30 in. The Fine Arts Museums of San Francisco, San Francisco, Gift of Mr. and Mrs. John D. Rockefeller 3rd

ness, that is to say, the momentary along with the transcendental. Soon enough, however, there would be stronger pulls against the harmonies of this vision. Significantly, in one of the later paintings of this first flatboat group, *Lighter Relieving a Steamboat Aground*, not only does the large machinery of a motor vessel intrude into the formerly edenic landscape, but it has also run aground. Nancy Rash has shown that this refers to a clash of party politics between the state and federal government. In 1846 President Polk vetoed the River and Harbor bill, which was designed to keep the nation's waterways cleared of debris and was supported by local Whigs as a necessity for unimpeded commerce. Here Bingham depicts progress grounded, and hints of disarray abound, in the prominently torn shirt, precariously balanced boxes, and the strong diagonals breaking the former purity of his pyramidal organization.[31] This was one of the first images of the period implying that the metaphoric "ship of state" was in trouble, a visual incident that would recur in paintings made by other artists done in the crisis years of the late 1850s and 1860s.

A second major sequence of riverboat pictures followed in 1849 and 1850; in all of these both the principal subject and the weight of the design have moved to the river's edge at the side of the canvas. The figures and architectural components still remain coherent arrangements of solid geometrical forms, although now Bingham pushes them into more dramatic asymmetrical configurations. Typical of this two-year period are *Watching the Cargo* (1849; State Historical Society of Missouri, Columbia), and *The Wood-Boat* (St. Louis Art Museum), *Fishing on the Mississippi* (Nelson-Atkins Museum of Art, Kansas City, Mo.), and *Mississippi Boatman* (colorplate 10), all 1850. The last in one sense is a reworking of the principal figure in *Watching the Cargo* from the previous year, but unlike other Bingham revisions of subjects, it has been transformed in significant ways into a new picture altogether. The most obvious changes are the shift from a horizontal to vertical format and from three figures to one and the substitution of a much older face for the upright seated man.

The increased compactness well suits the solitude and heightened thoughtfulness of this image, now less of narrative genre and more of an individual portrait, or at least the distillation of a human type. In his isolation and relaxed but direct outward gaze, the boatman faces us as if posing for a camera, at the same time calm in the tested wisdom of old age and the durability of human experience. Equal to the larger compositions that preceded it, this painting demonstrates similar subtleties of formal and coloristic harmonies despite its evident simplicity. The angled volumes of torso and limbs play off the nearby geometries of the barrel, boxes, and brick. Behind, the looser cloud formations gently echo the descending diagonal silhouette of the old boatman's head and shoulder. Appropriate to these expressive economies of form, Bingham's palette concentrates on the three primary colors of red, yellow, and blue, obvi-

ous first in the man's cap, trousers, and striped shirt, then dispersed across the red dirt ground and soft yellow clouds in the deep blue sky. Stoic, enduring, mythic, the plain, vertical form of the boatman evokes the same purity of feeling we are to find in Robert Mills's envisioned obelisk design for the Washington Monument just then rising in the nation's capital (see fig. 48).

Another related group of paintings from this time shares many of the compositional conventions of the boatmen series while turning to somewhat different subjects. Replacing the spatial and emotional detachment of the earlier river scenes are transient frontiersmen and hunters in *The Squatters* (Museum of Fine Arts, Boston) and *Shooting for the Beef* (The Brooklyn Museum), both of 1850; game players have moved indoors in *The Checker Players* (1850; Detroit Institute of Arts); and most obviously, the political characters and caricatures gaining visibility in both Bingham's and the nation's life in these critical years, depicted in *The Country Politician* (1849; Fine Arts Museums of San Francisco) and *Canvassing for a Vote* (1851–52; The Nelson-Atkins Museum of Art, Kansas City, Missouri).

However, the biggest stylistic changes occur in Bingham's American work in the last sequence of pictures he painted during the early 1850s. The most famous and ambitious canvases of this period are the election series, including *The County Election* (fig. 42), *Stump Speaking* (1853–54), and *The Verdict of the People* (1854–55; both Boatman's Bankshares, Inc., St. Louis).[32] In addition, there are other thematic diversions with paintings such as *Daniel*

Figure 42. George Caleb Bingham, *The County Election*, 1851–52. Oil on canvas, 35⁷⁄₁₆ x 48³⁄₄ in. The St. Louis Art Museum

Boone Escorting Settlers through the Cumberland Gap (fig. 38) and *Landscape with Waterwheel and Boy Fishing* (1853; Museum of Fine Arts, Boston). In the election series the artist essayed some of his largest canvases and group assemblages, still employing strong asymmetrical designs, but now with highly complicated and compacted figural clusters, dense in narrative content, journalistic and moral commentary—almost visual polemics regarding the most democratic activities of the political process. Bingham himself had run for state office in this period, and his art became a complex blend of personal autobiography with regional and national history. Numerous historians have pointed out his extensive use of old master print sources for many of his figural poses and gestures, but this is not the high classicism of balance and order; rather we see baroque drama and compression and rococo agitation and contrivance.

Bingham's *Daniel Boone* was a further excursion into artifice and nostalgia, as he conflated early American mythology with his own family history, the biblical Flight into Egypt by the Holy Family, and allusions to Greek and Roman statuary. By contrast, *Landscape with Waterwheel* returned to his landscape scenes of a decade before but with a rococo lushness and picturesque volatility. Although still devoted to intensely American subjects, these later works over a critical decade's evolution intuitively reflect the heightened state of disintegration in the national fabric, as the consequences unfolded from the fateful and ironic Compromise of 1850. As an art of national expression, Bingham's great paintings of this hour achieved their own compromise between the ideal and the real, but only for the time being.

Frederic Edwin Church

Time's sweet passage and the promise of American history were themes also very much on the mind of Frederic Edwin Church. Born in Noah Webster's Hartford, Church would make his own significant contribution to shaping a national language of expression. Although a generation younger than Lane and Bingham, he gained artistic maturity early and produced as original and important a body of work as theirs during these same crucial years just around 1850. Church also created a heroic visual vocabulary for a tumultuous moment in the nation's affairs. Showing exceptional artistic promise as a young man, he gained through the fortuitous intercession of the major Hartford collector Daniel Wadsworth the opportunity to study with Thomas Cole in Catskill, New York. During a key two-year period from 1844 to 1846 the aspiring painter learned the art of landscape from the senior master of the preceding generation, and Church not only inherited Cole's mantle of leadership but emerged, through his prodigious technical skill and intellectual imagination, as arguably America's greatest artist at mid-century.

During this early period Church defined his own artistic style first in Cole's shadow, then in conscious memorial homage, and finally in the creation of an original vision—mythic, optimistic, nationalist—worthy of an expansive, still united nation. Like his peers Lane, Bingham, Thoreau, and Whitman, he celebrated both the physical and the spiritual power of American nature. Like Melville, Hawthorne, and Stowe he addressed issues of morality, individual and national purpose, and art's redemptive authority. As with his fellow painters, we may divide Church's artistic output in these mid-century years into a few clear thematic groupings. For example, works emulating Cole's subjects, compositions, and painting manner dominate the later 1840s, whether depicting allegorical history—*Hooker and Company Journeying through the Wilderness from Plymouth to Hartford, in 1836* (1846; Wadsworth Atheneum, Hartford)—or natural history—*Storm in the Mountains* (1847; Cleveland Museum of Art). Cole's passing inspired a number of artistic tributes, among the best known being Church's *To the Memory of Cole* (1848; Des Moines Women's Club) and Durand's *Kindred Spirits* (fig. 31). Attention by Church to the native landscape in its generic elements as well as special topological character continued in such paintings as *New England Scenery* (1851; George Walter Vincent Smith Museum, Springfield, Mass.), *Home by the Lake* (Collection of JoAnn and Julian Ganz, Jr.), and *The Natural Bridge, Virginia* (Bayly Art Museum at the University of Virginia), both of 1852. In this group Church created the artistic foundations for a subsequent masterpiece such as *Niagara* (1857; Corcoran Gallery of Art, Washington, D.C.).

But perhaps his most influential achievement was the intense fresh vision of his dawn and twilight pictures, with at least a dozen concentrated in the early 1850s. Many of these were of unsurpassed technical finish, strikingly beautiful, and some were among his most important early works. Highlights of this chronology include *Twilight, "Short arbiter 'twixt day and night"* (1850; fig. 43) and *Mount Ktaadn* (1853; colorplate 11).[33] Generally paralleling the development of Fitz Hugh Lane's art through the same period, these images tend to stress at the outset narrative or allegorical content, explicit New England locations, and the cooler, softer palette of early morning or evening. Historians have argued that Church's sunrise pictures painted in the later forties and early fifties reflect that moment's sense of optimism and promise, the possibility and regeneration associated with the beginning of a new day.

By the mid-fifties these scenes became notably more strident in their coloration, somewhat more generalized in their location, more dramatic, and even agitated in their interpretation of nature. To be sure, as many have recognized, some of these heightened effects were the consequence of the newly available hot red cadmium pigments artists now had at their disposal. But by 1856, when Church painted *Twilight (Sunset)* (Albany Institute of History and Art)

Figure 43. Frederic Edwin Church, *Twilight, "Short arbiter 'twixt day and night,"* 1850. Oil on canvas, 32¼ x 48 in. The Newark Museum

and *Sunset* (fig. 44), his attention had turned almost obsessively to the intense flares of sunset and a juxtaposition of cadmiums now expressing tension rather than serenity. The entire sequence would culminate in Church's great apocalyptic vision of *Twilight in the Wilderness* (1860; Cleveland Museum of Art), painted on the eve of the Civil War and just after the unsettling publication of Charles Darwin's *On the Origin of Species,* whose reverberations were felt in America, as elsewhere, soon after its appearance in 1859. The lurid sunset conveys a vivid hour of dramatic change in nature, in keeping with the larger political and spiritual crises abroad in the land. The notion of a peaceful evening sunset and its suggestion that just as beautiful a day would follow in a natural and dependable cycle yielded by the end of the fifties to one of threatening turbulence. Where Church perceived America in *Mount Ktaadn* in 1853 as a new Eden at the moment of Genesis, he saw the nation in his 1860 *Twilight* consumed by the fires of the Apocalypse at a time of terrible judgment. As such, his sunset paintings were not only marvels of acute scientific observation, but they were also among the most powerful and original visual metaphors of the age.

But Church undertook another important artistic enterprise in the mid-fifties with his first exploratory trip to northern South America in 1853 and a series of expansive Andean landscapes painted in counterpoint to his northern vistas. Again, he established an essential pictorial vocabulary expressing an heroic vision of New World art and science. Such grandeur of emotion, abundance of nature, and spatial breadth characterize such works as *The Cordilleras: Sunrise* (New York market) and *Tequendama Falls, near Bogata, New Granada* (Cincinnati Art Museum), both 1854, *Cotopaxi* (fig. 45), and *The Andes of Ecuador* (Reynolda House, Winston-Salem, North Carolina), both 1855.[34] Their spiritual self-confidence and order well suited antebellum and pre-Darwinian America, and found common voice at this time with the contemporaneous expressions of Melville, Thoreau, and Whitman. Church was able to sustain his convictions into his summary South American canvas, *The Heart of the Andes* (1859; The Metropolitan Museum of Art, New York), but in painting a later version of *Cotopaxi* in 1862 (Detroit Institute of Arts), he found his literal and emotional landscape exploding in cosmic fires.

Figure 44. Frederic Edwin Church, *Sunset*, 1856. Oil on canvas, 24 x 36 in. Munson-Williams-Proctor Institute, Utica, New York, Proctor Collection (PC 21)

Figure 45. Frederic
Edwin Church,
Cotopaxi, 1855.
Oil on canvas,
28 x 42⅛ in.
National Museum
of American Art,
Smithsonian
Institution,
Washington, D.C.,
Gift of Mrs. Frank
R. McCoy

It was Church's great triumph that he found in his raw, red pigments colors that caught nature's most delicate moments of transience as well as the deeper chords of national sentiment. Along with the other seers of this time he transformed the conventions of his art as he addressed the shifting gravities of unity and discord.

The Writers' Renaissance: Melville, Thoreau, and Whitman

WHAT LINKED the best artists and writers around 1850 was their lofty moral reach, often matched by a bold new freeing of imagination and form. F. O. Matthiessen, in his defining book of 1941 about the literary culture of this period, gave us the memorable title *American Renaissance*, which ever since has been associated with his work and this subject.[35] What stimulated his undertaking was the realization that an unprecedented "number of our past masterpieces were produced in one extraordinarily concentrated moment of expression," namely the half-decade of 1850 55.[36] Relevant to our discussion here, his list included Hawthorne's *The Scarlet Letter* (1851), Melville's *Moby-Dick* (1851), Thoreau's *Walden* (1854), and Whitman's first edition of *Leaves of Grass* (1855), to which other cultural historians have since argued for the addition of Harriet Beecher Stowe's *Uncle Tom's Cabin* (1852).[37] However configured, the group was an unprecedented flourishing, prompting Matthiessen to claim, "You might search all the rest of American literature without being able to collect a group of books equal to these in imaginative vitality."[38]

Written during the gathering intensity of World War II, Matthiessen's work can be read as growing out of a heightened moment of nationalist fervor and self-consciousness, itself a period of powerful American writing by Frost, Faulkner, and Hemingway, among others. Such factors surely facilitated the retrospective scrutiny of an earlier age of great creativity and contributed critically to the serious modern study of American literature. Indeed, Matthiessen was among the first wave of scholars and academics who gave independent respectability to the field and its teaching alongside the established study of English literature. Even more important, his broader concerns with painting and culture made his book one of the fountainheads for the interdisciplinary college-level programs founded then and since in American studies and civilization.

While *American Renaissance* took as its premise the remarkable confluence of several landmarks in literature, Matthiessen in his consideration of Emerson turned to a brief discussion of the theories and sculpture of Horatio Greenough, and in the final sections on Whitman he wrote pointedly about the sunny genre pictures of William Sidney Mount, the expansive landscapes of Albert Bierstadt, and the solid realism of Eakins and Homer.

Indeed, Matthiessen's book must have been one of the first devoted to American literature that contained illustrations of contemporaneous paintings, including three by Mount and two by Eakins. Although the latter correlates with Whitman's mature years later in the century, Mount's images shared with Bingham's the plein air order and optimism of mid-century. In particular, Matthiessen cited, in conjunction with Mount's landscapes *Coming to the Point* and *Long Island Farmhouses* from the later 1840s, what he called Whitman's three-lined "Farm Picture" from *Leaves of Grass*:

> Through the ample door of the peaceful country barn,
> A sunlit pasture field with cattle and horses feeding,
> And haze and vista, and far horizon fading away.[39]

Matthiessen further perceived the larger connection of Whitman's national vistas to the concurrent flourishing of landscape painting, although the still obscure careers of Lane, Church, and many of the luminists were virtually unknown to Whitman at the time of his writing. Ultimately, Matthiessen's study concentrates primarily on the central figures of Emerson, Thoreau, Hawthorne, Melville, and Whitman but extends both beyond their works of the early 1850s to their full careers and to their modern legacy in the writings of Henry James, T. S. Eliot, and Ezra Pound. But Matthiessen's ideas remain an important touchstone for our discussion here of that mid-century turning point, which, thanks to him, has been most familiarly celebrated up to now by America's great writers.

Disparate as these writers and their major books were, what are some of the elements they shared to forge such a sense of cultural achievement? Running through almost all these works was, in an age of contesting forces, the mediation between reportage and symbolic abstraction. With Hawthorne, Stowe, and Melville we encounter stories of high moral and spiritual, even religious, power, where good and evil, black and white, light and dark, are interlocked in conflict. Surely Melville and Whitman share an expansive cosmic vision, while Thoreau and Whitman manipulate in vital new ways the conventions of their genre, one turning a narrative journal and the other verse into autobiographical expression as original as Franklin's a half century earlier and Henry Adams's a half century later.

For his part, Nathaniel Hawthorne explicitly introduced the personal self into *The Scarlet Letter* with his autobiographical preface, "The Custom House," as a beginning to the novel. From this account of his own term as a local customs inspector in Salem he moved into a story grounded both in Puritan history and in the actuality of ordinary human experience. The force of the novel derives from his combination of probing psychological realism and universal moral truths, of basic facts and suggestive allegory, of immediate and timeless human dilemmas. In calling his story "A Romance," Hawthorne was signaling an enterprise of imaginative transformation of reality, wherein we are haunted equally by the dreams of sleep and of our waking hours.

Human suffering and redemption were also at the heart of Harriet Beecher Stowe's novel *Uncle Tom's Cabin*, which has only in recent decades been proposed for consideration in the basic canon of American literature. In fact, Matthiessen makes only a passing reference to what was one of the most popular and influential books of its day. He does so in relation to Emerson, who was uneasy "over his restricted audience when he compared the response of his few hundreds or thousands to the mass that greeted *Uncle Tom's Cabin*. He perceived also how it was that book's distinction to have been 'read equally in the parlor and the kitchen and the nursery.'"[10]

Stowe's book, which had appeared in magazine installments during 1851, was published in its entirety on March 20, 1852; ten thousand copies sold within the first week, three hundred thousand within a year.[41] One senses that Matthiessen shared Emerson's unease at such popularity as somehow contrary to high art, a paradox that has traditionally worried Americans about their culture. But this is exactly one of Stowe's great distinctive achievements: that her novel could bridge popular culture and visionary expression, that she could be descriptive and prophetic at the same time. Secondly, she epitomized the interest of women in public affairs and entry into American letters, yet she went beyond any limited preoccupation with her gender. Perhaps above all, she engaged the present rather than past history and in particular addressed the most provocative element at the heart of American history and life, from Jefferson to Martin Luther King: race. To be sure, modern critics have noted her disposition to condescension and stereotyping, which flaws the intentions of her antislavery tract, yet we should remember that neither were Lincoln's views about African-Americans and slavery pure or ideal in the 1850s. But as president a decade later, readying the Emancipation Proclamation, Lincoln was able to greet Stowe at the White House in 1862 with the celebrated remark, "So you're the little woman who wrote the book that started this great war!"[42]

This inciting book arose out of the confluence of several activities and interests in prior years: her early religious and moral education at home (her father, Lyman Beecher, and her brother Henry Ward Beecher were both ministers and outspoken abolitionists) and at the Hartford Female Seminary; the beginnings of her literary efforts during the nearly two decades her family spent in the border city of Cincinnati, which led to the first publication of her stories in the 1840s; and finally her intense feelings precipitated by passage of the Fugitive Slave Act in the Compromise of 1850. Life in the new West in the years before 1851, when she returned to the East Coast, offered a raw picture of the nation's class and race tensions, to which she responded with an observant eye and moral fervor. By January 1851 she announced that she was "projecting a sketch for the Era of the capabilities of liberated blacks to take care of themselves." And shortly after, she spoke with even more committed intensity: "Up to this year I have always felt that I had no particular call to meddle with this subject, and I dreaded to expose even my own mind to the full force of its exciting power. But I feel now that the time is come when even a woman or a child who can speak a word for freedom and humanity is bound to speak."[43]

Although Cincinnati provided her with glimpses of black life and problems, Stowe as a northerner had less firsthand familiarity with her subject than she wished. For realism of circumstances and character she wrote to Frederick Douglass to secure information about blacks working on a southern plantation: "I wish to be able to make a picture that shall be graphic & true to nature in its details." She also made use of the escape stories of slaves to ground this "study of the negro character."[44] Certainly one of the most notable accounts published was Douglass's own autobiography, whose first version appeared as the *Narrative of the Life of Frederick Douglass, an American Slave* in 1845 and which he would rework and expand ten years later as *My Bondage and My Freedom*. In her ability to combine fact and allegory, Stowe triumphed in creating an exciting story with indelible and enduring characters, treated with deep feeling as well as wit. Her careful descriptions of locales and events have direct parallels in the genre landscapes of William Sidney Mount and were surely ingredients in the popular appeal her story immediately had.

But just as Mount conveys a sense of sympathy and dignity in his rendering of black figures, Stowe too shaped deeper themes that went beyond recounting incidents of daily life. For example, Mount implicitly understood the similar marginalization of blacks, women, and children in American life when he painted the powerful image of *Eel Spearing at Setauket* (fig. 30), where the monumental composition balances the black woman and youth with each other and with the landscape. For her part, Stowe forces us to think about the comparable evils of slavery and capitalism and, for a modern audience, the comparable aspirations of women and blacks. In her "sketch for the Era" she wrote about the capabilities not just of blacks but of humanity in general.

Herman Melville

Melville shared with Stowe the creation of lasting personifications of evil in Captain Ahab and Simon Legree, respectively. Both wrote epic adventures with a panoramic reach and universal themes, balancing nihilism and redemption, and in contrasting ways they used the symbolic passage of water for a deeply American vision. For Stowe, of course, her novel's setting was the great central American rivers joining the polar opposites of north and south; for Melville the vast Pacific was at once an expanding region of sea trade and an imaginative horizon of adventure, self-discovery, and personal freedom. During these same years Frederic Church was metaphorically extending the geographic and mental reach of the United States the length of the western hemisphere, from the arctic north to the equatorial south. For artist and writer alike, America in the 1850s was a place of heroic possibilities: Church would have agreed with Stowe that this was "a country whose products embrace all between the tropics and the poles!" But as the painter's landscapes shifted from tranquil to turbulent, he would also have concurred that "This is an age . . . when nations are trembling and convulsed. A mighty influence is abroad."[45] The nation was going to have to confront the dark truths of evil in a coming day of judgment, and Stowe, Melville, and Church all expressed the conflict in biblical absolutes.

If Stowe's novel forever changed the way her countrymen thought about American life, Melville's equally changed the way we think about literature. While *Moby-Dick* is in other ways very different from *Uncle Tom's Cabin*, both used literature to embrace a religious fervor. Melville too wrote a story grounded in the daily life and circumstances of mid-century America. On one level, the details of his whaling voyage spoke to the expansionist national vision; on another, literary historians have pointed out the concurrence of *Moby-Dick's* artistic revolution with the country's political crisis.[46] Melville's obsession with language contributed to elevating his book to a cerebral and abstract plane all its own. His opening chapter initiates a traveling of the mind as much as of the body. After naming himself in the famous opening line, the authorial narrator has found "nothing particular to interest me on shore." He proposes to "see the watery part of the world," and the subsequent paragraphs unfold with images of water: "The spleen, and regulating the circulation . . . damp, drizzly November . . . your insular city of the Manhattoes, belted round by wharves as Indian isles by coral reefs—commerce surrounds it with her surf . . . streets take you waterward . . . the Battery . . . is washed by waves . . . crowds of water-gazers. . . . Circumambulate the city . . . mortal men fixed in ocean reveries . . . striving to get a still better seaward peep . . . pacing straight for the water . . . get just as nigh the water as they possibly can . . . the magnetic virtue of the needles of the compasses of all those ships . . . by a pool in the stream. There is magic in it . . . lead you to water, if water there be . . . a thirst in the great American desert." All this concludes with that memorable line among so many: "Yes, as everyone knows, meditation and water are wedded forever."[47]

This fierce ocean reverie extending standard literary forms grew out of Melville's earlier, firsthand experiences of sea travel to Liverpool in 1839 and to the Pacific two years later. These voyages provided him with a mix of adventure, anecdotal incidents, and ethnographic and social observations, which formed the basis of his first published stories, *Typee* and *Omoo* in 1847, *Mardi* and *Redburn* in 1849, and *White-Jacket* in 1850. Historians believe his friendship with Hawthorne that year was a critical stimulus to Melville's new spiritual and artistic reach in writing *Moby-Dick*. In fact, dedicated to his friend, "In token of my admiration for his genius, This Book is Inscribed to Nathaniel Hawthorne," it was also to be a work about suffering, epiphany, and redemption. But transcending previous novels, it explored language both as the recording of facts and as an embodiment of artistic creation itself. In this latter capacity his story evoked the elemental forces of religion, from the dramas of Creation to the Day of Judgment. F. O. Matthiessen called attention to this rich play of opposites in the book: reporting and allegory, matter and spirit, land and sea, calm and storm, "the fleece of innocence with ferocity."[48] As we have seen, such a union between observation and idea likewise informed the art of Hawthorne, Stowe, Lane, Bingham, and Church, as it also did that of Thoreau and Whitman. Needless to say, an enormous secondary literature exists regarding *Moby-Dick*, and this is not the place to engage it, but rather to stress those central aspects that Melville's achievement shares with other contemporary expressions defining this singular moment in the nation's life and culture.

Several passages will indicate the book's power of imagery and form. Chapter 37, "Sunset," for example, immediately calls to mind Frederic Church's contemporaneous twilight vistas, both in its allusions to the conventions of landscape painting and in its exclamatory vision. First of all, parenthetical notes establish the setting at the head of the chapter, a form that suggests a theatrical composition; the scene is the interior of a cabin where Ahab is gazing out the stern windows. This establishes both a viewer and a view, the latter framed like a picture within the window. The narrative opens by meditating again on the mysterious open sea: "I leave a white and turbid wake; pale waters, paler cheeks, where'er I sail. The envious billows sidelong swell to whelm my track. . . ." Then our attention is turned to the horizon and the sublime passage of the setting sun: "Yonder, by the ever-brimming goblet's rim, the warm waves blush like wine. The gold brow plumbs the blue. The diver sun—slow dived from noon—goes down; my soul mounts up!"[49] As in Fitz Hugh Lane's evening scenes, we move from observation to contemplation of nature's larger cycle. We are witness to a

poignant and dramatic moment of time's transition, glowing in the painter's colors of wine, gold, and blue. And, as in luminist painting, space and light become
charged with expressive feeling and spiritual meaning.

Just as we know Lane had himself hauled up a mast in a bosun's chair in
order to get a more panoramic view for his seascapes, so Melville's voyager on
the whale ship describes how "the three mast-heads are kept manned from sunrise to sun-set. . . . In the serene weather of the tropics it is exceedingly pleasant—the mast-head; nay, to a dreamy meditative man it is delightful. . . . There
you stand, lost in the infinite series of the sea, with nothing ruffled but the
waves. The traced ship indolently rolls; the drowsy trade winds blow; everything resolves you into languor." Such a passage is also a reminder that
Melville's melodic prose is often matched to the lulling rhythms of the sea itself,
as well as the driftings of the dreaming mind. An equally memorable sequence
occurs at the beginning of Chapter 51, "The Spirit-Spout," where the alliteration of sounds perfectly captures the deep ocean rhythms: "It was while gliding
through these latter waters that one serene and moonlight night, when all the
waves rolled by like scrolls of silver; and by their soft, suffusing seethings, made
what seemed a silvery silence, not a solitude: on such a silent night a silvery jet
was seen far in advance of the white bubbles at the bow. Lit up by the moon, it
looked celestial; seemed some plumed and glittering god uprising from the
sea."[50]

But *Moby-Dick* asserts the presence of words as having not only sound,
shape, and texture, but accumulates them as names, facts, and evidence of
knowledge. The oft-cited Chapter 32, "Cetology," also opens on the ocean as a
vast cosmos: "Already we are boldly launched upon the deep; but soon we shall
be lost in its unshored, harborless immensities." This calls for the artifice of language to classify and clarify: "Now the various species of whales need some sort
of popular comprehensive classification," and immediately there follow subtle
images of the craft of writing: "an easy outline . . . no ordinary letter-sorter in
the Post-office is equal to it. . . . What am I that I should essay to hook the nose
of this leviathan! . . . I have swam through libraries and sailed through oceans."
Melville plays further with the task of giving organization to his subject by
interweaving related references to other structural systems, namely architecture
and anatomy: "I am the architect, not the builder . . . to have one's hands among
the unspeakable foundations, ribs, and very pelvis of the world; this is a fearful
thing." All this leads to his well-known differentiation of whales by book sizes:
"According to magnitude I divide the whales into three primary BOOKS (subdi-
visible into CHAPTERS), and these shall comprehend them all, both small and
large. I. The FOLIO WHALE; II. the OCTAVO WHALE; III. the DUODECIMAL
WHALE."[51] Standing for all subjects, and even for the immensity of America we
might say, this cataloguing records the probing search for self-discovery and

learning. Its interior imagery of books within a book, like Whitman's inter-changeable leaves of grass and paper a couple of years later, pay tribute ulti-mately to the art of letters and to artistic creativity itself.

Henry David Thoreau, Journal Keeper

Melville shared with Thoreau the joint investigation of experience and imagina-tion and with Whitman a meditation on the American cosmos. All three looked at nature but thought about nation, and they did so in writing of unprecedent-ed intensity, grandeur, and inventiveness. Thoreau and Whitman likewise bear a certain kinship to their artistic counterparts: In both *Walden* and Lane's mature luminist paintings we find a similar distillation of sentiment and abstracted form; while the exultant, all-embracing vision of *Leaves of Grass* is akin to Church's geographic panoramas. Or compare Bingham's reductive geometries to Thoreau's familiar command to "Simplify, simplify."[52]

Although *Walden* was not published until 1854, Thoreau had largely drafted it by 1849 and was refining it through 1851. As with Melville, this was the culmination of an intense period of creative output: In 1848 Thoreau pub-lished the initial section of his essay on "Ktaadn and the Maine Woods," based on his first two of four excursions into the northern interior (1838, 1846, 1853, 1857); and in 1849 *A Week on the Concord and Merrimack Rivers* appeared. Throughout, he maintained the active literary productivity of his Journal, with historians citing the critical time around 1851, when these notations become more consciously philosophical, crafted, and substantial. Although Melville was nominally writing fiction and Thoreau forms of journalism, both itemized the elements of nature, meditated on their craft as art, and wrote about person-al journeys of exploration, one to the far reaches of the Pacific and the other to the introspective depths of a pond near home. Each repeatedly employed metaphors of the horizon. While autobiographical experience was the genesis of both writers' works, Thoreau naturally recorded his Journal observations from a personal point of view and intentionally stated at the outset of *Walden* that "In most books, the I, or first person, is omitted; in this it will be retained."[53] He would, of course, play throughout with the interrelationship of the I as indi-vidual and the seeing eye.

Thoreau accounted for his life by various measurements of the calendar. He had begun his Journal as a fresh Harvard graduate in 1837, the year of Emerson's address on the "American Scholar," and its many volumes over his lifetime accumulated like so many books of days. Until 1850 the entries were fre-quently sporadic, but during that year they gradually became more regular and sequential, as they more purposefully analyzed the self in relation to nature, and were written with an increasing sense of literary form and style.[54] This has led historians to see the Journal as draft material for parts of both *A Week* and *Walden*, although recent criticism has begun to celebrate the writings of the Journal as an equally distinguished literary achievement in its own right. One obvious reason for its less popular reputation is its great length and coverage, but focus on the critical period of the early 1850s has provided new insight into the complex interrelationships among his several enterprises.[55]

Where the Journal took its form from daily entries, *A Week* described more defined and linear travel through space and time, now the larger unit announced by the title. Originally called an "Excursion," this river voyage reminds us of the reflective passage of time seen contemporaneously in Bingham's drifting boatmen pictures. Both the observation of nature's face and ordinary daily incidents became an opportunity for exploring the process and possibilities of the imagination, for uncovering distilled truths on a higher plane. In *Walden* this voyaging became even more abstracted, as walking self-consciously was like an act of writing or reading, recording or responding to the text of nature around him. Thoreau also more artificially shaped *Walden* as travel inward and more literally as well as metaphorically circumscribed by the general circle of Walden Pond. In this regard we might recall Melville's opening musing on "your insular city of the Manhattoes" and his urging to "circumambulate the city of a dreamy Sabbath afternoon."[56] As we know, Thoreau's circlings took some time to distill, and here a number of the themes running through his Journal anticipate the subjects formalized in the writing of *Walden*.

First, there are the recurring references to walking and its connection to thinking: already in early January 1851 Thoreau notes "the Adam who daily takes a turn in his garden," and the need to understand "the art of taking walks daily—not exercise—the legs or body merely—nor barely to recruit the spirits but positively to exercise both body & spirit." A day or so later he added, "When we can no longer ramble in the fields of Nature, we ramble in the fields of thought & literature."[57] The following month he began to play with the real and the imaginative: "Walking in the woods it may be some afternoon the shadow of the wings of a thought flits across the landscape of my mind." Later he celebrates one of his favorite personifications: "Traveller! I love his title. A Traveller is to be reverenced as such—His profession is the best symbol of our life," and, "A traveller who looks at things with an impartial eye may see what the oldest inhabitant has not observed." In his last observation for the year Thoreau saw the image as one of essentials, including the virtue of self-reliance, as he associated "Denuded pines . . . So stands a man. . . . The lonely traveller."[58]

On occasion, Thoreau used observations of the animal world to make other philosophical points about learning from nature: "You must creep before you can run—you must run before you can fly." But it was mostly the awareness of self and the stretching of the mind that he repeatedly found exhilarating: "Let me forever go in search of myself. . . . You must walk sometimes perfectly free. . . . Flights of imagination . . . So a man is said to soar in his thought."[59] Like Melville's linking of his explorations with bookmaking, Thoreau was also increasingly conscious of his own literary enterprise, as he contemplated various forms of observation and the art of writing itself: "The poet must be continuously watching the moods of his mind as the astronomer watches the aspects of the heavens. . . . For roads I think that a poet cannot tolerate more than a foot-path through the fields—That is wide enough & for purposes of winged poesy suffices. . . . Resolve to read no book—to take no walk—to undertake no enterprise but such as you can endure to give an account to yourself. . . . Those sentences are good and well discharged which are like so many little resiliencies from the spring floor of our life."[60]

As numerous critics have noted, Thoreau's imagery often correlates with luminist painting, especially his seeking of the expansive horizon and the elevated point of view, what H. Daniel Peck refers to as his "horizontal vision of nature," his recordings of fog as both unifying and revelatory, and above all his infatuation with the suggestive effects of sunlight and moonlight.[61] This immersion in nature, most notably in the expanses of American space and light, matches the central aesthetics of landscape painting and constitutes a second pervasive theme that resonates throughout the Journal at this time. Thoreau uses several metaphors for the merging of self with the natural world: "We have a waterfall which corresponds even to a Niagara somewhere within us. . . . There is no doubt a perfect analogy between the life of the human being and that of the vegetable. . . . man sends down a tap root to the centre of things. . . . As with the roots of the Plant so with the roots of the Mind. . . . I now descend round the corner of the grain field. . . . I seem to be nearer to the origin of things. . . . I seem to be more constantly merged in nature."[62] We also recognize in these phrases echoes of the writings of Emerson and Thomas Cole, who prominently articulated similar thoughts about nature a decade and a half earlier.

Thoreau made observations not only close-up but also by surveying distant expanses, and he loved recording both the particularities of individual tree types and their extended imaginative aspects. For example, "The birch is the surveyor's tree—It makes the best stakes to look at through the sights of a compass. . . . Their white bark was not made in vain." And elsewhere, "I am sure that my eye rested with pleasure on the white pines now reflecting a silvery light."[63] Thus, the trees became a means of measuring space, they offered aesthetic delight, and they heightened one's perspective powers. At the same time, marking trees in the distance was but part of Thoreau's frequent awareness of the horizon in his travels, and the noun or its variant appears regularly throughout 1851: "Bear my head through atmospheres and over heights unknown. . . . I am thankfull that we have yet so much room in America. . . . Westward is Heaven or rather heavenward is the west. . . . All distant landscapes—seen from hill tops are veritable pictures. . . . 'Tis distance lends enchantment to the view.' . . . The prospect of a vast horizon must be accessible in our neighborhood. Where men of enlarged views may be educated. . . . We experience pleasure when an elevated field or even road in which we may be walking—holds level toward the horizon. . . . It is worth the while to see the *Mts* in the horizon once a day."[64] Let us recall the countless visual equivalents of such phrases in the landscape views of almost all Hudson River School and luminist painters working in this mid-century period.

Closely related for Thoreau to "lifting your horizon" were his repeated images of sunlight and moonlight, also with their multiple counterparts in the canvases of Cole, Lane, Gifford, Heade, Church, and other contemporaries. With Lane's subtle twilight pictures and Church's nuanced sunset paintings in mind, or the latter's meticulous drawings annotated with precise notations of color and time of day, we find Thoreau recording the conditions of sunlight with equal sensitivity and evocativeness: "There was a remarkable sunset a mother of pearl sky seen over the Price farm. . . . The fields are blushing with the red species as the western sky at evening. . . . A gorgeous sunset after rain with horizontal bars of red sashes to the western window. . . . I saw the seal of evening on the river. There was a quiet beauty in the landscape at that hour which my senses were prepared to appreciate. . . . Standing on distant hills you see the heavens reflected the evening sky in some low lake or river in the valley. . . . The most beautiful thing in Nature is the sun reflected from a tear-ful [sic] cloud. . . . I love to see any redness in the vegetation. . . . It asks a bright sun on it to make it show to best advantage . . . as if the fires of the day had just been put out in the west and the burnt territory was sending out volumes of dun & lurid smoke to heaven. . . . this red vision excites me, stirs my blood—makes my thoughts flow—& I have new & indescribable fancies."[65]

Moonlight was almost equally appealing to Thoreau, for it was both a reflection of the sun as well as part of the day's endless cycle: "Now we are getting into moonlight. . . . And proves how remarkable a lesser light can be when a greater has departed. . . . Tis true she was eclipsed by the sun—but now she acquires an almost equal respect & worship by reflecting & representing him. . . . I remember the last moon shining through a creamy atmosphere—with a tear in the eye of nature. . . . The stars of poetry & history—unexplored nature looking down on the scene. This is my world now. . . . The landscape seen from the slightest elevation by moonlight . . . Moonlight is peculiarly favorable to reflection. . . . the moon is not to be judged alone by the quantity of light she sends us, but also by her influence on the earth. . . . is not the poet who walks by night conscious of a tide in his thought which is to be referred to lunar influence."[66] But the relationship between sun and moon was also part of another larger theme preoccupying Thoreau, that of cycles or circles, one which would become a unifying abstraction in his composition of *Walden* a few years later. Not only did the two celestial bodies move in orbits linked to each other, but their shapes possessed the same pure geometry: "The sun that lights this world from with out shines in at a window—but the moon is like a lamp within an apartment. It shines for us. . . . The bright sheen of the moon is constantly travelling with us. . . . the reflection of its disk in the rippled water by our boatside appears like gold pieces falling on the river's counter.—This coin is incessantly poured forth as from some unseen horn of plenty at our side."[67]

He further noted the larger cycles of the seasons, a sequence he would use to define the shape of *Walden*: "Nature is a great imitator & loves to repeat herself. . . . So you get not the absolute time but the true time of the season. . . . Suggesting amid all these signs of Autumn—falling leaves & frost—that the life of nature—by which she eternally flourishes, is untouched. . . . I lie on my back with joy under its boughs. While its leaves fall—its blossoms spring. The autumn is in deed [sic] a spring. All the year is a spring." As we know, *Walden* begins in March and concludes the following spring. Even nearing the end of a year in mid-December, he could write, "As for the weather, all seasons are pretty much alike to one who is actively at work in the woods."[68] A smaller circling image to reappear in his more formal later narrative was that of "a large hawk circling over a pine wood below me." In the same entry he went on to talk about "the poetry of motion" and "that America Yacht of the air that never makes a tack—though it rounds the globe itself . . . Flights of imagination . . . So a man is said to soar in his thought." Again, near the end of the year he enriches and deepens his several metaphors: "How swiftly the earth appears to revolve at sunset—which at midday appears to rest on its axle. . . . The man is blessed who every day is permitted to behold anything so pure & serene as the western sky at sunset—while revolutions vex the world."[69]

Walden as Art and Autobiography

Literary scholars have thoroughly documented many passages in the Journal that found their way, transformed and reshaped, into *Walden*. What we should briefly pursue here are Thoreau's recurring themes and their ongoing connections to wider aesthetic concerns of the period. With regard to form, Thoreau chose to organize his book around the cycle of a year, which he treated as both experienced reality and as artifice. That is, while he actually went to Walden Pond between 1845 and 1847, he wrote his account retrospectively almost a decade later, conflating his two years there into one standing for the whole. He blandly concluded his final narrative chapter: "Thus was my first year's life in the woods completed; and the second year was similar to it."[70] That he followed this with another section called "Conclusion" indicates he was doing more than keeping a day book but was rather seeking a more symbolic and abstract level of meaning. Indeed, one result is that his "year" at Walden is intended to represent a whole lifetime, a full circle of the seasons, the voyage of life. Thus, its design especially made it an American autobiography with an originality that recalls Benjamin Franklin and anticipates Henry Adams.

This autobiographical self is at the heart of *Walden*, as observer, reader, and writer: Thoreau's opening paragraph indicates he wrote and lived alone and was now "a sojourner in civilized life again," although he hastens to understate that he did not have to journey far: "I have travelled a good deal in Concord." Ostensibly, "My purpose in going to Walden Pond was . . . to transact some private business." Again he stressed, "I have thought that Walden Pond would be a good place for business. . . . it is a good port and a good foundation."[71] Presumably, here he will be able to sail forth and build imaginatively. One immediate theme that was on his mind was the freedom of the self, which had physical and spiritual, as well as political dimensions: he pointedly notes more than once that he "took up [his] abode in the woods . . . on Independence Day, or the fourth of July, 1845," and elsewhere asserts that "the only true America is that country where you are at liberty to pursue such a mode of life as may enable you to do without these [tea, and coffee, and meat everyday], and where the state does not endeavor to compel you to sustain the slavery and war and other superfluous expenses. . . ."[72] We must remember that Thoreau wrote these lines against the background of the Compromise of 1850 and the Kansas-Nebraska Act of 1854, which makes us realize that Walden also stands in part for America itself. Again, near the beginning he says, "there are so many keen and subtle masters that enslave both north and south . . . but worst of all when you are the slave-driver of yourself." Like Harriet Beecher Stowe, he also hints that contemporary industrialization and capitalism are imprisoning: "And if the railroads are not built, how shall we get to heaven in season? But if we stay at home and mind our business, who will want railroads? We do not ride on the railroad; it rides upon us." This idea comes full circle in his Conclusion, where he writes, "you are but confined to the most significant and vital experiences. . . . It is life near the bone where it is sweetest. . . . Superfluous wealth can buy superfluities only. Money is not required to buy one necessary of the soul."[73]

Walden, then, is everywhere a self-conscious creative act, as we pick up from the interspersed references to books and art, for example: "Books must be read as deliberately and reservedly as they were written. . . . The book exists for us perchance which will explain our miracles and reveal new ones." (Both of these lines come from the chapter entitled "Reading.") Later he adds, "You want room for your thoughts to get into sailing trim and run a course or two before they make their port. . . . our sentences wanted room to unfold and form their columns in the interval. . . . Ah, many a tale their color told! And gradually from week to week the character of each tree came out, and it admired itself reflected in the smooth mirror of the lake. Each morning the manager of this gallery substituted some new picture, distinguished by more brilliant or harmonious coloring, for the old upon the walls."[74]

As with his Journal entries, there are frequent phrases that correlate with the composition and content of contemporary American landscape painting. Church or Duncanson comes to mind with the following passage: "A lake like this is never smoother than at such a time; and the clear portion of the air above it being shallow and darkened by clouds, the water, full of light and reflections, becomes a lower heaven itself so much the more important." We can visualize a painting by Cole, Gifford, or Kensett here: "By standing on tiptoe I could catch a glimpse of some of the peaks of the still bluer and more distant mountain ranges in the north-west, those true-blue coins of heaven's own mint." We think of Lane or Mount when Thoreau writes, "The morning, which is the most memorable season of the day, is the awakening hour. . . . Poetry and art, and the fairest and most memorable of the actions of men, date from such an hour . . . . let me have a draught of undiluted morning air."[75] One landscape convention was the presence of the lone fisherman at the side of a stream or quiet lake. A scale-giving device to suggest nature's immensity and a surrogate for the author and observer, the figure takes a place within the larger harmony of the surroundings. Water becomes a metaphor for a higher transcendental order: "Time is but the stream I go a-fishing in. . . . Its thin current slides away, but eternity remains. I would drink deeper; fish in the sky, whose bottom is pebbly with stars. . . . It seemed as if I might next cast my line upward into the air, as well as downward into this element which was scarcely more dense. Thus I caught two fishes as it were with one hook. . . . Walden is blue at one time and green at another. . . . Lying between the earth and the heavens, it partakes of the color of both. . . . In such transparent and seemingly bottomless water, reflecting the clouds, I seemed to be floating through the air as in a balloon, and their swimming impressed me as a kind of flight or hovering. . . . Shall I go to heaven or a-fishing?"[76]

But perhaps *Walden*'s dominant imagery is that of the circle, whose clarity and purity matches the similar geometric order and serenity of paintings by Duncanson, Lane, and Bingham. Thoreau brings it up in numerous guises—the calendar and the seasons, the setting and rising sun, the globe, the town, and of course the pond itself. First, he admits to the abstraction of the year in "for convenience, putting the experience of two years into one," and later stating that "My days were not days of the week. . . . The phenomena of the year take place every day on the pond on a small scale. . . . The day is an epitome of the year. The night is winter, the morning and evening are the spring and fall, and the noon is the summer." When he is finished at Walden, "Perhaps it seemed to me that I had several more lives to live," as if there will be other cycles to complete.[77] The passage of the seasons was another inspiration to Thoreau: "I enjoy the friendship of the seasons. . . . The indescribable innocence and beneficence of Nature,—of sun and wind and rain, of summer and winter,—such health, such cheer, they afford forever! . . . the absolute progress of the seasons . . . As every season seems best to us in its turn, so the coming in of spring is like the creation of Cosmos out of Chaos and the realization of the Golden Age. . . . In a pleasant spring morning all men's sins are forgiven. . . . We can never have enough of Nature."[78]

Though he took note of a "hawk sailing over some farmer's yard" and "the circle of the town," it was Walden Pond itself that "was made deep and pure for a symbol." In one permutation, "It is earth's eye; looking into which the beholder measures the depth of his own nature." Elsewhere, he referred to "the color of its iris." When he measured the pond, "I was surprised at its general regularity. . . . The regularity of the bottom and its conformity to the shores and the range of the neighboring hills were so perfect." Out on the water, "I used to raise the echoes by striking with a paddle on the side of my boat, filling the surrounding woods with circling and dilating sound. . . . The forest has never so good a setting, nor is so distinctly beautiful, as when seen from the middle of a small lake amid hills which rise from the water's edge."[79] He amplified this metaphor: "it had the appearance of an amphitheatre. . . . The largest pond is as sensitive to atmospheric changes as the globule of mercury in its tube. . . . One might suppose that it was called, originally, *Walled-in* Pond. The Pond was my well ready dug." It was at once personal and cosmic: "I have my horizon bounded by woods all to myself. . . . I have, as it were, my own sun and moon and stars, and a little world all to myself. . . . The pure Walden water is mingled with the sacred water of the Ganges. . . . Our voyaging is only great-circle sailing."[80]

In *Walden*'s final pages Thoreau returns to his favorite imagery of the sun's orb at a time of day and season in passage: "the setting sun is reflected from the windows of the alms-house as brightly as from the rich man's abode; the snow melts before its door as early in the spring." With a joy and optimism characteristic of this season in America, he closes his book with the lines, "Only that day dawns to which we are awake. There is more day to dawn. The sun is but a morning star."[81]

Walt Whitman

Joy and optimism also characterize Walt Whitman's equally original outpouring of *Leaves of Grass*, extroverted in contrast to Thoreau's introspection and unbounded in form instead of distilled and reductive. If Thoreau's work stands

Figure 46. Thomas
Eakins, *Walt Whitman*,
1887. Oil on canvas,
30 x 24 in. The
Pennsylvania Academy
of the Fine Arts,
Philadelphia, General
Fund Purchase

with Lane's and Bingham's in their shared clarity of design, Whitman's aligns
with Church's in its exuberant, all-embracing outlook. Whitman's long poem
was as radical in form as its content. As we know, it blurred poetry and prose
and overturned most standard literary conventions of punctuation, grammar,
meter, and narrative logic. Like Jefferson's Monticello and Peale's family portrait, *Leaves of Grass* was also a form of ongoing autobiography, which Whitman
added to and modified over much of his life. From its first edition in 1855 the
book underwent at least eight more formal editions until the so-called Deathbed
Edition in 1891. Correspondingly, its tone and contents changed from the early
positive vision to the more ambivalent and anxious tenor of poems added during the Civil War, Lincoln's assassination, Reconstruction, and the ills of the
poet's old age. At the same time, Whitman also saw his life merged with that of
America; his ambivalences and conflicts were those of the nation's, and his revolution in writing corresponded to the larger upheavals in the country's politics
and culture.

     As with Melville and Thoreau, there exists an enormous body of secondary literature on Whitman, from many illuminating biographies to probing studies of all aspects of his themes.[82] What we want to highlight here are some of the principal distinguishing elements of *Leaves of Grass* itself, its circumstances and presentation as well as the actual text. The first edition was bound in bright green leather with embossed vine motifs, a play on the double meaning of the title's subject, that is, the verdant landscape and the pages of a book. Facing the title page was a photograph of Whitman, in lieu of his name, identifying him as author. He appears as a jaunty workingman, a reminder of his prior working career as a journalist and an assertion of the common democratic man, who now replaces the refined and polished formality of prior poets and poetry. Below the title are printed only the place and year of publication. We know Whitman designed, arranged, and paid for the book's printing in Brooklyn, intentionally launching its publication on July Fourth, 1855, just as Lewis and Clark a half century before and Thoreau a year previous had associated their acts with Independence Day. Only on the verso of the title page does the author's name appear holding the copyright, but as "Walter Whitman," another reminder of the transformed informal poet waiting in the text ahead. In short, Whitman will invent a new self and language for his country and time.

He further embellished this act of invention by writing and publishing several enthusiastic reviews of his book and by shamelessly quoting Emerson's famous lines written to him about it: "I find it the most extraordinary piece of wit and wisdom that America has yet contributed. . . . I greet you at the beginning of a great career."[83] Without any table of contents or headings, Whitman immediately establishes his personal voice with a lengthy prose introduction, broken into lines according to its internal rhythms and almost indistinguishable from the free verse that follows. Just as Thoreau was aware of writing against the background of the Union's moves toward dissolution, so Whitman began by declaring, "The United States themselves are essentially the greatest poem. . . . Here is not merely a nation but a teeming nation of nations." Then follow many of the phrases, images, and colloquialisms that he will elaborate on in his subsequent verse: "the genius of the United States . . . the common people . . . the freshness and candor of their physiognomy . . . the fluency of their speech . . . unrhymed poetry. . . . The American poets are to enclose old and new for America."[84]

There follows the first of his well-known inventories, a run-on celebration of American places: "The blue breadth over the inland sea off Massachusetts and Maine and over Manhattan bay and over Champlain and Erie and over Ontario and Huron and Michigan and Superior, and over the Texan and Mexican and Floridian and Cuban seas and over the seas off California and Oregon. . . . " This is but half of the sentence, with only one comma at its center. Its flow and rhythm rather take their cadence from the inhalation and exhalation of the human breath, an early assertion of Whitman's disregard for traditional sentence structure and appearance. A few lines later he enumerates the variety of American trees and birds, having claimed that the job of the American poet is to incarnate "its geography and natural life and rivers and lakes."[85] At this moment in the mid-1850s Whitman had great faith in the present and the future, for himself and for America: "The greatest poet is today . . . himself the age transfigured." He saw his calling to provide no less than a new art appropriate to the energies and self-confidence of a democratic America: "A great poem is for ages and ages in common. . . . A new order shall rise and they shall be the priests of man, and every man shall be his own priest. . . . The English language befriends the grand American expression. . . . it is brawny enough and limber and full enough." He concluded by saying, "The proof of a poet is that his country absorbs him as affectionately as he has absorbed it."[86]

This then led directly to the famous opening lines of the major poem, "Song of Myself," which occupies a good half of his volume:

> I celebrate myself,
> And what I assume you shall assume,
> For every atom belonging to me as good belongs to you.

Here in the single opening noun is the grand "I" who embraces all and, in doing so, aspires to write for the whole American union. The lines conclude with "you," which Whitman has inventively charged with both the singular and the plural, the intimate and the worldly.[87] Union with others was a notion he returned to often: "In all people I see myself. . . . Do I contradict myself? Very well then. . . . I contradict myself; I am large. . . . I contain multitudes." He took it up again in the succeeding poem, "A Song for Occupations": "If you meet some stranger in the street and love him or her, do I often not meet strangers in the street and love them? . . . I am this day just as much in love with them as you. But I am eternally in love with you and with all my fellows upon the earth."[88]

Love, of course, was part of the larger, recurring theme of sexuality. Whitman broke new ground in addressing women equally with men and in his advocacy of liberated sexuality. His references move freely between opposite and same-sex relationships, as a further recasting of democratic equality and union: "Urge and urge and urge, Always the procreant urge of the world. . . . You settled your head athwart my hips and gently turned over upon me, And parted the shirt from my bosom-bone, and plunged your tongue to my barestript heart. . . . I am the mate and companion of people, all just as immortal and fathomless as myself. . . . for me mine male and female . . . Who need be afraid of the merge? Undrape. . . ."[89] Perhaps best known is section 11 in "Song of Myself" which begins:

> Twenty-eight young men bathe by the shore,
> Twenty-eight young men, and all so friendly,
> Twenty-eight years of womanly life, and all so lonesome.

The passage begins with the male presence but soon introduces the female. In a following line Whitman emphasizes water as a sensuous element: "You splash in the water there." His subsequent description of details suggests both purification and eroticism:

> The beards of the young men glistening with wet, it ran from
>   their long hair,
> Little streams passed all over their bodies,
> An unseen hand also passed over their bodies,
> It descended trembling from their temples and ribs.

The number twenty-eight, of course, carries associations with the lunar and menstrual cycle, and although he returns to the male figure at the end, the imagery has become more sexually charged, climaxing in allusions to arousal and ejaculation:

> The young men float on their backs, their white bellies swell to
>   the sun . . .
> They do not know who puffs and declines with pendant and
>   bending arch,
> They do not think whom they souse with spray.[90]

Elsewhere Whitman continued to move freely between female and male sexuality: "I am the poet of the woman the same as the man, And I say it is as great to be a woman as to be a man. . . . Press close barebosomed night! Press close magnetic nourishing night! . . . Smile O voluptuous coolbreathed earth! . . . . Smile, for your lover comes!. . . . Thruster holding me tight and that I hold tight!. . . . rock me in billowy drowse, Dash me with amorous wet. . . . I believe in the flesh and the appetites." Just as mother earth had an attraction, so also could an animal: "A gigantic beauty of a stallion, fresh and responsive to my caresses. . . . His nostrils dilate. . . . my heels embrace him. . . . his well built limbs tremble with pleasure." Given Whitman's own complex sexuality, his metaphors often hint of repression as much as expression, of voyeurism as well as desire. "My lovers suffocate me! Crowding my lips, and thick in the pores of my skin, Jostling me through streets and public halls . . . coming naked to me at night."[91]

Variations of these phrases appear in the shorter poems that follow. "A Song for Occupations" opens with "Come closer to me, Push close my lovers and take the best I possess, Yield closer and closer and give me the best you possess." The opening section of "The Sleepers" includes, "The married couple sleep calmly in their bed. . . . The sisters sleep lovingly side by side in their bed, The men sleep lovingly side by side in theirs." Likewise, he also reintroduced the eroticism of the male swimmer: "I see a beautiful gigantic swimmer swimming naked. . . . I see his white body. . . . His beautiful body is borne in the circling eddies. . . ." Among the early lines interspersed in "I Sing the Body Electric" are, "The bodies of men and women engirth me, and I engirth them. . . . The male is perfect and that of the female is perfect. . . . The swimmer naked in the swimmingbath . . . seen as he swims through the salt transparent greenshine, or lies on his back and rolls silently with the heave of the water . . . The wrestle of wrestlers . . . two apprentice-boys, quite grown, lusty, goodnatured, nativeborn, out on the vacant lot at sundown after work. . . . The natural perfect and varied attitudes . . . the bent head, the curved neck, the counting: Suchlike I love. . . . And swim with the swimmer, and wrestle with wrestlers, and march in line with the firemen. . . ."[92]

When Whitman used a phrase like "procreant urge," however, he had in his mind not just its sexual connotation but in an interchangeable sense the impulse of artistic creativity. Whitman hoped his poetic energies would embrace all regions of America and be a positive force in the face of growing conflicts. As much about the political state of America in the mid-fifties, *Leaves of Grass* also expresses faith and confidence in the healing power of poetry itself. An early line states: "Stop this day and night with me and you shall possess the origin of all poems," and later he adds, "I am the poet of the body, And I am the poet of the soul." In addition, he proclaimed his poetry as both forward-looking and democratic: "Endless unfolding of words of ages! And mine a word of the modern . . . a word en masse." In "Song for Occupations" Whitman takes note of the mechanics of printing: "I was chilled with the cold types and cylinder and wet paper between us." Near the close of his volume he returns to honor words and language: "Great is language. . . . it is the mightiest of the sciences, It is the fulness and color and form and diversity of the earth. . . . and of men and women . . . and of all qualities and processes . . . Great is the English speech. . . . What speech is so great as the English?"[93]

Of course, spoken and written speech throughout received Whitman's manipulative and transforming attention. F. O. Matthiessen was one of the earliest to estimate that Whitman deployed in the first edition of *Leaves of Grass* a vocabulary of over thirteen thousand words, of which little more than a half were used only once.[94] Many of these were invented, others were adapted technical or foreign words, still others colloquial or unexpected in their use, as if

Whitman were responding to Noah Webster's impulse to capture the American vocabulary. A sampling includes: "Ya-honk, clack of sticks, omnific, sextillions, eleves, gymnosophist, teokallis, chuff of your hand, accoucheur, etui, ennuyees, douceurs, cache and cache again, erysipalite."[95] Closely related was Whitman's exclamatory catalogues of names. One section itemized professions: "contralto, carpenter, pilot, mate, duck-shooter, deacons, spinning-girl, farmer, lunatic, jour painter, quadroon girl, machinist, young fellow, half-breed." Shortly after, he added: "A farmer, mechanic, or artist. . . . a gentleman, sailor, lover or quaker, A prisoner, fancy-man, rowdy, lawyer, physician or priest." Naturally, nicknames pleased him: "a Hoosier, a Badger, a Buckeye." But we also find minerals: "gneiss and coal and long-threaded moss and fruits and grains and esculent roots"; animals: "panther, buck, rattlesnake, otter, alligator, black bear"; states and cities: "We walk the roads of Ohio and Massachusetts and Virginia and Wisconsin and New York and New Orleans and Texas and Montreal and San Francisco and Charleston and Savannah and Mexico."[96]

We are made aware of words not just for their own sake, but for their sounds as well, another reminder of the driving force of Whitman's personal, physical voice. One favorite device was that of alliteration, especially when it served the imagery presented, as in: "Sea of stretched ground-swells! Sea breathing broad and convulsive breaths! Sea of the brine of life! Sea of unshovelled and always-ready graves! Howler and scooper of storms! Capricious and dainty sea!" Another was the repetition of a word or phrase beginning sequential lines. For example, "In vain" introduced nine lines in a row, and "Where" begins some thirty-one lines with but a few interruptions. Often he eliminated punctuation almost entirely in order to achieve a breathless accumulation of sensations: "Storming enjoying planning loving cautioning, Backing and filling, appearing and disappearing . . . Books friendships philosophers priests action pleasure pride beat up and down seeking to give satisfaction."[97] Such linguistic originality not only made Whitman singularly modern in Victorian America, literary historians have shown us how much his writing has been a source of inspiration and precedent for much of modern poetry in the twentieth century.

In contemplating the contrasts between Melville, Thoreau, and Whitman, we face once more the paradoxes of America at mid-century, a moment we could call expansive as well as introspective, orderly as well as explosive. Referring more to the dichotomies in luminist paintings of the period, Barbara Novak once used the terms "Grand Opera and the Still Small Voice" and "Sound and Silence: Changing Concepts of the Sublime."[98] At once in opposition and interdependent, these antiphonal voices were heard as much in literature and art as in contemporary politics. The polarities held in balance for several astonishing years, before the country yielded to the struggles of the 1860s and those that followed through the rest of the century.

The Architect's Abstractions: Robert Mills

WE CANNOT argue that the neoclassical style, so dominant in American architecture at mid-century, was by any means as innovative as American writing at the same time. By definition, it was a derivative movement, yet the revival of Greek and Roman forms had enormous and pervasive impact and carried powerful symbolic value for Americans in the decades before the Civil War. What is significant is that neoclassicism can be said to have reached its culmination in the decade of the 1850s. Indeed, by then other revival styles, such as the Egyptian and the Gothic, were already gaining in appeal, and by the next decade no single manner so universally dominated architectural forms as neoclassicism had in the first half of the century. Certainly, ancient styles had been a part of national architectural expression since the beginning of the republic—Thomas Jefferson's Monticello, the Virginia State Capitol, and the University of Virginia, and Benjamin Latrobe's banks and Baltimore Cathedral come to mind as obvious examples. But as William H. Pierson, Jr., has so eloquently demonstrated, neoclassicism became by mid-century a truly national style, popular across most of the United States as it was then, that is, in all of the country east of the Mississippi.[99]

Just as Daniel Webster sought to emulate in his congressional speeches the language and phraseology of the ancient Roman senate, so architects tried through archaeology and firsthand visits to make use of original ancient structures for many types of American buildings, private as well as public, statehouses and courthouses, banks and academic buildings, churches of various denominations and domestic dwellings. Rotundas, colonnades, and temple forms served all of these purposes, and the dignified effect of ancient marble could be replicated equally in stone, masonry, or painted wood, depending on

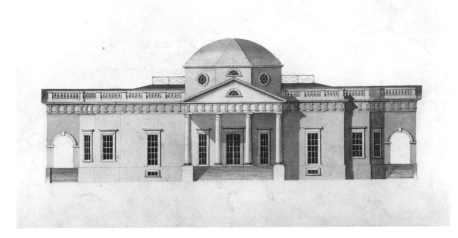

Figure 47. Robert Mills, Drawing of Monticello, 1803. Ink and wash on paper. Massachusetts Historical Society, Boston

financial practicality, class need, and symbolic intent. Americans believed that on national soil arose no less than a reincarnation of the values and virtues of ancient republican order and democratic practices. Not surprisingly, the 1850s was the last period when the country could so widely sustain such self-confidence, heroic possibility, and sheer idealism, and Greek temple variations more often than not served the newly built capitals in the western states as they joined the union, in both the North and the South.

Aside from the associations with ancient precedents, there was the appealing purity of materials and design, the clarity of expression, the sense of simplicity and endurance, which could, in Whitman's phrase, "contain multitudes." In short, the Greek revival perfectly suited self-image, regional image, and national image. Part of its universality resided in the reductive geometry of its essential forms—the circles and spheres we have already found in Thoreau, the triangles and receding planes in Bingham, or interlocking horizontals and verticals in Lane. All reflected aspirations for order, harmony, and permanence held by the country until the balances shifted and the compromises collapsed.

One architect in particular embodied the perfection of the Greek-revival style and above all employed it with an unsurpassed creativity, sophistication, and expressive force worthy of the moment. That was Robert Mills, held up as the first major professionally trained architect to be born in the country. A native of Charleston, South Carolina (b. 1781), he apprenticed as a young man with James Hoban, Thomas Jefferson, and Benjamin Latrobe and began designing his own first significant works as early as 1812. Among the best known are his Monumental Church (1812) in Richmond, Virginia, and the Fireproof Building (1822) in Charleston.[100] These displayed a clean, bold simplicity and a dramatic control of solid massings and voids. Mills moved in 1830 to Washington, D.C., where he gained some of the most important national commissions during the following two decades.

He undertook the renovation of the old House Chamber, worked on designs for a new city prison, and in 1841 drew up plans for development of the Mall and a building for the new Smithsonian Institution.[101] Undoubtedly, the structures for which Mills is most justly remembered are the new Patent Office, General Post Office, and Treasury Building, all begun in the later 1830s and completed in 1842. They were all monumental buildings, each occupying a city block, and probably the most impressive to be constructed in the heart of the capital city after the White House and the U.S. Capitol. With large-scale temple-front entrances and colonnades, the architecture well suited all the increased functional needs of each institution and provided appropriate symbolic imagery of national growth and power. The cleanly sculpted walls and expansive interior spaces all projected a sense of democracy in action; it is revealing that the governmental functions requiring new edifices at this time were those of the nation's expanding commerce, communications, and technology. For example, the patents and models of inventions submitted by citizens, formerly housed in the basement of the Library of Congress, had escalated so dramatically in number that the country now needed a vast new building to contain and catalogue them. Mills's commissions in a larger sense reflected the rapid increases in the country's population, additions of territory, industrialization, and prosperity in the decades approaching mid-century.

The Washington Monument

Perhaps of all Mills's designs the one that most embodied the combined aspirations and frustrations of this mid-century moment, and the only one actually under construction in the early 1850s, was the Washington National Monument (fig. 48). As completed, it was one of the most austere and reductive of all neoclassical works, a piece of monumental sculpture as much as an architectural design, set in the heart of the capital's public spaces as a symbol of commemoration and of national continuity. As historians tell us, memorials and proposals for memorials in honor of Washington began to appear at the time of his death in 1799. Mills himself had already executed one of the most imposing, his Washington Monument for Baltimore, which was constructed between 1813 and 1838.[102] Drawing on his knowledge of plates in books he knew from Thomas Jefferson's library, as well as more immediate familiarity with European precedents such as Trajan's Column in Rome and the Vendôme Column in Paris, Mills designed a massive cubic base from which his cylindrical column rose. This culminated in a solid rectangular capital, surmounted by a drum and cupola and finally a statue of Washington himself. The mix here of the figural form and simplified geometric masses evolved through a number of preceding

Figure 48. Robert Mills, Washington National Monument, 1848–54, 1880–84. Washington, D.C.

designs that were much more elaborate in their narrative content and architectural embellishments. One such early proposal for Baltimore included a series of surrounding balconies, sculptural reliefs at the base depicting Revolutionary War events, and at the top an elaborate sculpture of Washington driving a chariot guided by Liberty. Through subsequent drawings Mills gradually stripped the column of this visual elaboration and reduced the topmost sculpture to a single figure, which showed Washington resigning his commission at Annapolis. Although some impetus doubtless came from financial constraints, the final results were more powerful and suggestive. The same process would occur with his Washington effort in the city of Washington.

In the meantime Mills submitted drawings for the Bunker Hill Monument in Boston, a project that was ultimately built by Solomon Willard.

As conceived by both architects, however, this was to be a plain obelisk, an allusion to the civilization of ancient Egypt and its notions of immortality. This
stark symbolic form would, of course, anticipate the final shaping of the
Washington National Monument. When he arrived in the capital city in 1830,
Mills was already discussing with Congress a memorial to the first president.
Again, his initial conceptions included extensive allegorical decoration and
complex architectural elements, such as a pyramid with four obelisks and a statue, along with a spiral ascending ramp. At one moment Mills even explored
Gothic-revival details in an alternative scheme.[103] Most of his designs envisioned a shaft, whether cubic or cylindrical, rising from a contrasting circular or
square base, combinations that had various ancient sources, but which Mills's
biographers suggest he recalled from his early work with Latrobe, in particular
the older architect's Frank's Island Lighthouse in Louisiana at the mouth of the
Mississippi. For Mills's other mentor, Jefferson, the lighthouse had both the
practicality of a major structural marker and the symbolism of a beacon.[104] The
commemorative form that Mills sought to distill for Washington likewise
required symbolic power and authority.

Ever since the centennial of Washington's birth in 1832, Mills had given
sporadic attention to possible plans for a memorial. His drawings were accepted in 1845, and by 1848 Congress granted an area of land near the Potomac,
which L'Enfant had envisioned as a site for a monument on his original plans for
the capital. A ceremony for the laying of the cornerstone took place on the
Fourth of July in 1849, with a commitment of resources and optimism that were
to unravel as the 1850s moved on. Mills initially envisioned an ambitious edifice
of massive scale and complex components, such as a great circular pantheon
base recalling Hadrian's tomb in Rome, in which Washington's tomb would be
installed, and other elements drawn from Egyptian and Greek precedents, all
combined to project a suitable imagery of national pride and heroic immortality.
There was to be an elaborate program of allegorical and portrait sculpture, plus
a colossal statue of Washington placed within a rotunda and decorative paintings depicting scenes of the Republic's founding.[105] Symbolically, construction
was to take place with stones contributed from all the states of the union.

Soon financial setbacks and political squabbling began to intrude, and
the monument as erected was greatly scaled back, without any massive colon-
naded base or decorative sculpture. The strong impulses for a grand historical
and allegorical edifice now yielded to a simple but paradoxically more expressive memorial to the Father of the Country. Mills added a strong pyramidal conclusion to the summit of the shaft in order to augment the visual sense of its
soaring height. As we know today, the monument sits directly on the site; the
rise of ground sloping up to its base has replaced the originally intended stone
pantheon, and a ring of flags circling the area hints at the one-time plans for a

colonnade. Despite the final minimalism, the structure represents the essence of Mills's passionate efforts to introduce "a *correct* taste in architecture into our country" for "the *whole Union*."[106] Its clean and legible solid geometry reaches for a transcendental harmony we have seen in the best visual and literary expression of the time, and we may propose that this one work represented the culmination of such aspirations held by Americans at mid-century.

But those aspirations increasingly fragmented and conflicted with one another as the fifties wore on. Progress on construction slowed, public interest and official dedication—so enthusiastic and unified at the laying of the cornerstone—began to wane, and contributions of money as well as materials also slackened. Finally, construction came to a halt in 1854 (the year of the Kansas-Nebraska Act, let us recall); growing regionalist tensions led to states refusing to contribute native stones. The deaths of some members of the original organizing committee meant more loss in momentum, and Mills himself became diverted with new work on the Capitol and additions to his Treasury Building. Then in 1855 criticism from the Know-Nothing party polarized political support for the monument, and undoubtedly affected by such pressures, Mills suffered a stroke and died that same year. His ideals and those of the country so eloquently embodied in this project were truncated when construction of the shaft stopped as it reached 153 feet, barely one third of its intended height.

Standing at one end of the Mall, the Washington National Monument was intended to anchor the great axes of the L'Enfant plan, with the President's House to the north and the Capitol Building to the east, a bold sculptural homage to the nation's patriarchy facing its active seat of government in a dynamic tension of past and present. But because of unreconcilable regionalist disagreements, the national clock stopped, and it would take more than two decades for the resources and the will of the union to resume work on the Washington Monument. Only with the national centennial in 1876 did sentiment return for completing work on the structure, albeit with a stone of a slightly different color, visible even today in the upper portion of the shaft. We might say that the assertive masculine image of national fatherhood stood impotent and emasculated in 1855. The country's sense of direction was fragmented, and the last half of the decade saw it move uncontrollably toward civil war. But politics was only one force undoing the ideals and optimism of mid-century; the decade also concluded with the intellectual assault of Charles Darwin's publication *On the Origin of Species*, which undermined the spiritual authority of nature and the confidence in absolutes people had had in preceding years. In addition, the gathering steam of industry would rise to new dominance during the second half of the century, transforming American life and geography. Even the idea and reality of the frontier, so much an image of promise and possibility in both 1800 and 1850, was to expire on the western horizon by century's end.

PART THREE

Circa 1900:
Disorientation

Memoirs, Music, and Meditations

AS THE nineteenth century turned to the twentieth, American consciousness ranged in multiple directions, geographic and imaginative, looking backward (in Edward Bellamy's phrase) as well as forward, looking upward to the skyscraper and downward from the airplane, inward to the sphere of the self and outward to other hemispheres. The impulse of nostalgia mingled with that of anticipation, with each in part generated by anxiety. The uncertainties of the present raised concerns about what the new century would bring, even as it stimulated the pursuits of retrospection and memory. There was reason to feel uneasy. Earlier nineteenth-century ideas of order and progress appeared challenged or disrupted by social, economic, and political upheavals. The growing awareness of Darwin during the second half of the century undermined the spiritual foundations of nature and showed that the haphazard, the uncertain, and the accidental were significant factors in the human condition. The efforts of Reconstruction in the decade after the Civil War eventually failed in psychological as well as social terms. By century's end, the United States Census Bureau had officially declared the closing of the American frontier, as settlements and transportation uninterruptedly reached across the continent to the Pacific coast. First in the 1870s and again in the 1890s bank failures and severe financial crises accompanied depressions both economic and moral. Accelerating immigration rates reached new highs in the opening decade of the new century, transforming the growth, density, and character of life in New York and other large cities of the country. The memory of Lincoln's traumatic loss remained strong, but new shocks to the national structure came with the additional presidential assassinations of James Garfield in 1881 and William McKinley in 1901. An even greater mark of that year as a turning point was the death of Queen Victoria, whose name had come to be identified throughout the

English-speaking world with the entire age now gone.

In the years around the turn of the century America was a nation in flux, marked as much by a sense of old ways ending as by new innovations portending the future. With western expansion coming to a close, the country now turned elsewhere to expand its presence, signaled by the short Spanish-American War in 1898 over Cuba. The following year the United States reaffirmed its Monroe Doctrine with a so-called New Manifest Destiny of territorial reach, first annexing Hawaii, Puerto Rico, Guam, and the Philippines. In 1900 came the purchase of the Danish West Indies, in 1901 the designation of Cuba as a protectorate, and in 1903 the annexation of the Panama Canal Zone. Then came control over American Samoa and the struggle for free trade in the Far East, led by Adams's friend John Hay through the Open Door Policy to China. In the year of Victoria's death, 1901, the United States reached agreement with Great Britain for the right to build the Panama Canal, an enterprise that would transform, symbolically and physically, relationships between the continents and the hemispheres.

There were other energies at work in these years as well. Invented in the mid-1870s, the telephone became a significant new means of communication by the new century. Equally important as a means of conflating time and distance was the wireless telegraph. Guglielmo Marconi constructed the first transmission station for wireless communication in 1897, and three years later the first transatlantic wireless message was sent from England to the United States. During the same period Thomas Edison's invention of the lightbulb came to transform the appearance and experience of urban spaces especially, as electrification and incandescent lights helped to illuminate cities around the clock. We need only look at the early night photographs of New York by Alfred Stieglitz in the late nineties, or the urban landscapes of the Ash Can School painted in the early years of the twentieth century, to see the compelling visual effects.

In addition, New York opened its first subway line in 1904, an operation that would have a radical effect not only on transportation for large numbers of people but also on the economic and architectural development of the city. The notion of building both above and below street level dated back to previous decades in the nineteenth century, with elevated rail lines proposed as early as the 1840s and designs for underground travel conceived not long after. The building of els along many of New York's avenues reached its heyday around 1880, and their operation is still a familiar if noisy presence in many parts of the city. However, the inevitable congestion above ground only accelerated planning for subway travel. Various forms of pneumatic-tube construction and differing means of propulsion, including steam and electricity, were explored by the end of the century. Ground was broken on the first subway line early in 1900, two years after the historic consolidation of Manhattan with the sur-

rounding boroughs into the modern entity of New York City. The opening of the subway on October 27, 1904, thus came to symbolize urban unity, aspirations, and economic growth. Even more, the new visions of speed and motion were seen as signs of modernism itself, with their artistic counterparts in the urban imagery of fragmentation and simultaneity painted by John Marin and Joseph Stella. It is also no coincidence that the subway and skyscraper construction paralleled one another: This moment, as historians have pointed out, saw completion of the Flatiron Building (1902) and the Times Tower (1904).[1] Thus the two powerful axes of motion through the density of the modern city would be the vertical provided by the elevator and the horizontal provided by the subway.

Just as far-reaching in impact, though less immediately visible, were the profound revolutions taking place in the science of matter with the discovery of new elements and laws of physics. Henry Adams was to find a metaphor for these new forces in the great dynamos on display at the world's fairs of 1893 and 1900: "To Adams the dynamo became a symbol of infinity. As he grew accustomed to the great gallery of machines, he began to feel the forty-foot dynamos as a moral force. . . ."[2]

Others were more fearful of the strong currents of change and saw disintegration and collapse in the waning years of the old century. Indeed, the period came to be called "fin de siècle" in recognition of a widespread sense of foreboding. The term came from a French play of 1888, and was soon identified with the decade of the nineties as a time of endings.[3] Associated with that notion were feelings of malaise, decay, and paranoia. Accelerated immigration aggravated class polarities and racial animosities, prostitution and poverty, slums and disease, urban unrest and social alienation. In Germany books were published with such portentous titles as *The Last Days of Mankind* (by Karl Kraus) and *Concerning the Last Things* (by Otto Weininger). Where the end of the eighteenth century had seen the upheavals of the American and French Revolutions, the onset of the twentieth century brought gathering intimations of new war on an international scale. As his mind tried to adjust to the growing evidence of disorder, Adams had to admit, "at last in 1900, a new avalanche of unknown forces had fallen on it, which required new mental powers to control."[4]

If nostalgia and reflection were common modes of response at this time, American writers pursued several variations in their narratives. For example, Mark Twain's late short stories are notable for their turn to deep bitterness and disillusionment. Stephen Crane's *Red Badge of Courage* (1895), although acknowledged primarily for its modernist terse realism, is also a sentimental, impressionistic look back at valor and mortality in the Civil War, at a time when the age of Lincoln and the survival of the nation had accumulated special

Figure 49. Edward Steichen, *The Flatiron Building, Evening*, 1905. Gum-bichromate toned blue-green over platinum print. The Metropolitan Museum of Art, New York, Gift of Alfred Stieglitz, 1933

poignance. The novelist William Dean Howells's *A Traveller from Altruria* (1894) took the course of escapism with an imaginary futurist tale. Probably the best known of this genre was Edward Bellamy's *Looking Backward* (1888), set in the millennial year 2000. Respectively, Howells and Bellamy focused on two contemporary preoccupations, social constraints and economic inequalities. As Howells wrote, "If a man got out of work, he turned his hand to something else; if a man failed in business, he started in again in some other direction; as a last resort, in both cases, he went West, pre-empted a quarter section of public land and grew up in the country. Now the country is grown up; the public land is gone; business is full on all sides. . . ."[5] For Bellamy it was the dark side of industrialization, a mass-production economy and unequal distribution of capital, that needed reforming. It is no accident that utopian visions should emerge in the very years when Americans saw the demise of their continental frontier. Critics have pointed out that between the date of Bellamy's novel and the turn of the century more than two hundred utopian books were published, forming one of the most popular literary genres of the period.[6] Bellamy spoke for many when he wrote in a postscript: "All thoughtful men agree that the present aspect of society is portentous of great changes." Though critical in intent, he ultimately wanted his novel to affirm "man's essential nobleness . . . the Golden Age lies before us and not behind us, and is not far away."[7]

Henry James

Was it a golden age or, in the dispirited words of Henry James, "the triumph of the superficial and the apotheosis of the raw"?[8] This was the ambivalence of 1900, quite different in its tensions from the unpredictability of 1800. Then, the instabilities of Washington's death, the contested two-party election, and fragility of the government at home and abroad were overcome by the far-reaching optimism and sense of possibility shared by the country's leaders and populace. By 1900 the acceleration of change was equal cause for expectation and for dismay. The latter dominated Henry James's reaction to America in 1904, when he returned, after a twenty-year absence as an expatriate, to tour and assess his native land. Arriving in August, he visited many sections of the country over the following eleven months and recorded his observations in notes, letters, and eventually *The American Scene*, published soon after his return to England. Like Thoreau's *Walden*, James's book was far more than a journal—throughout he obsessively referred to himself as "the restless analyst"[9]—and its shape does not reflect his actual itinerary or chronology. After his arrival in New York, he traveled to New England in the early autumn and went south during the winter, but he made periodic return stays in New York City, visited Chicago in the early spring on his way to the West Coast, and went back and

Figure 50. John Singer
Sargent, *Henry James,*
1913. Oil on canvas,
33 x 26 in. National
Portrait Gallery,
London

forth between New England and several mid-Atlantic cities before leaving for England on July 5.

To give coherence and focus to his book, really an extended essay, James concentrated on New England first and followed with a long major section on New York, a framing return to Newport and Boston, and a series of chapters gradually moving south, through Philadelphia, Baltimore, Richmond, Charleston, Savannah, and Florida. He makes only passing reference to Chicago or his West Coast experiences. He was not interested in recording contemporary events, politics, or personalities. Although he dined with Mark Twain on the evening of his arrival, paid short visits to William Dean Howells in Kittery

Point, Maine, and to Charles Eliot Norton in Cambridge, and stayed for a week or more with his brother William James in New Hampshire, Edith Wharton in Massachusetts and New York, and Henry Adams in Washington, they are only obliquely identified. Suggestively, he termed the nation's capital "the City of Conversation" and commented, "Washington talks about herself, and about almost nothing else."[10] Rather, it was the impact of history on the country in his time away, especially the changes to the built environment, that concerned him most. Philadelphia struck him as a city of society, but even more he responded to "its admirable comprehensive flatness. . . . The absence of the note of the perpetual perpendicular, the New York, the Chicago note. . . ."[11]

By contrast, Richmond, as capital of the Old South, expressed the irrevocable burden of the Civil War: "the final massacres, the blood, the flames, the tears; they are chalked with the sinister red mark at sight of which the sensitive nerve of association forever winces. . . . I was tasting of the very bitterness of the immense, grotesque, defeated project—the project, extravagant, fantastic, and to-day pathetic in its folly, of a vast Slave State. . . . such passive, such pathetic victims of fate, as so played upon and betrayed, so beaten and bruised, by the burden of their condition." In some of his most elegiac language James went on: "The collapse of the old order, the humiliation of defeat, the bereavement and bankruptcy involved, represented, with its obscure miseries and tragedies, the social revolution the most unrecorded and undepicted, in proportion to its magnitude, that ever was."[12]

Washington in turn was easy to see in terms of carved spaces and forms: "the great park-aspect gained, and became nobly artificial, by the very complexity of the plan of the place—the perpetual perspectives, the converging, radiating avenues, the frequent circles and crossways. . . . This clustered, yet at the same time oddly scattered, city, a general impression of high granite steps, of light grey colonnades . . . overweighted by a single Dome and overaccentuated by a single Shaft . . . figments of the upper air." This last was of course Robert Mills's prominent final commission, which James went on to characterize cleverly in this conversational city, as "the fine Washington Obelisk . . . not a little as if some loud monosyllable had been uttered, in a preoccupied company. . . ."[13]

While James took offense most with the architectural disfiguring of the once-familiar face of America, he was alternatively capable of lyric passages memorializing the felt air and light of different places. The nuances of atmosphere he observed in cities and countryside were equally sensitive. The New Hampshire fall first caught his attention: "This light, from whatever source proceeding, cast an irresistible spell, bathed the picture in the confessed resignation of early autumn, the charming sadness that resigned itself with a silent smile." In a voice recalling Thoreau's, he added, "The apple-tree, in New England, plays the part of the olive in Italy, charges itself with the effect of detail. . . . its office in early autumn is to scatter coral and gold."[14] In the Hudson River valley he sensed "an atmosphere draping it indeed in luminous mystery, hanging it about with sun-shot silver. . . . the strong silver light, all simplifying and ennobling, in which I see West Point. . . . the geography of the ideal, in the long perspective of the poetry of association. . . . type and tone good enough for Claude or Turner, if they could have walked by these rivers instead of their thin rivers of France and Italy." At Concord, Massachusetts, he recorded "the extraordinary sweetness of the river . . . under the autumn sun . . . the sense of this full, slow, sleepy, meadowy flood."[15]

The Rhode Island shore at Newport was a favorite haunt for James, for both its social and its visual appeal: "The charm was there again. . . . under a chastened light and in a purple sea, the dainty isle of Aquidneck . . . a whole world that called out to the long afternoons of youth, a world with its scale so measured and intended and happy, its detail so finished and pencilled and stippled . . . I had followed the beautiful 'ocean drive' to its uttermost reach and back without meeting either another vehicle or a single rider, let alone a single pedestrian. . . . a quiet, mild waterside sense, not that of the bold, bluff outer sea, but one which shores and strands and small coast things played a greater part . . . the intimate Newport delicacy . . . the low, densely shrubbed and perfectly finished little headlands." He preferred landscapes that were gentle in scale, open and still, and always saw the defining possibilities of light: "The American air . . . lends a felicity to all the exactitudes of architecture and sculpture, favors sharp effects, disengages differences, preserves light, defines projected shadows."[16]

Correspondingly, he also found the urban atmosphere distinctive, as when "the mellower light prevailed, somehow, *all* that fine Philadelphia morning," or in Baltimore, "the air seemed from the first to breathe upon it a pledge of no bruises." Reaching Washington, he found "everything washed over, at the mention of the name, by the rare light, half green, half golden, of the lovely leafy moment"; he "found Mount Vernon exquisite. . . . The light of nature was there, splendid and serene; the Potomac opened out in the grandest manner; the bluff above the river, before the sweep of its horizon, raised its head for the historic crown."[17] The cities of the deep south summoned an imagery of warmer tones and temperatures. For example, in Charleston, "the day announced itself as warm and radiant, and, keeping its promise to the end, squared itself there as the golden frame of an interesting picture. . . . The golden afternoon, the low, silvery, seaward horizon, as of wide, sleepy, game-haunted inlets and reed-smothered banks, possible site of some Venice that had never mustered, the luxury, in the mild air, of shrub and plant and blossom that the pale North can but distantly envy." Finally, Palm Beach offered "the velvet air, the colour of the sea, the 'royal' palms, clustered here and there, and, in their nobleness of beauty, their single sublime distinction, putting every other mark and sign to the blush. . . ."[18]

Lest we be lulled into reading James as merely an eloquent travelogue, we need to see these glowing vignettes in counterpoint to the primary sources for his displeasure with the American scene, namely what he would have called the suppression of history by the banal transformations of urban planning and architecture. Returning to Boston was especially poignant for him, because there he found a mix of preservation and renewal. On the one hand, there was "the old charm of Mount Vernon Street . . . this ancient grace was not only still to be felt, but was charged, for depth of interest, with intenser ghostly presences, the rich growth of time. . . . This was exactly the kind of impression to be desired and welcomed. . . . such a clear Boston bravery . . . the happiest street-scene the country could show . . . Oh, the wide benignity of brick, the goodly, friendly, ruddy fronts, the felicity of scale, the solid *seat* of everything." On the other hand, "in the Boston neighbourhoods, the work of time loomed large. . . . What was taking place was a perpetual repudiation of the past. . . . there had been an old conscious commemorated life too, and it was this that had become the victim of repression. . . . It is the huge democratic broom that has made the clearance." Even his beloved old university was changing, and he was not sure for the better: "It massed there in multiplied forms, with new and strange architectures looming through the dark; it appeared to have wandered wide and to be stretching forth, in many directions, long, acquisitive arms. This vision [was] of a great dim, clustered but restlessly expansive Harvard. . . ." Back around Beacon Hill, "memory met that pang of loss. . . . I found but a gaping void, the brutal effacement, at a stroke, of every related object, of the whole precious past. . . . It was as if the bottom had fallen out of one's own biography, and one plunged backward into space without meeting anything."[19]

But James saved his most despairing language for New York, which he termed "the terrible town" and "the whole immense promiscuity." In his first paragraph of impressions upon arrival, he noted "the waterside squalor of the great city" and the "odd consciousness of roughness superimposed upon smoothness." He was offended by the easy erasure and discarding of the past: "Were I not afraid of appearing to strike to excess the so-called pessimistic note, I should really make much of the interesting, appealing, touching vision of waste—that flung its odd melancholy mantle even over one's walks through the parts of town supposedly noblest and fairest."[20] Sadness edges his voice: "The whole costly up-town demonstration was a record, in the last analysis, of individual loneliness; whence came, precisely, its insistent testimony to waste. . . . It spoke with that huge process of historic waste that the place in general keeps putting before you."[21]

Another driving theme was commerce, "the overwhelming preponderance, wherever he turns and twists, of the unmitigated 'business man' face." New York was "the most extravagant of cities . . . in the bigness and bravery and insolence, especially, of everything that rushed and shrieked . . . One has the sense that the monster grows and grows." Prophetically, he saw the dehumanizing side of the modern city as "some colossal set of clockworks, some steel-souled machine-room of brandished arms and hammering fists and opening and closing jaws. The immeasurable bridges are but as the horizontal sheaths of pistons working at high pressure, day and night."[22]

He railed against "those monsters of the mere market . . . the whole play of wealth and energy and untutored liberty, of the movement of a breathless civilization." Even the Metropolitan Museum to James was primarily a demonstration of wealth and possessions: "acquisition if need be on the highest terms—may, during the years to come, bask here as in a climate it has never before enjoyed. There was money in the air, ever so much money. . . . And the money was to be all for the most exquisite things—for *all* the most exquisite except creation, which was to be off the scene altogether." He summarized sadly, "the faculty of making money is in America the commonest of all and fairly runs the streets."[23]

The tyranny of the "'business man' face" was to be new and up to date at all costs: "the newness of New York—unlike even that of Boston, I seemed to discern—had this mark of its very own. . . . The very sign of its energy is that it doesn't believe in itself. . . . Its mission would appear to be, exactly, to gild the temporary, with its gold. . . . with a fresh shrug, a shrug of its splendid cynicism." In lower Manhattan, which James hardly recognized, "a house, or a row, is 'coming down'; and you gasp. . . . the actual past that we are now sweeping away . . . this vision of eternal waste." Everywhere he saw the density of crass facades and a superficiality of taste, and concluded, "New York really, I think, is all formidable foreground; or, if it be not, there is more than enough of this pressure of the present. . . ."[24]

His central image of change over the two decades he had been abroad was, of course, the skyscraper, made possible by such technological advances as the elevator and iron-cage construction: "the multitudinous sky-scrapers standing up to the view, from the water, like extravagant pins in a cushion already overplanted . . . they are impudently new and still more impudently 'novel'—this in common with so many other terrible things in America—and they are triumphant payers of dividends. . . . Crowned not only with no history, but with no credible possibility of time for history, and consecrated by no uses save the commercial at any cost, they are simply the most piercing notes in that concert. . . . sky-scrapers are the last word of economic ingenuity." The massing of the "tall buildings" everywhere was tasteless, crowded, and chaotic: "the white towers, all new and crude and commercial and over-windowed as they are . . . huge constructed and compressed communities, throbbing, through its myriad arteries and pores, with a single passion . . . the confusion carried to chaos for any intelligence, any perception; a welter of objects and sounds in which relief, detachment, dignity, meaning, perished utterly and lost all rights." Complaint piled upon complaint: "There was no escape from the ubiquitous alien into the future, or even into the present; there was an escape but into the past. . . . there are flaws and defacements enough. . . . The tall building, grossly tall and grossly ugly, has failed of an admirable chance of distinguished consideration for it, and the dignity of many of its peaceful fronts has succumbed to the presence of those industries whose foremost need is to make 'a good thing' of them."[25]

Again, there was a poignant sense of betrayal and loss in the new construction around James's favorite Washington Square area: "the lamentable little Arch of Triumph which bestrides these beginnings of Washington Square—lamentable because of its poor and lonely and unsupported and unaffiliated state. With this melancholy monument it could make no terms at all. . . . neighboring Sixth Avenue, overstraddled though it might be with feats of engineering." Worst of all was "a high, square, impersonal structure, proclaiming its lack of interest with a crudity all its own, so blocks, at the right moment for its own success, the view of the past, that effect for me, in Washington Place, was of having been amputated of half my history."[26]

Then he drew one of his indelible metaphors: "New York may indeed be jagged, in her long leanness, where she lies looking at the sky in the manner of some colossal hair-comb turned upward and so deprived of half its teeth. . . . the big vulgar 'apartment hotels' that are having their own way, so unchallenged, with the whole question of composition and picture. The fatal 'tall' pecuniary enterprise rises where it will, and in the candid glee of new worlds to conquer . . . . the sky-line, eternal victim of the artless jumble, submits again to the type of the broken hair-comb turned up."[27]

James was troubled by the disregard for precedent or sense of design: "the great city is projected into its future as, practically, a huge, continuous fifty-floored conspiracy against the very idea of the ancient graces." Specific elements were unsuccessful, as "window upon window, at any cost, is a condition never to be reconciled with any grace of building. . . . each light having a superlative value as an aid to the transaction of business and the conclusion of sharp bargains"; and, "the very name of architecture perishes, for the fire-escapes look like abashed afterthoughts, staircases and communications forgotten in the construction."[28] Even for the grandest of hotels James had critical phrases: "the endless labyrinth of the Waldorf-Astoria . . . enlightened contemplation of a pandemonium"; as he did for New York's systematic street plan: "this original sin of the longitudinal avenues perpetually, yet meanly intersected . . . its pettifogging consistency . . . The electric cars, with their double track, are everywhere almost as tight a fit in the narrow channel of the roadway as the projectile in the bore of a gun." Similarly, the park "has had to have something for everybody, since everybody arrives famished. . . . It has had to have a feature at any price. . . . it being inevitably too self-conscious, being afraid to be just vague and frank and quiet." Lastly, along with the growth of architecture came the influx of the masses, "hundreds and hundreds of people in circulation. . . . the alien was as truly in possession."[29]

Louis Sullivan

Henry James had been caught in the pivotal dilemma between nostalgia and modernism. He had literally left America in the nineteenth century and returned in the twentieth, and he was unable to reconcile the two. A contemporary of his negotiated the transition more successfully, however, and was as responsible as anyone for making architecture a positive and essential expression of the modern vision. It is revealing that James barely mentioned Chicago in *The American Scene* or the architecture of Louis Sullivan, who was responsible for creating some of the finest "tall buildings" in the last decade of the nineteenth century. Surely, many of the buildings designed by him and other Chicago contemporaries attained the very aesthetic quality, coherence, and expressiveness James generally found lacking elsewhere. Sullivan also unashamedly propounded the democratic nature of modern architecture, and his leadership in taking buildings upward further prophesied the coming significance of the vertical axis in twentieth-century thought. Just three years into the new century man would lift off the ground in an airplane, the beginning of man's exploration of the heavens, of human aspirations turned in the direction of the cosmos.[30]

Born in Boston, Sullivan received his first architectural training in the early 1870s at the Massachusetts Institute of Technology, followed by brief apprenticeships with Furness & Hewitt in Philadelphia and William Le Baron Jenney in Chicago. At mid-decade he was in France for study at the École des Beaux-Arts and a summer of travel before he returned to Chicago to establish a career. During the 1880s Sullivan was first an employee of Dankmar Adler, soon a partner, and then a principal through the early nineties. The year 1895 was an important turning point: The partnership dissolved; one of its greatest buildings—the Guaranty in Buffalo (fig. 51)—was completed; and Sullivan launched his independent practice and brought his career to its peak. Two of his most important writings were published in this period: "The Tall Building Artistically Considered" appeared in *Lippincott's* magazine in 1896, and "Kindergarten Chats" came out in a builder's journal during the course of 1901.

The former has been one of Sullivan's most quoted essays and includes his famous passage on the divided but interrelated functions of each part of his tall office buildings. He wrote the piece just after finishing the Guaranty Building, itself a reworking of his classic Wainwright Building in St. Louis of

1890–91, and just as he was beginning designs for the Schlesinger & Meyer (later Carson, Pirie, Scott) Department Store, constructed in Chicago from 1899 to 1903–4 (fig. 52). Because it is such a concise articulation of his philosophy, the key paragraph is worth quoting in full:

Figure 51.
Sullivan and
Adler,
Guaranty
Building,
1895. Buffalo,
New York

Wanted—1st, a story below-ground, containing . . . the plant for power, heating, lighting, etc.; 2nd, a ground floor . . . devoted to stores, banks or other establishments requiring large area, ample spacing, ample light, and great freedom of access. 3rd, a second

Figure 52. Louis Sullivan, Schlesinger & Meyer Department Store (now Carson, Pirie, Scott Store), 1899. Chicago, Illinois

story readily accessible by stairways—this space usually in large subdivisions, with corresponding liberality in structural spacing and expanse of glass and breadth of external openings. 4th, above this an indefinite number of stories of offices just like all the other offices—an office being similar to a cell in a honeycomb, merely a compartment, nothing more. 5th, the last, at the top of this pile is placed a space or story that, as related to the life and usefulness of the structure, is purely physiological in its nature—namely, the attic. In this, the circulatory system completes itself and makes its grand turn, ascending and descending. The space is filled with tanks, pipes, valves, sheaves, and mechanical etcetera that supplement and complement the force-originating plant hidden below-ground in the cellar. Finally, or at the beginning rather, there must be on the ground floor a main aperture or entrance common to all the occupants or patrons of the building.[31]

We recognize here many of the now-familiar ideas associated with Sullivan's thinking, especially form expressing function and the principle of an organic whole, which he likened elsewhere to the metaphor of a growing tree. Naturally, the new technology of metal-frame construction permitted a revolutionary flexibility in a building's support over earlier systems of load-bearing walls, while the invention of the elevator soon made possible easy access to the "indefinite number of stories" above. As architectural historians have pointed out, Sullivan at this crucial moment transformed the inert cubic block into an energetic tall building, which he called a "modern poem."[32] Would that Henry James had been able to engage this poetry instead of the dull prosody he confronted in New York. Where James primarily saw the American scene as decaying and oppressively anonymous (certainly accurate in part as a forecast of what the city would become by the end of the twentieth century), Sullivan arrived at a more optimistic and humane ambition for architecture: "a sane and pure accounting of Democracy, a philosophy founded upon Man, thereby setting forth, in clear and human terms, the integrity and responsibility and accountability of the Individual,—in short, a new, a real philosophy of the People."[33]

A National Music

There were several other realms of culture around 1900 where strong originality, the American spirit, and individuality were also on the rise. One such area was American music, which experienced two remarkable developments at the turn of the century, in many ways complementary to one another. These were, respectively, the highly inventive symphonic writings of Charles Ives and the creation of a new popular form of music in Scott Joplin's ragtime. High and low, fine and vernacular, both expressions sought to incorporate indigenous voices and modern energies into their rhythms. For his part, Ives is best known for his use of musical quotations from other sources in his work. He drew freely not only on elements from European romantic composers for his own symphonies, but more importantly on popular native forms, such as hymns, marches, songs, fiddle tunes, and college songs and cheers.[34] Music historians divide his career into three principal phases: an apprenticeship that included his education at Yale and early employment in New York between 1894 and 1902, a key period of artistic adaptation and innovation from 1902 to 1908, and the later decades of his maturity.

The years just before and after 1900 were significant for Ives in a number of respects. He gave up his job as an organist to work independently and experimentally; he married a woman with the felicitous name Harmony Twitchell; and he moved steadily from reliance on direct musical quotations to a process of clever rephrasing, adaptation, and synthesis. With his European borrowings, Ives freed himself from imitation to pay musical homage as a colleague; much of the success of his American quotations relied on the surprise of fresh contexts and the recognition by his audiences of familiar notes in new guises.[35] Characteristic were two major early works, his First Symphony (1897/1898–1902) and his Second Symphony (1900–1902). The former contains sequential allusions to Anton Dvořák's "New World" Symphony, which had premiered to great acclaim in New York during 1893, and to Tchaikovsky's romantic compositions. Although Ives also incorporated two American hymn tunes in the First Symphony, the Second made much greater use of national music, especially vernacular songs by Stephen Foster, such as "De Camptown Races," and other familiar melodies, including "Turkey in the Straw" and "Columbia, The Gem of the Ocean."[36]

After this, Ives turned increasingly to American themes and created in his shorter as well as longer pieces a new music nationalist in both content and form. Now in such works as *Emerson*; *Lincoln, the Great Commoner*; *The "St. Gaudens" in Boston Common*; *Decoration Day*; *Washington's Birthday*; and *The Fourth of July*, he referred to obvious traditional subjects and heroic figures in musical expressions that were recognizably lively, familiar, and democratically understood. His could be called the first thoroughly American symphonies, which critics found as experimental and bold as the early-twentieth-century work of his European contemporaries Arnold Schoenberg and Igor Stravinsky.[37] Foster and others had been important voices of vernacular song, but Ives grafted European symphonic models onto an idiosyncratic American utterance that expressed all the vitality and freedom of the age.

Only a few years older than Ives, Scott Joplin was born in 1868 and moved with his family north to St. Louis in the mid-1880s. By the century's turn he too would have helped to shape a new development in American music, namely ragtime, the precursor of much jazz, swing, and popular music to follow in the twentieth century. By the time of the Columbian Exposition in Chicago in 1893, ragtime had made a public appearance. Coming from a musical family, Joplin began to teach piano and compose songs during the nineties. He published his own first piano rags in 1899, the best known from that period being the *Maple Leaf Rag*. One biographer speculates that the title may refer to the symbol of Canada and earlier aspirations of slave freedom, while the term *rag* derives from the syncopated rhythms, or ragged time, of the music.[38] Like Ives, Joplin drew for inspiration from older musical traditions, in his case from African-American melodies and the colloquial song and band compositions of his youth. At the same time, the irrepressible rhythms and virtuoso improvisations of ragtime also spoke to the energetic life of the nation in the early years of the new century, as embodied in its young president, Theodore Roosevelt. It was T. R. who in 1899 pronounced, "I wish to preach . . . the doctrine of the strenuous life."[39]

The association may go further. Soon after becoming president, T. R. invited the great black educator Booker T. Washington to the White House, an event that evidently moved Joplin in 1903 to attempt composing a ragtime opera called *Guest of Honor*. Although the opera was a failure, ragtime by then had become widely popular, and the *Maple Leaf Rag* was among many rag tunes played in the Roosevelt White House.[40] About 1907 Joplin left Missouri for Chicago and then New York, where his music soon invigorated the clubs and theaters of the Tin Pan Alley era. Indigenous and exuberant, his joyful noise was one of the essential manifestations of American culture as emphatically national and modern at the same time.

Douglass, Washington, and Du Bois

Mention of Joplin at this juncture is a reminder of the confluence of three of the country's most famous African-American figures and their critical presence in national culture in these same years. Frederick Douglass, the self-educated escaped slave and later eminent abolitionist and orator, was by the time of his death at the end of the century perhaps the best-known black in the country. His three autobiographies spanned its second half. The first, *Narrative of the Life of Frederick Douglass, an American Slave*, considered his strongest because it was the most terse and vivid, was published in 1845; a much longer revision, *My Bondage and My Freedom*, appeared ten years later. He amplified an even fuller version, *Life and Times of Frederick Douglass*, in 1881 and published it in 1893.

Together, these books constitute the most powerful and eloquent stance taken on behalf of human freedom and rights to that date. It is fitting that Douglass collapsed and died after attending a women's rights gathering in the nation's capital early in 1895, where he was introduced by the leading suffragist Susan B. Anthony. Just as his career came to this dramatic close, two other influential individuals, Booker T. Washington and W. E. B. Du Bois, were rising to their own prominence.

Indeed, in the same year as Douglass's death Washington reached national fame as a prominent black leader with his speech at the Atlanta Exposition, which was both praised and criticized. In it he sought cooperation among northern capitalists, progressive southern whites, and blacks to create educational advancement and economic growth for blacks. He advocated self-improvement, hard work, and mutual support, worthy goals for black pride, but his willingness to compromise on certain restraints on voting rights and integration in order to secure economic investments was soon challenged as a means of keeping blacks in their place and encouraging them to work more than think.[41] Likewise, his dinner at the White House with Teddy Roosevelt upset whites and blacks alike, although it led to support and patronage over the next few years and to the flourishing of Tuskegee Institute. Born a Virginia slave, Washington went on to an education at the Hampton Institute and then in 1881 to the leadership of Tuskegee in Alabama, living the quintessential American success story. Ironically, his fight for the integrity and economic prosperity of his race took place just as talk of white supremacy, lynchings, segregation, and black disenfranchisement reached a new crescendo. As the ultimate legacy of Reconstruction's failure, the "separate but equal" doctrine, which would haunt the country well into the coming century, was declared by the Supreme Court in 1896 in *Plessy v. Ferguson.* To some Washington's efforts were practical achievements in adverse times; to others they were self-serving and shamefully compromising.

At the turn of the century he was the foremost leader of a black educational institution, and like Douglass before him he undertook to write his autobiography in more than one version. More precisely, he supervised, edited, and dictated his narrative, first with *The Story of My Life and Work* (1900) and then, during the next year, *Up from Slavery.* In this enterprise he made a name and a life for himself, literally, since, born as an unnamed slave, he was able to choose his name and subsequently to write his life story. The name he chose, Booker Washington, of course referred to the Father of the Country and a fellow Virginian, while his first name incorporates "book," which he came to write. As one critic has noted, Washington gained the freedom to identify and define himself, and, as the title of his principal autobiography indicated, his life's trajectory was upward from slavery to mastery of himself.[42]

By 1903 this approach to black aspirations was under challenge, and leaders were polarized over the racial question. Criticism came foremost from the slightly younger William E. B. Du Bois, seen by some as the intellectual heir of Douglass and an ardent, eloquent champion of self-reliance and unfettered dreams for African-Americans. Du Bois found limiting Washington's reliance on reconciliation, humility, thrift, and hard work.[43] The first African-American to receive a Ph.D. in history from Harvard (he also studied philosophy with William James), he brought a balance of scholarly rigor and intense personal feeling to his arguments, which soon elevated him to a position of undisputed prominence during the early twentieth century. Du Bois's thinking steadily crystallized with the publication of his books, *The Suppression of the African Slave Trade to the United States of America, 1638–1870* (1896); *The Philadelphia Negro* (1899); and the assemblage of essays constituting his autobiography, *The Souls of Black Folk* (1903). The poetic, passionate style of the last prompted Henry James to call it "the only 'Southern' book of any distinction published for many a year."[44]

Du Bois began his book with two sentences that include his most often quoted line: "Herein lie buried many things which if read with patience may show the strange meaning of being black here in the dawning of the Twentieth Century. This meaning is not without interest to you, Gentle Reader; for the problem of the Twentieth Century is the problem of the color-line." He repeated the phrase and elaborated on it at the start of his second chapter: "The problem of the twentieth century is the problem of the color-line, the relation of the darker to the lighter races of men in Asia and Africa, in America and the islands of the sea."[45] His inquiry was as much philosophical as political, and the tension between the two informed much of his rhetoric as he sought to articulate himself in relation to American society. And, as he asserted, that proposition has engaged all of us up to the threshold of the twenty-first century.

The third chapter of *Souls of Black Folk* confronted Booker T. Washington's position head-on: "Mr. Washington represents in Negro thought the old attitude of adjustment and submission. . . . This is an age of unusual economic development, and Mr. Washington's programme naturally takes an economic cast, becoming a gospel of Work and Money to such an extent as apparently almost completely to overshadow the higher aims of life."[46] In his own lived and written life, Du Bois argued for blacks to make the best of it on their own, to hold their own aspirations as well as reach them. He frequently used an imagery of natural growth to gain "the higher aims of life": "Now a rising group of people are not lifted bodily from the ground like an inert solid mass, but rather stretch upward like a living plant with its roots still clinging in the mould." He combined that image with an even more deeply felt sympathy for the spiritual power of African-American music as another metaphor of black aspiration: "We could hear dimly across the fields a rhythmic cadence of song,—soft, thrilling, powerful, that swelled and died sorrowfully in our ears. . . . The Music of Negro religion is that plaintive rhythmic melody, with its touching minor cadences, which, despite caricature and defilement, still remains the most original and beautiful expression of human life and longing yet born on American soil."[47]

Du Bois's biographers have drawn comparisons with Henry Adams and the contradictions expressed by the latter's *Education*. Both individuals mixed personal and national history, meditations on economics, society, and culture. They felt the tensions between political life and the imagination, between acting and thinking, although Adams perhaps indulged himself more in constant ironic speculation.[48] Both, of course, attempted to define the central ideas of the new age, and race in its different senses would be for each an issue of modernism. They also shared with Henry James a love of language and belief in the creative enterprise of autobiographical expression. Yet another writer turned to constructing his autobiography at this time—Mark Twain—with a similar devotion to the experience and power of words.

Mark Twain

Although despair informs Mark Twain's late stories, such as "The Mysterious Stranger," which he struggled to complete between 1897 and 1905, he worked on his autobiography with enthusiasm over the same period.[49] During the seventies and eighties he wrote down fragments, and in the late nineties abroad he recorded memories of his youth on his uncle's farm; between 1904 and 1906, abroad again, he wrote and dictated extensive sections about his later life: "Finally in Florence, in 1904, I hit upon the right way to do an Autobiography: Start it at no particular time of your life; wander at your free will all over your life; talk only about the thing which interests you for the moment." This he did, with all his familiar serious wit: "The whole scheme of this autobiography . . . is a system which follows no charted course. It is a system which is a complete and purposed jumble—a course which begins nowhere, follows no specified route, and can never reach an end while I am alive. . . . This Autobiography of mine is a mirror and I am looking at myself in it all the time."[50] Originally he wanted his narrative published as he had recorded it, rather than in chronological order, as if to assert the primacy of imagination and language.

He began playfully with ambiguities about his authorial stance, birthplace, and credibility of recollection: "In this Autobiography I shall keep in mind the fact that I am speaking from the grave . . . because I shall be dead when the book issues from the press. . . . I can speak thence freely. . . . I was born . . . in the almost invisible village of Florida, Monroe County, Missouri. . . . my faculties are decaying now and soon I shall be so I cannot remember any but the things that never happened."[51] In more ways than one, his book would be a newly created life—just as his pseudonym was a creation—and throughout he intermixed nostalgia and recollection with meditations on writers, books, and the craft of writing itself. From the vantage point of the century's turn as he approached age seventy, Mark Twain anxiously dwelt on family deaths, which we sense he could counter only through the redemptive acts of recollection and fabrication.

He vividly recalled the picture of life on his uncle's farm in a passage of pure poetic sensations: "I can call back the solemn twilight and mystery of the deep woods. . . . I can call it back and make it as real as it ever was. . . . I can see the blue clusters of wild grapes hanging among the foliage of the saplings, and I remember the taste of them and the smell. I know how the wild blackberries looked . . . and I can feel the thumping rain, upon my head, of hickory nuts and walnuts. . . . I know the taste of maple sap. . . . I know how a boy looks behind a yard-long slice of that melon, and I know how it feels; for I have been there." This sense of sheer consciousness, descriptive eloquence, and linguistic melody confirms the bold inventive modernity of Twain's project. Again he stresses the private act of rumination: "The reader, if he will look deep down in his secret heart, will find—but never mind what he will find there. I am not writing his autobiography but mine."[52]

Two of his primary themes are interwoven throughout the text, the poignant loss of family members and the active pleasures of literature. Of the former he first noted that "when my mother died in October 1890 she was well along in her eighty-eighth year, a mighty age. . . . What becomes of the multitudinous photographs which one's mind takes of people? Out of the million which my mental camera must have taken . . ." Then in later years new deaths recalled older ones: "Murat Halstead is dead. . . . he devoted about sixty years to diligent, hard slaving at editorial work. His life and mine make a curious contrast. From the time that my father died, March 24, 1847, when I was past eleven years old. . . . I worked—not diligently, not willingly, but fretfully, lazily, repiningly, complainingly, disgustedly, and always shirking the work when I was not watched."[53] In later life his favorite daughter died: "Susy passed from life in the Hartford home the 18th of August, 1896. . . . It is one of the mysteries of our nature that a man, all unprepared, can receive a thunder-stroke like that and live. . . . The mind has a dumb sense of vast loss—that is all." On Christmas Eve in 1909, four months before Mark Twain's own death, he lost another daughter who had been epileptic: "*Jean is dead.* Has any one ever tried to put upon paper all the little happenings connected with a dear one—happenings of the twenty-four hours preceding the sudden and unexpected death of that dear one?" He felt the losses accumulate: "In England, thirteen years ago, my wife and I were stabbed to the heart with a cablegram which said, 'Susy was mercifully released today'. . . . I lost Susy thirteen years ago; I lost her mother—her incomparable mother!—five and half years ago; Clara has gone away to live in Europe; and now I have lost Jean. How poor I am, who was once so rich! Seven months ago Mr. Rogers died—one of the best friends I ever had."[54]

As he mentioned, the loss of his ailing wife, Olivia, occurred in 1904, between the deaths of his daughters, and we can understand the impact his mounting grief and sense of failure must have had on his work. In 1906 he wrote: "Tomorrow will be the 5th of June, a day which marks the disaster of my life—the death of my wife. It occurred two years ago, in Florence, Italy. . . . The dictating of this autobiography, which was begun in Florence in the beginning of 1904, was soon suspended because of the anxieties of the time, and I was never moved to resume the work until January 1906. . . . She was my life, and she is gone; she was my riches, and I am a pauper." He conveyed the anguished mood of his last years in the book's final paragraphs: "Night is closing down; the rim of the sun barely shows above the sky line of the hills. . . . From my windows I saw the hearse and the carriages wind along the road and gradually grow vague and spectral in the falling snow and presently disappear. Jean was gone out of my life and would not come back any more."[55]

In counterbalance to this frame of mind were Twain's frequent references to the sustaining pleasures of books and words. He had no use for "another nuisance, which was an Unabridged Dictionary. . . . it wasn't a good dictionary, anyway—didn't have any modern words in—only had obsolete ones that they used to use when Noah Webster was a child." On another occasion he admitted to having "an adversion to good spelling for sixty years . . . there was not a thing I could do creditably except spell according to the book. . . . this is because the ability to spell correctly is a talent, not an acquirement. There is some dignity about an acquirement, because it is a product of your own labor." He often engaged his family's reactions to his writing: "The children always helped their mother to edit my books in manuscript. She would sit on the porch at the farm and read aloud, with her pencil in hand. . . . It had furnished three of us with good entertainment." Elsewhere, he "pleaded against the assumption that a book is not properly property because it is founded upon ideas and is built of ideas from its cellar to its roof." He described the commitment needed for writing: "There is one great trouble about dictating an autobiography and that is the multiplicity of texts. . . . still you must choose; there is no help for it. . . . It is a lofty and reckless daring which I suppose is exhibited in no field but one—the field of literature. . . . a profession which requires no apprenticeship, no experience, no training—nothing whatever but conscious talent and a lion's courage."[56]

He commented on authors he admired: "Kipling's words always stir me now, stir me more than do any other living man's. . . . I am not acquainted with my own books but I know Kipling's—at any rate I know them better than I know anybody else's books. They never grow pale to me; they keep their color; they are always fresh. . . . It was on a bench in Washington Square that I saw the most of Louis Stevenson. . . . [Bret] Harte was good company and a thin but pleasant talker. . . . he must not be classed with Thomas Bailey Aldrich." And near the end of his life Mark Twain received honorary degrees from Oxford, Yale, and the University of Missouri, which amused him: "It pleased me beyond measure when Yale made me a Master of Arts, because I didn't know anything about art; I had another convulsion of pleasure when Yale made me a Doctor of Literature, because I was not competent to doctor anybody's literature but my own, and couldn't even keep my own in a healthy condition without my wife's help. I rejoiced again when Missouri University made me a Doctor of Laws, because it was all clear profit, I not knowing anything about laws except how to evade them and not get caught."[57] Like the best autobiographies of his time, Mark Twain's was more than a recording of facts or an account of history, but an examining of self as a pursuit of imagination and freedom.

Cassatt, Jewett, Chopin

By the close of the nineteenth century, not only had African-Americans risen to national prominence, but this was also a period that saw women flourishing in a variety of callings, many with international distinction. Susan B. Anthony was in the forefront of women's suffrage. Bertha Potter Palmer in Chicago and Louisine Havemeyer in New York assembled the first significant collections of French Impressionist paintings in the country. Beatrix Jones Farrand was a leading landscape architect, and Celia Thaxter and Candace Wheeler were well-known gardeners. A number of women established successful reputations as artists, among them figure or landscape painters such as Maria Oakey Dewing, Lydia Emmet, Frances Coates Jones, Helen Turner, Elizabeth Lowell, Alice Barber Stephens, and in portraiture, Cecilia Beaux.[58] Foremost in prominence was the Philadelphian Mary Cassatt, the first American artist to be accepted into the French Impressionist circle and to exhibit with them formally.

After training at the Pennsylvania Academy of the Fine Arts, Cassatt went to Paris, where she was to remain for much of her life. There she met Edgar Degas, who gave her encouragement and collaborated on several early pictures. By the late 1870s she was well established and accepted among French colleagues, and over the next couple of decades she painted both probing portraits of visiting family members and subtly composed genre paintings, many set in theater or opera interiors. Some resemble Degas's work in their psychological suggestiveness and compressed spatial arrangements, while others retain the

Figure 53. Mary
Cassatt, *Portrait of
Mrs. Havemeyer and
Her Daughter Electra*,
1895. Pastel on
paper, 24 x 30½ in.
The Shelburne
Museum, Shelburne,
Vermont

firm directness and solid realism of the American tradition. By the mid-nineties
Cassatt reached a peak of technical inventiveness and virtuosity. She was one
of two American women called upon to decorate the women's building with a
large-scale mural at the Chicago Columbian Exposition in 1893, and the following year she completed one of her best known and boldest canvases, *The Boating
Party* (National Gallery of Art, Washington). Though clearly reminiscent of
similar treatments by Manet and Monet a generation earlier, her picture possessed a highly individual color scheme of flat, bright yellows and blues, a close-
up point of view, and a cropped composition with a very high horizon line.

The striking overall effect is closely related to another of Cassatt's most
innovative enterprises, her venture into producing colored acquatints with the
flattened patternings, delicate coloring, and asymmetrical designs of Japanese
prints, so popular with many of her contemporaries at this time. Her prints were
extraordinarily complex and challenging in their execution, and they remain
among the highest graphic achievements of this generation. Yet a further
endeavor was her pursuit and mastery of the medium of pastel, a process of
drawing on paper with colored powders, which was also very demanding in
touch and execution, at its best having the bright spontaneity of watercolor and
the substance of oil paint. While she is perhaps best known for her imagery of
mothers with children, more significant is her presentation of women who are

industrious, contemplative, actively engaged, and conscious of themselves. Cassatt's versatility in different mediums was rarely equaled by any of her peers; along with her achievements as an artist, she also played a key role as adviser to Mrs. Havemeyer and Mrs. Potter Palmer in the early acquisition of works by Degas and other French Impressionists.

Two women in this period made significant marks as writers of fiction. Until recently, Sarah Orne Jewett has usually been treated as a writer of sentimental and regional subjects, while Kate Chopin in turn has undergone a revival of interest for her story of a strong woman's life. In fact, different as the two authors and their novels are—one writing about the Maine coast, the other about New Orleans—both writers were determined, independent-minded individuals who wrote about self-reliant, isolated, and psychologically interesting figures. Jewett's *Country of the Pointed Firs* (1896) was a sequence of vividly drawn sketches in short chapters of a woman, Almira Todd, visiting some offshore Maine islands. Simple but moving themes unfold: a family reunion, a disappointed lover in exile, the imaginings of an old seafarer, stalwart older women, and the sensuous growth of gardens. While Jewett brings alive the picturesque scenes of the coastal Maine landscape and island village life, what gives her story strength are the hints of inner life in her characters, along with the physical and symbolic presence of the sea as a space for contemplation.

Born at mid-century in southern Maine, Jewett was often left alone during her childhood, sustained by reading from her family's large library and by a love of nature.[59] It is easy to see how this shaping environment led to the thoughtful women and sensual gardens that occupy her later stories. She collected her early tales of Maine in *Deephaven* in 1877, and the vigorous and wise country women who appear in them anticipate the spiritual strength of Almira Todd in *The Country of the Pointed Firs*. Several factors in Jewett's life during the nineties were likely stimulants to her writing that novel. First, a sense of loss and isolation came with the series of deaths among close family and friends: her mother and James Russell Lowell in 1891, Celia Thaxter in 1893, and Oliver Wendell Holmes a year later. Then, in 1895, Jewett spent the summer on Islesboro with its lush island gardens just off the central Maine coast. The next year she serialized publication of her novel in the *Atlantic* magazine.

What strikes us is not so much any intricate or tightly woven narrative, but rather subtly accumulating impressions and repeated themes. The powerful sensations of flower and herb gardens were one: "If Mrs. Todd had occasion to step into the far corner of her herb plot, she trod heavily upon thyme, and made its fragrant presence known. . . . There were some strange and pungent odors that roused a dim sense and remembrance of something in the forgotten past. . . . the strange fragrance of the mysterious herb blew in from the little garden." From the first page to the last, the sea and the horizon were likewise evocative images. For example, high windows were "knowing eyes that watched the harbor and the far sea-line beyond. . . . The bay-sheltered islands and the great sea beyond stretched away to the far horizon southward and eastward. . . . a shadow had fallen on the darkening shore. . . . The sun-burst upon that outermost island made it seem like a sudden revelation of the world."[60] Walking over the island with friends, the narrator "could see the ocean that circled this and a hundred other bits of island ground, the mainland shore and all the far horizons. It gave a sudden sense of space, for nothing stopped the eye or hedged one in,— that sense of liberty in space and time which great prospects always give."[61]

Similar phrases follow: "a far-off look that sought the horizon; one often sees it in seafaring families . . . always watching for distant sails or the first loom of the land. . . . my friends plunged into a borderless sea of reminiscences." On another walk with Mrs. Todd, the visitor "reached the top of a hill, and suddenly there lay spread out before us a wonderful great view of well-cleared fields that swept down to a wide water of a bay. Beyond this were distant shores like another country in the midday haze which half hid the hills beyond, and the faraway pale blue mountains on the northern horizon."[62]

Leaving the island at the end of the summer is a poignant separation, and the novel's final paragraph is one of the receding view, in which ultimately only the horizon is left: "When I looked back again, the islands and the headland had run together and Dunnet Landing and all its coasts were lost to sight."[63]

Jewett's novel is so slender that the reader is almost surprised to come across its emotional nuances and gentle psychological characterizations. The central figure of Mrs. Todd "kept up an air of secrecy. . . . as if love and hate and jealousy and adverse winds at sea might also find their proper remedies among the curious wild-looking plants . . . all that lay deepest in her heart . . . the sorrowful, large figure of Mrs. Todd." Of Captain Littlepage, "a sudden sense of his sufferings at the hands of the ignorant came to my help," and of William, "I began to discover that he and his sister could not speak their deeper feelings before each other. . . . William mastered his timidity and began to sing. His voice was a little faint and frail, like the family daguerreotypes. . . . It was the silent man's real and only means of expression." A distillation of thought comes toward the end of summer: "I often wondered a great deal about the inner life and thought of these self-contained old fishermen; their minds seemed to be fixed upon nature and the elements rather than upon any contrivances of man, like politics or theology."[64]

Holding many of these sketches together are the notes of human isolation and self-awareness, frequently experienced through moments of dreaming and reflection. Once on the island, the narrator "spent many days there quite undisturbed. . . . I had lost myself completely in work." Soon she becomes aware of a more solemn mood in others, especially Mrs. Todd: "There was something lonely and solitary about her great determined shape. . . . An absolute, archaic grief possessed this countrywoman . . . with her sorrows and the remoteness of daily life." In conversation another woman laments, "I have lost my hope. You must tell those that ask how 'tis with me,' she said, 'an' tell them I want to be alone.'" As summer proceeds, a melancholy awareness of other human lives tinges the observations: "There are paths trodden to the shrines of solitude the world over,—the world cannot forget them, try as it may. . . . But as I stood alone on the island, in the sea breeze, suddenly there came a sound of distant voices . . . . poor Joanna must have heard the like on many and many a summer after-noon, and must have welcomed the good cheer in spite of hopelessness and win-ter weather, and all the sorry and disappointment in the world."[65]

Islands were related metaphors of solitariness: "The hot midsummer sun makes prisons of these small islands that are a paradise in early June. . . . The air was very sweet; one could not help wishing to be a citizen of such a complete and tiny continent and home of fisherfolk. . . . I wondered why she had been set to shine on this lonely island of the northern coast. It must have been to keep the balance true. . . . My thoughts flew back to the lonely woman on her outer island; what separation from humankind she must have felt, what terror and sadness." At the end, the summer visitor worries about the "return to the world in which I feared to find myself a foreigner. . . . So we die before our own eyes; so we see some chapters of our lives come to their natural end."[66] Jewett's accomplishment was to suggest the limitations along with the possibilities of both physical and spiritual contact among human beings. At a time of intensify-ing urbanization and industrialization in America, she revealed an enlarged sense of the self in relation to others and to nature in that small country world.

Significantly, Kate Chopin's original title for her novel *The Awakening* (1899) was "A Solitary Soul." It, too, has at its center a stalwart, self-reliant woman as a principal character, and early in the story the author tells us this will be an awakening of a woman's sexual and psychological consciousness: "Mrs. Pontellier was beginning to realize her position in the universe as a human being, and to recognize her relations as an individual to the world within and about her."[67] Chopin herself was an unconventional, liberated woman, who refused to marry in favor of her writing career; no more than her novel's char-acter did she care for confinement or abuse, and this assertion of personal free-dom informs much of the book. Edna Pontellier lives an independent life from her husband, and at the end she separates from her lover as well after she admits, "It was you who awoke me last summer out of a life-long stupid dream."[68]

This imagery of emotional arousal recurs frequently: "She perceived that her will had blazed up, stubborn and resistant. . . . Edna began to feel like one who awakens gradually out of a dream, a delicious, grotesque, impossible dream, to feel again the realities pressing into her soul. . . . For the first time she recognized anew the symptoms of infatuation. . . . the poignancy of the revelation . . . her impassioned, newly awakened being . . . She reminded him of some beautiful, sleek animal waking up in the sun." We follow the increasing engagement of Edna's passion and intellect: "There was Robert's reproach itself felt by a quicker, fiercer, more overpowering love, which had awakened within her toward him. Above all, there was understanding. She felt as if a mist had been lifted from her eyes, enabling her to look upon and comprehend the significance of life, that monster made up of beauty and brutality."[69]

As with Jewett, Chopin evokes the symbolic universality of the shoreline and open water expanding to the horizon. The novel concludes with Edna taking—and taking hold of—her life by walking out from the beach and drowning herself: "The voice of the sea is seductive, never ceasing, whispering, clamoring, murmuring, inviting the soul to wander in abysses of solitude. . . . she was there beside the sea, absolutely alone . . . and for the first time in her life she stood naked in the open air. . . . How strange it seemed to stand naked under the sky! how delicious! She felt like some new-born creature, opening its eyes in a familiar world that it had never known. . . . The touch of the sea is sensuous, enfolding the body in its soft, close embrace. . . . She did not look back now, but went on and on. . . . She looked into the distance. . . ."[70] It was an ultimate act of freeing and possessing the self.

"The Awakening" was an appropriate phrase for the anxious creativity arising throughout all the arts just around 1900. In the background a sea change was taking place in the social and political order. This was certainly the turning point when the modern sensibility was born.

Inner Sight:
Saint-Gaudens,
Homer, Peto, and Eakins

COINCIDENTALLY, four major works of art with quite different subjects by different artists all date from 1903–4: Augustus Saint-Gaudens's *Sherman Monument* in New York City's Grand Army Plaza, Winslow Homer's *Kissing the Moon,* John F. Peto's *Old Companions,* and Thomas Eakins's *Mrs. Edith Mahon.* It is provocative to ask what shared ideas or overlapping themes are revealed by these contemporaneous expressions in commemorative sculpture, landscape, still life, and portraiture. Recurring within the output of these artists was the obsession with mortality, nostalgia for a lost past, a psychological sensibility, and the impulse toward abstraction. Moreover, these four major examples were in several instances at the heart of a larger, intense production of works amplifying such thematic concerns in the years on either side of 1900.

Augustus Saint-Gaudens

Although born abroad, Saint-Gaudens grew up in New York, where he was first apprenticed to a cameo cutter and later studied at the National Academy of Design. From the former experience he developed a lifelong ability to conceptualize and create sculpture in terms of expressive relief; from the latter he acquired a broad formal education in drafting, modeling, and appreciating classical precedents. He amplified all this with further training at the École des Beaux-Arts in 1867 and with travel to Rome and other major cities on the Continent. His appreciation for narrative and historical subjects, combined with the exposure to classical and Renaissance monumental sculptures in these great urban spaces, inspired many of Saint-Gaudens's own public commissions after he returned to the United States in the early seventies.

As a youth he had seen Lincoln in New York and watched Union troops

go off to the Civil War, and now as an adult reaching the high point of his career, Saint-Gaudens and his generation were increasingly aware that those war veterans were now dying off. By the turn of the century, with presidential assassinations jolting the nation once again, nostalgia for America's heroic youth and its earlier leaders was pervasive. Beginning in the late 1870s with the *Admiral Farragut Monument* (Madison Square Park, New York), and followed by the *Standing Lincoln* in Chicago in the later eighties and the *Shaw Memorial* (fig.

Figure 54. Augustus Saint-Gaudens, *The General William Tecumseh Sherman Memorial*, 1892–1903. Bronze, over life-size. Grand Army Plaza, Central Park, New York

Figure 55. Augustus Saint-Gaudens, *The Robert Gould Shaw Memorial*, 1884–97. Boston, Massachusetts

55), finally dedicated in Boston in 1897 after many years of work, Saint-Gaudens devoted much of the century's last decade to designing, modifying, and perfecting the details of his culminating masterpiece in the equestrian monument to the Union general William Tecumseh Sherman. Together, these gave eloquent expression to the need for glorifying and memorializing the triumphs of an earlier age, brought into relief by the worries of the present.

The *Sherman* was Saint-Gaudens's last great ensemble, the more impressive because its final stages of work coincided with the discovery that he was suffering from intestinal cancer. He had begun work on the project in the late eighties, when he had the opportunity to make a bust of Sherman from life at the time both men were in New York. During many hours of sitting the sculptor established a sympathetic intimacy with the Civil War general and had a chance to distill many pertinent facts and associations with his career into the subsequent sculpture. Saint-Gaudens continued to adjust and refine the figures in his Paris studio, and he exhibited plaster models at the Salon of 1899 and the

Universal Exposition the following year.[71] The final plasters were at last ready for casting in Paris in 1901, and the bronzes were shipped back to the artist at his home in Cornish, New Hampshire, where he could try various placements of the gilded grouping against the local hillside, in anticipation of locating it permanently in New York.

Before that installation took place, however, he faced an argument with the Sherman family, for Saint-Gaudens himself had hoped to place the monument in Riverside Park, appropriately, he thought, near Grant's tomb. Eventually, all agreed on the Central Park site at the corner of Fifth Avenue and Fifty-Ninth Street, where it could be seen fully in the round. Indeed, of all his major memorials, this was the most sculpturally realized in all dimensions and was equally commanding from several points of view. The *Shaw Memorial*, which preceded it, also combined an equestrian figure with the allegorical figure of Victory, but Saint-Gaudens framed them along with the black marching regiment in a proscenium stage intended to be viewed from the front. Although its substantial architectural framework by Stanford White gave the whole a solid three-dimensional framework, and the layers of figures were a tour de force of high-relief carving, the narrative and symbolic power of the monument occurs largely within the private enclosure of the forms. With the *Sherman* Saint-Gaudens liberated Victory from a confined relief floating within the compressed space to a fully modeled and independent figure, which complements both the form and the meaning of the equestrian portrait nearby.

The arrangement brought together a lifetime of artistic images evolving within his own work and absorbed from his years of studious observation in European museums and city spaces. The allegorical figure of Victory who guides the mounted general has, of course, precedents in the angels of mourning and triumphal figures that appear on ancient classical arches and altar reliefs. In addition, Saint-Gaudens had the opportunity to see such famous examples in the Louvre as the Hellenistic *Nike of Samothrace* and Delacroix's *Liberty at the Barricades*. In turn, the equestrian form likewise took him back to the Roman statue of Marcus Aurelius on the Capitoline Hill in Rome and its well-known artistic descendants from the Renaissance, Donatello's *Gattamelata* in Padua and Verrocchio's *Colleoni* in Venice.

What transforms Saint-Gaudens's achievement is his sophisticated fusion of idealism, realism, and abstraction, respectively, seen in the historical allusions, sensitive portraiture, and purity of expressive form. We are immediately aware of the visual integration of the three principal elements: abstract geometric base and pedestal, the general mounted on his horse, and the Victory walking in front. Saint-Gaudens decorated the pedestal with a water-leaf molding and bronze olive wreaths—classical allusions to honor and triumph—and with a pine branch, which refers to Sherman's march through Georgia to the sea.

Victory carries a palm branch and her head bears a laurel crown; she was perhaps the most fully realized version of several related incarnations throughout his career, from the *Amor Caritas* of 1880 (Saint-Gaudens National Historic Site, Cornish, N.H.) to the unsurpassed 1907 Liberty coin. As for the general's likeness, the sculptor began with his first-hand impressions of more than a decade earlier and had an unclothed model pose astride a barrel to ensure an accurate rendering of Sherman on his mount.

On the one hand, the three thin steps establish a gentle transition between the adjacent ground and rising volume of the pedestal; on the other, the sculpture stands elevated in fact and emotion from the viewer. The ground rises slightly under the horse and rider toward the front of the base, and with Victory's out-thrust arm, the subtle effect is of both forward and upward motion. Sherman's expression is grave, dignified, and concentrated as he looks to the inevitable end of strife at the horizon. While the windswept forms of Victory's drapery and wings and Sherman's cape unite the two in their movement together, his upright posture with right arm and hat lowered to his side give their pace a purposeful and measured restraint. Throughout Saint-Gaudens has orchestrated the visual rhythms of vertical and diagonal forms, in the torsos and legs of figures and horse, the balance of flowing tail behind and raised arm in front, in one compositional unity of historical action and symbolic power. The crisp, almost starburst, silhouette of heads and limbs radiating out from the central mass exudes a liveliness visible from all sides of the monument, as we are drawn in to contemplate the prospects of mortality and immortality.

Henry James described the "dauntless refinement of the Sherman image." But he could not help seeing it against "the comparative vulgarity of the environment" and summarized: "The best thing in the picture, obviously, is Saint-Gaudens's great outdoor group, splendid in its golden elegance and doing more for the scene (by thus giving the beholder a point of such dignity for his orientation) than all its other elements together."[72] James above all was one who could admire refinement and elegance, but in addition this memorial piece captured the period's nostalgia for past virtues and brooded over the sense of loss. On the threshold of a war to be fought for the first time in the air, this was a culminating reminder of one of the last wars to have been fought on foot and horseback. At this uneasy juncture Saint-Gaudens was able to convey through palpable form resonant abstract ideas.

Winslow Homer

Winslow Homer's 1904 painting *Kissing the Moon* (colorplate 12; fig. 56) also combined realism and a sense of abstraction, individuality, and universality. Although seemingly direct and clear in its nominal subject of three men in a

Figure 56. Winslow
Homer, *Kissing the Moon*,
1904. Oil on canvas,
30¼ x 40⅜ in. Addison
Gallery of American
Art, Phillips Academy,
Andover, Massachusetts,
Bequest of Candace
C. Stimson (see
colorplate 12)

dory at sea, there is about the picture ultimately something strangely inexplicable and detached. Caught between two massive troughs of waves, the boat is almost invisible save for a short section of an oar and the suggestion of a gunwhale in the lower-left corner. This is all that ties these figures to their solid, familiar world of a larger vessel or to shore and home. They are literally "at sea" in the several suggestive senses of the phrase: to be on a sea voyage, perhaps in search of fish, to be lost or bewildered, to be in open waters. No land is in sight at either side or on the horizon; even if it were there, our viewpoint and that of the dory are too low to see it. Moreover, the staring profiles and frozen postures of the men yield no hint of their purpose or course. They are linked in form and composition only to the otherworldly sphere of the full moon, just intersected by the crest of a wave and so providing the picture's title.

One of Homer's great masterpieces of his later years, this painting has received relatively little attention by comparison with other works of the same period.[73] Nevertheless, *Kissing the Moon* has appeared in every important publication on Homer and has often received astute, brief commentary, beginning in his lifetime. The artist's first biographer, William Howe Downes, knew him personally and in 1911 wrote a short observant description of the picture just a few years after its completion.[74] Downes noted several of the image's key elements:

the striking contrasts in scale between men and water, the details or forms concealed, the idea of buoyancy, and the "novelty of the design." Among Homer's modern biographers Albert Ten Eyck Gardner was the first to stress the artist's awareness of Japanese prints in the composing of many of his later works.[75] First exposed to japonaiserie on his early trip to Paris in the later 1860s, Homer often thereafter made use of such graphic devices as asymmetrical designs, cropping, flat patterning, bold contrasts of foreground and background, unusually low or elevated points of view, and spatial compression. Gardner pointed out the striking similarity of Hokusai's *Great Wave* as a likely inspiration for *Kissing the Moon*. In the Japanese wood block two small boats are partially visible as they cut through the towering waves cresting in the foreground, while the peak of Mount Fuji rises on the horizon, drawing our attention as the moon did for Homer. Where Downes chose the word "novel," Gardner likewise saw these compositional devices as "unconventional."

Philip Beam, who gathered much new biographical information relating to Homer's late work at Prout's Neck, Maine, wrote little more than a sentence about this painting, describing it as "a wonderfully simple and natural yet unusual composition," but he called attention to the one identifiable figure in the boat as that of the artist's grown nephew Charlie, son of his brother Arthur, indicating that the painting was a personal, even autobiographical, expression for the artist.[76] Homer must have created an intentional contrast between the one recognizable face and the nearly or fully obscured features of the two men opposite. In fact, the partial profile of the middle figure mediates between an explicit portrait on the left and a totally anonymous head to the right; his position also serves as a visual fulcrum at about the same area where we would find the oarlocks, another balancing point for the rising and falling vessel in the waves. His glance engages young Homer's, while the head on the right turns to face the moon, a sequence leading us from the near to the far, the immediate to the cosmic. This last probably explains what Beam and so many other observers have found unusual here, that is, Homer's dramatic conflation of space in the linking of the near foreground to a body actually a quarter of a million miles away. Equally powerful is Homer's rendering of a human situation begun out of firsthand experience but elevated to an abstracted and universalized plane.

Another Homer biographer writing a year later, James Thomas Flexner, likewise devoted only a paragraph to this work. He saw it as a part of Homer's simplifying process, and characterized it as "paradoxical . . . mysterious, still. . . . the realm of a dream. The men sit ramrod straight as the waves lift in peaks all around them; the moon shines, but it is the light of the setting sun that gives their heads their ruddy glow."[77] Each viewer has attempted to explicate the veiled silence and deep-sea rhythms in these forms, at once described and incorporated in the large flowing brushwork itself.

During the 1990s a younger generation of scholars has undertaken a new intensive study of Homer, both pursuing these formal investigations and adding fresh insights to the allusive content. Bruce Robertson, for instance, has discussed *Kissing the Moon* as a subliminal precedent for *Right and Left* (1909; National Gallery of Art, Washington, D.C.) four years later, even considering them as informal pendants with interlocking meanings. Certainly, both works rely on balances of form and subject matter, the latter with two ducks shot in flight, but also contrasting the immediate foreground viewpoint with distant forms on an obscured horizon. He explains the drifting stillness of the men in the earlier painting and their frozen stares as scanning the ocean for ducks, which the hunters actually fire upon in the later canvas. Yet we see no sign of shotguns or concealed immanence of death, only the trancelike postures, a mysterious emptiness, and the gentle face of the moon. Robertson does call attention to one concern of recent Homer scholarship, the potential sexual associations suggested here by the title. As he says, the title "refers overtly to the viewpoint of men: seen so low, the waves seem to kiss the moon. But the evocative sexuality of the title suggests that the men are about to kiss the globe of the moon, flushed warmly gold by the setting sun."[78]

Concurrently, Nicolai Cikovsky was arguing another interest of recent art history, the autobiographical subtext running through much of Homer's mature art. He has added a couple of important insights to our reading of this painting: that it was compositionally related to a painting the artist began the following year but did not finish, *Shooting the Rapids, Saguenay River* (1905; The Metropolitan Museum of Art, New York), and that Homer shaped his signature within the curving wave at the picture's lower right.[79] First, this tells us that he saw these men in a challenging, if not threatening, situation of possibly being overwhelmed by the turbulent waves, and secondly, that the painter placed himself via his signature in the low, watery vantage point of surging foam. Cumulatively, all these comments confirm the unsure reaction we have to this image and the realization of Homer's uneasy relation to his subject. Two points we can be certain about: its highly personal, even psychological, nature, and its new abstractions of spatial treatment, both powerful signs of the modern as they were evident by 1904.

But this one major work was not an isolated expression; rather it highlighted a whole series of formal experimentations Homer concentrated on during the years before and after 1900. One of these was his employment of the square format, a configuration he first tried with a watercolor of 1885, *Rest* (private collection), but now used to dramatic effect in some of his most important late seascapes: *Cannon Rock* (1895; The Metropolitan Museum of Art), *On a Lee Shore* (fig. 57), and *Driftwood* (1909; Museum of Fine Arts, Boston).[80] Normally we think of the traditional shape of a landscape as that of a rectangle, usually

Figure 57. Winslow Homer, *On a Lee Shore*, 1900. Oil on canvas, 39 x 39 in. Museum of Art, Rhode Island School of Design, Providence, Jesse Metcalf Fund

horizontal but sometimes vertical, as reflecting nature's plains or valleys and analogous to the view through a window or stage set. So the square stands out as somehow arbitrary, a conscious artifice that calls attention to its framing edges and to the surface it contains. Within this shape Homer clearly exploited the balancing of opposites, near and far, light and dark, water and rock, liquid and solid, as purely formal forces locked together, much like the perfect right angles framing them. He also flattened his spatial recession by making us aware of the strength of paint and brushwork crossing the canvas surface, in places almost independent of its descriptive function. Thus this choice of pure geometry crucially helped Homer at this point move his art from the objective to the subjective, from the realm of nature to the realm of art.

A second formal pursuit of the later nineties was his exploration of monochrome, sometimes in variants of dark greens, sometimes in browns, and sometimes in grays. If we ordinarily see the world in color, and Homer certainly did, especially with the brilliant blues, reds, and yellows he experienced in

Florida and the Caribbean, or the corresponding dark greens, blues, and purples of the northern landscape in Canada and the Adirondacks, then monochromy seems startlingly reductive and abstract. Of course, Homer had worked on and off in black and white since the beginning of his career, producing wood engravings for *Harper's* magazine during the Civil War; large-scale charcoal drawings during his two-year trip to Cullercoats on the North Sea coast of England in the early 1880s, some of his strongest work to that date; and later in that decade, after his return to Maine, executing several fine etchings after his oil compositions. After his brother Charles gave him one of the new Eastman Kodak No. 1 cameras, Homer took a number of photographs on his fishing trips to Canada and Florida in the mid-nineties.[81]

About the same time, he turned to painting a few unusual watercolors and oils in nearly monochrome black and white. His first effort was inspired by a visit in 1893 to the international world's fair, the Columbian Exposition, in Chicago, the so-called White City, where he responded not to the grand Beaux-Arts architecture or the multitudes of visitors but to the surreal illumination of the grounds by artificial lighting at night. Like Henry Adams, Homer intuitively sensed the new and transforming power of electricity, and his only painting of the visit, *The Fountains at Night, World's Columbian Exposition* (fig. 58), was a nocturne of darks and lights. Photography may have played some role in the ink-wash watercolors he executed two years later, variously depicting two or three men in canoes fishing, but their intent clearly seems less to record a narrative situation than to create a reflective tone poem.[82] Art historians have recognized them as quite new and original in his work at this time, and their delicacy and

Figure 58. Winslow Homer, *The Fountains at Night, World's Columbian Exposition,* 1893. Oil on canvas, $16^{15}/_{16}$ x $25^{1}/_{16}$ in. Bowdoin College Museum of Art, Brunswick, Maine, Bequest of Mrs. Charles Savage Homer, Jr.

Figure 59. Winslow
Homer, *The Artist's
Studio in an Afternoon
Fog*, 1894. Oil on
canvas, 24 x 30¼ in.
Memorial Art Gallery
of the University of
Rochester, New York,
R. T. Miller Fund

privacy suggest a focusing on pure issues of form, expression, and imagination
that in fact mark the great innovative creativity of his last period of work.

An important monochrome painting leading into this period was *The
Artist's Studio in an Afternoon Fog* (fig. 59), which directly relates to his owner-
ship and study of Michel Chevreul's book on color theory, *Laws of the Contrast
of Colour and Their Application to the Arts*. He made use of the manual through
much of his career, describing it to a friend at the end of his life as his Bible.
Chevreul stressed the interaction of nature's colors when perceived by the
human eye and advised that in recording them one had to be sensitive to
the total effect rather than just to independent details. Another major idea was
the abstract, expressive role of color in capturing the essential feeling, more than
the descriptive facts, of a scene.[83] Both the sense of overall coloristic harmony
and the emotional power were key elements in *The Artist's Studio*. The light and
atmospheric conditions of a dense Maine fog obviously blur and distort the various masses of buildings, water, and ledges into flattened areas of color, all visually unified by the eerie moisture as variant tonalities of browns, tans, and grays.

We know from the actual site that Homer manipulated his perspective
and placement of principal masses in the painting, most notably the foreground
diagonal ledge, which cannot be seen in this relationship to the water and build-

ing profiles behind. Homer has also conflated the spatial recession and juxta-posed the contrasting dark masses with each other and the silvery light above. In a sense, this picture unified what the artist saw with what he created, the exterior and interior life joined. The place where he made his art has here liter-ally become its own subject, shrouded appropriately in a mysterious light, in an act of intense feeling as well as intellect. The result was one of his most abstract and cerebral expressions, which would characterize the distinct concerns of his late career and have a brooding echo in the somber *Cape Trinity, Saguenay River* (Regis Collection, Minneapolis, Minn.) a decade later.

A third process in Homer's selection and handling of subjects during the later nineties was an intense exploration of seriality in his watercolors. While we are now aware that he frequently rethought and revisited subjects through-out his mature career, in this late phase he more consciously and systematically undertook closely related sequences of images. As early as 1889, for example, he painted at least four similar versions of *Leaping Trout*.[84] Helen Cooper was among the first to analyze the sequence he did of deer by the water's edge; one dates from 1889 and three followed together in 1892. Likewise, there is an early treatment from 1885 of black coral divers in the Caribbean, which leads to at least three similar watercolors in 1898–99. One of the largest groups shows broad white sloops in Nassau and Key West, dating from 1899 and 1903.[85] The details are not identical from image to image within each series—the deer shown are male and female, and locations shift from Florida to the Caribbean—nor does Homer engage in a linear narrative. But he does appear to have been inter-ested in pursuing related moments and shifting points of view, in almost cine-matic fashion. Such seriality indeed relates to concurrent experiments in early motion photography by contemporaries such as Étienne-Jules Marey, Eadweard Muybridge, and Thomas Eakins and reminds us that the invention of "moving pictures" dates from these very years.

At the same time Homer also made several oil paintings of waves break-ing on the rocky Prout's Neck shore with a comparable close scrutiny of one area, perhaps not as an intended series in itself but as slightly different investi-gations of compositional forms, textures, and balances. Even more so than the watercolors, these canvases have no ostensible narrative or anecdotal story and are almost always devoid of the human presence. Beginning with *Sunlight on the Coast* (1890; Toledo Museum of Art) and continuing intensively at mid-decade with *Weatherbeaten* (1894; Portland Museum of Art, Maine), *Northeaster* (1895) and *Maine Coast* (1896; both The Metropolitan Museum of Art), these were images of reductive, elemental forces in degrees of conflict and equilibrium with each other. Even more than the battle of waves with rocks, these pictures lead us to respond to the sheer strength of design, the tactile presence of paint, and the raw physical energy of nature. With these works it is evident that Homer

Figure 60. Winslow
Homer, *The Gulf
Stream,* 1899. Oil on
canvas, 28⅛ x 49⅛
in. The Metropolitan
Museum of Art,
New York, Catherine
Lorillard Wolfe
Collection, Wolfe
Fund, 1906 (see
colorplate 13)

was moving decisively beyond the descriptive realism of his earlier years to artistic issues on the threshold of modernism.

When we turn to Homer's single great paintings at the turn of the century, in this context we discover that even his most legible images carry deeper and often not always fully explicable meanings. This was no more so than in perhaps his most famous picture, *The Gulf Stream* (1899; colorplate 13; fig. 60). Given its date, it was certainly about endings, not just the century's close but also the looming plight of the black man, alone and adrift, framed by circling sharks and an approaching waterspout. Furthermore, on a personal level this bleak drama came to occupy Homer during the year immediately after his father's death. Similarly, he had painted a precarious scene of life and death in the balance, *The Life Line* (1885; Philadelphia Museum of Art), in the months after his mother's death, and clearly the loss of Homer's father marked another finality. Besides its evident personal associations, other contexts of meaning have suggested themselves as scholars scrutinize this image with all its artistic, historical, and even religious evocations. Certainly, it takes its place in the substantial romantic tradition of allegorical and historical dramas at sea: Gericault's *Raft of the Medusa* (1824), Delacroix's *Barque of Dante* (1822), and Turner's *Slave Ship* (1840), which was acquired by the Museum of Fine Arts in Boston only a few years before Homer began his painting. Its principal American precedent, John Singleton Copley's *Watson and the Shark* (1778), was also on view in Boston and also depicted a scene alluding to the slave trade and set in Cuban waters. The threat of death, the abandoned black man, and enveloping dark waters were all romantic themes Homer made his own at this critical moment in his and the nation's life.

As we have already seen, the question of the black race's relationship to the rest of American society was brought to the fore by such figures as Douglass, Washington, and Du Bois, so Homer's embattled image in 1899 intuitively spoke to that historical moment. Government policy encoded racism anew in the 1890s, and the Caribbean setting of *The Gulf Stream* expressed America's heightened imperialism abroad at the same time. It is also conceivable, as some have argued, that Homer, unmarried, alone, and set apart, identified with the isolated black as outsider. At sixty-three, with illness just a few years away and his death a little over a decade later, Homer understandably may have felt cast adrift and facing an uncertain destiny. On yet another level, certain details suggest religious connotations; though Homer was not an overtly religious person, he well knew the symbolic visual iconography to express ideas about mortality and transcendence. Nicolai Cikovsky has enumerated some of the crucial details: the large cleat on the foredeck in the shape of a cross, the broken mast similar to a funerary column, the open hatch in the shape of a tomb with the sugarcanes looking like ropes to lower the body into the tomb. To these

Figure 61. Winslow Homer, *Searchlight, Harbor Entrance, Santiago de Cuba*, 1901. Oil on canvas, 30⅛ x 50½ in. The Metropolitan Museum of Art, New York, Gift of George A. Hearn, 1906 (06.1282)

Figure 62. Winslow
Homer, *Diamond
Shoal*, 1905.
Watercolor on paper,
13⅞ x 21¾ in.
Private collection

we may add the passages of red in the surrounding waves, alluding to blood, and
the universal life force of water providing the hope of regeneration. Mention of
the snakelike forms of the canes on the deck, another interpreter has reminded
us, along with the light blue of the Gulf Stream's warm flow, locates this specifically in the route of the sugar and slave trades between Africa and the
Americas.[86] Consciously nor not, the canvas carries insights into the state of
America and of the artist. We know the latter for certain, since *The Gulf Stream*
was the one painting Homer chose to be photographed beside him in his studio,
thus linking its complex imagery with his own self-image.

Cikovsky has gone on to argue that if *The Gulf Stream* represents the old
and the passing, then *Searchlight, Harbor Entrance, Santiago de Cuba* (1901; fig.
61) signals the new and the coming. Although just two years apart, one
belonged to the nineteenth century, in its representational realism, while the
other stood at the outset of the twentieth century, with its greater abstraction
in both form and idea. Human figures were absent, as was increasingly the case
in Homer's late works, and his subject was layered and oblique. Ostensibly, he
was responding to events in the recent Spanish-American War: the searchlight
illuminated the harbor, so Americans might seek any vessels attempting to leave
for open water, although all we see is the stark intersection of old cannon with
the loom of light. Just as the composition itself consists primarily of silhouetted
horizontals and verticals, so the earlier world of the battlement and gun barrel
reinforce the earthly horizon, while the modern searchlight reaches skyward.[87]
Like *Kissing the Moon*, it was a picture of near-monochromatic coloring dark

blues, almost as cold and empty as a lunar landscape. That association is evident in the complementary presence of the three-quarter moon at the upper left, which casts, we presume, the bright patch of light on the rampart below. It is the moon's light that illuminates the bank of moisture sweeping the horizon and fuses the two forms of unearthly lighting. In both *The Gulf Stream* and *Searchlight* our eye is drawn to the far horizon, but in the former it is to signs of foreboding and in the latter to a sense of mystery and possibility.

As Homer became ill in his last years, often his horizons become inverted or closed off. One such example was *Cape Trinity, Saguenay River* (Regis Collection, Minneapolis), which occupied him from 1904 to 1909. The bold, looming cliffs over the river, where Homer had often fished during previous years, dominate the composition, painted in a palette of dark blues, blacks, and white highlights. The headland presses forward to the picture plane, and save for the moonlit clouds above and their reflections on the water, the spatial and emotional environment seems claustrophobic and gloomy. An arbitrary touch of blood-red paint appears on the river surface at the lower left, perhaps, we have to wonder, as some private or unconscious hint of mortality. Prolonged illness during the summer of 1906 interrupted his work on this canvas, and again in the early summer of 1908 Homer suffered a mild stroke. It is not hard to connect his vulnerable state of mind and body with the somber coloring and oppressive masses of this landscape, as psychological as it is real.

The other work of this period that suggests intimations of uncertain fate was his last dated watercolor, *Diamond Shoal* (1905; fig. 62). As with *Kissing the Moon* the year before and *Cape Trinity*, finished a few years after, our viewpoint is low in the water as the forms of nature rise above us. Even more aggressive is the thrust of the principal subject, here the schooner in a gale, bearing down on the viewer. This, of course, is an antecedent for Homer's last major oil, *Right and Left*, four years later, where our position is with the birds as shots explode toward us from the horizon. The lightship tossing in the background in *Diamond Shoal*, from which the watercolor takes its title, indicates that the setting was in the rough waters of the Atlantic off Cape Hatteras, where countless vessels over time had gone down. On board two sailors struggle to lower the mainsails in the suddenly rising wind in order to stabilize the vessel in the turbulent seas. Meanwhile, the ship rushes toward the dark, surging wave in the foreground, where Homer has placed his name in brush strokes like those of the watery crests nearby. With the massive bow almost upon us, we can only wonder about our imminent fate. When we summarize the principal elements running through much of Homer's late art—its symbolic content, spatial abstractions, and the anxious disequilibrium—we have left the long-familiar Homer as objective American realist for an artist with subjective and aesthetic concerns just as prophetic of modernism as his Post-Impressionist contemporaries in France.

John F. Peto

Similar, shifting undercurrents are evident in the equally introspective late work of John Frederick Peto and Thomas Eakins. Still-life painting, especially in Peto's hands, changed markedly in this period both in its subject matter and in its formal means. Peto was born in Philadelphia in 1854 and studied there at the Pennsylvania Academy of the Fine Arts in the late 1870s. A fellow student at the same time was William M. Harnett, who later went on to a much more visible and publicly successful career. Both learned the standard drawing and modeling techniques, using the extensive plaster-cast collection at the Academy, and soon emerged as friendly rivals with a clear eye on one another's work. Their earliest paintings were still lifes of fruit arrangements on tabletops, reminiscent of that flourishing subject matter during the 1850s in the hands of John F. Francis and Severin Roesen. But artists coming into their own after the Civil War in the shadow of Reconstruction and rising Victorian materialism found less appealing the earlier ideas about nature's bounty, the sense of youthful freshness, and the bright promise of growth. Concurrently, Peto and Harnett quickly turned to tabletop compositions of pipes and mugs, books and old candles, currency and newspapers, the bric-a-brac of daily affairs. While the objects painted by both artists remained rather similar over the next few years, and led later historians to confuse their artistic identities, each began to develop a distinctive style, Harnett's rather linear and precise, Peto's more painterly, textured, and sensuous. After Harnett's early death at the peak of his reputation in 1892, the reclusive Peto moved into prominence. By the end of the decade, his relatively subjective and imaginative approach yielded some of the most mysterious and evocative still-life inventions of the time, inventions that also show the stirring of a modern spirit.

Peto exhibited his works only about half a dozen times during his life, and by the late 1880s he had largely withdrawn to the Methodist resort community of Island Heights on the New Jersey shore, where he spent the rest of his life. His later work took on an introspective and private character, as if he found in the basic domestic objects around him all he needed to assemble his austere combinations of geometric forms, disquieting colors, and uncertain light sources. On one level his still lifes of old violins, leatherbound books, and quill pens seemed to be quiet songs of praise to the sister arts; on another they reflected the larger culture of collecting and material possessions in an America of rapid commercial growth, accumulations of wealth, banking scandals, and financial failures. Intuitively, Peto's art reflected both the immediate and the broader worlds about him.

During the late 1890s and early 1900s the settings, colors, and selection of objects gradually but decisively changed. Most revealing was Peto's transfor-

Figure 63. John F. Peto, *Card Rack with Jack of Hearts,* c. 1900. Oil on canvas, 30 x 25 in. The Cleveland Museum of Art, Purchase from the J. H. Wade Fund

mation of the traditional tabletop arrangement, in which he moved his objects, primarily old books, from the surface of a desk or chest to a shelf in a cupboard or on the wall. His viewpoint drew closer: instead of showing the full edge or corner of a table, as well as a sense of its recession into the background, he gives us only a cropped section pressed forward to the picture plane, with objects densely clustered in dark, impenetrable blackness. As Peto's career evolved, his colors became less objectively descriptive and more independently expressive. He tended to favor dark greens, intense blues, mustards, and slate grays, often in combinations that approach but do not reach an unnerving dissonance. Likewise, the objects of his artistic affection increasingly show the presence of age and suffering at the hands of time. Many belonged to earlier days: old lanterns and lighting devices, daguerreotypes and *cartes de visite*, battered pots and pans, and always frayed and broken books, all indices of nostalgia, for the worlds of either his parents and his grandparents or reflections of the late-nineteenth-century fashions of the colonial revival.

Peto's style of intense concentration and mystery culminated with *Old Companions* (colorplate 14) and several other bookshelf pictures from about 1904. Piled on a very shallow shelf are combinations of precariously stacked books and pamphlets, candles or oil lamps, and the occasional pipe, tobacco canister, or inkwell. Everything seems in danger of collapse and disorder; light often appears to emanate from different sources, casting contradictory shadows; and gritty textures throughout at once describe worn surfaces and convey a sense of physical as well as psychological exhaustion.

Another major formal development in Peto's later work was painting flat, illusionistic still lifes of wall boards and old doors. He took his objects from the receding tabletop and shallow shelf and painted them pinned or hung flush to the wall. One extensive series included large canvases of fishing or hunting gear, music instruments or painting equipment, and old lighting devices, hanging against door boards. A related series, known as letter racks, depicted arrangements of business and calling cards, envelopes and newspaper clippings, calendars and old family photographs, usually shown held to the painted wood panels with crisscrossing pink tapes. Peto and Harnett together attempted their earliest versions in this format in 1879, and while Harnett would undertake only one other letter rack a decade later, Peto became fascinated with the artistic and technical challenge of shallow illusionism, almost abstract patterns of color, and the two-dimensional geometric designs. Most of his earlier paintings of this type were autobiographical, incorporating visual references through photographs, written addresses, or printed cards to family, friends, patrons, or business associates. They became ingenious still-life portraits and personal histories of professional callings; at the same time they were studio explorations of color, shape, line, and texture beyond their coded signs of daily commerce or personal communications.

Peto completed one sequence of about a half dozen of these letter racks during the first half of the 1880s and did not return to the format until a decade later. When he did so, producing another half dozen or so between 1894 and 1906 (a year before his death), the later group was markedly different in mood and approach. Instead of bright coloring, light blond wood backgrounds, and specific references to family, friends, or business associates, the nineties canvases were gravely subdued, the wood panels very dark green or black, and the various paper fragments were left generalized or cryptic in their associations. Moreover, his brushwork was looser and more textured, the pinned tapes were worn and usually torn, and the emphasis on nails, scratches, and gouging was everywhere apparent. By the turn of the century Peto's forms had come to express the troubled concerns both of his deep inner self and of the nation at large. His more universalized imagery of the later paintings was able to convey the accumulating tribulations in his personal life as well as a wider melancholy permeating the country's turn-of-the-century mood.

Doubtless one reason for the graver mood emerging in Peto's later paintings was the death in 1895 of his father, Thomas Hope Peto, to whom the artist was deeply devoted. Peto senior was an honorary member of the Philadelphia Fire Department, and this association may have led his son to take up playing the cornet through acquaintance with such department activities as providing bands for parade music and community performances.[88] As a beginning painter, Peto found inspiration in the paperwork of his father's business as a supplier of fire supplies and equipment. In the myriad trade cards and advertisements, invoices, and inventories he may have found the precedents for all the signs, letters, and numerals that he made so central to his painting. When his father died, Peto painted a trompe l'oeil memorial plaque, a significant moment he turned into a work of art at once serious and playful.

But this autobiographical nature of Peto's art also became intertwined with later nineteenth-century American culture, in particular with the Lincoln cult and nostalgia for the Civil War era. We have already seen one manifestation of this in Saint-Gaudens's memorial sculptures and noted another in Crane's novel; in addition, Walt Whitman's devotion to the Lincoln myth intensified through the later editions of *Leaves of Grass*, and one of his later efforts was the poignant assemblage of his Civil War memories in *Specimen Days*. At a time when the veterans of that conflict were beginning to die as a generation, the country was engaged in a new call to arms in its fight with Spain over Cuba, and under Teddy Roosevelt the exercise of masculine power became both an individual and a national ideal.[89] Sacrifice and suffering became themes common to Peto's and the nation's losses.

One of his first Lincoln images was a rack picture of 1894, *Old Time Letter Rack* (Museum of Fine Arts, Boston), in which a *carte-de-visite*–sized photograph of the president sat at the center of the crossed tapes. Three years later, following the death of Peto's father, another Lincoln image in an oval format hung from a tack against an old board in *Reminiscences of 1865* (Wadsworth Atheneum, Hartford). Just above it was a tacked envelope with the phrase "Head of the House" partially written across it, and hung above both, cutting off the word "Head," was an aged bowie knife. The original blood-stained knife, said by the artist's family to have been picked up by Thomas Hope Peto on the Gettysburg battlefield, was kept in the Peto house, along with similar memorabilia and bric-a-brac, and appears as an evocative prop in a number of other late

Figure 64. John F. Peto, *Reminiscences of 1865*, after 1900. Oil on canvas, 30 x 20 in. The Minneapolis Institute of Arts, The Julia B. Bigelow Fund

paintings. For Peto the loss of two father figures must have occasioned a sadness of many depths.

In other variations he pursued additional expressive details on this motif: a second version of *Reminiscences of 1865* (after 1900; fig. 64) depicts two large nails illusionistically projecting from the back of the canvas into the viewer's space in the foreground. It is a startling image of aggressive violence and assaults us in a way analogous to Homer's rushing ship's prow or firing shotguns. In *Lincoln and the Star of David* (1904; private collection) a nail tears through the painted board, which nearby has a gouged star, both oblique suggestions of pain and martyrdom. One of the most intriguing Lincoln pictures, *Old Time Letter Rack* (1894; fig. 65), shows the Lincoln *carte* upended and stuck partway behind an envelope, thereby visually and metaphorically beheading the assassinated president. Nearby is another card with the word "Balcony" printed on it, presumably a coded reference to the site where John Wilkes Booth fired

Figure 65. John F. Peto, *Old Time Letter Rack*, c. 1894. Oil on canvas, 30 x 25⅛ in. The Manoogian Collection

his shots before he leapt to the stage in Ford's Theater to make his escape.[90]

For Peto this visual language expressing pain was not just psychological but physical as well. Sometime during the nineties he was diagnosed with Bright's Disease, a kidney ailment that became increasingly painful during his last years and led to his death in 1907. There were also family stories of an unscrupulous friend who manipulated an aunt's finances and property, drawing Peto into a protracted legal fight. Another senile aunt came to live with the family at Island Heights and had to be confined to an upstairs room in the house, while the artist attempted to keep on with his painting in the living room downstairs. By any account his last decade must have been difficult, and it is no wonder that his pictures of this period wrestle with the forces of darkness, injury, and deterioration. Like Homer, autobiography was never far from the surface, and in very different subjects both explored new expressive means that approached modernist abstraction and symbolism.

Thomas Eakins

Art as an extension of self was a dominant force as well in the later portraiture of Thomas Eakins. His depiction of *Mrs. Edith Mahon* (1904, fig. 66) was not only one of the sublime paintings of his career, but also, beneath its deceptive simplicity and subtlety, a summary of his major artistic concerns. In a challenging pose Eakins did not often use, the sitter looks directly out at the artist and at us, meeting any critical scrutiny with equanimity and self-control, neither confrontational nor apologetic. We all know in real life how hard it is to look someone else straight in the eyes, how often we would prefer to avert our glance and look over another's shoulder. By this directness of pose Eakins forged an almost magnetic link of connection between the sitter and himself. Indeed, the pained expression, the poignant sense of resignation yet perseverance, reflected both what he saw in this concert pianist and singer past her prime and what he felt as much in the professional and psychological difficulties of his own later years.

The light falls most strongly on Mrs. Mahon's upper chest and neck, the place where song would emanate, and on her face, which is highlighted by the eyes, the locus of intelligence and self-awareness. Otherwise, mysterious darkness surrounds her, and the light comes from no certain source or direction. This is a marked change from Eakins's earlier paintings of women in interiors, such as those of his sisters seated at the piano made in the 1870s just after his return to Philadelphia from study with Gérôme in France. In these pictures we see full figures realized in clear if confined spaces, in the midst of playing or pausing at the piano. Despite their hushed tone and sense of concentration, one is aware of restrained action, a vignette of Victorian leisure activity, and a descriptive sensibility. While Eakins continued to paint occasional full-length portraits in his last decades, he increasingly focused on the torso and the head as essential reflections of character and inner life. Trained in anatomy at Jefferson Medical College and in draftsmanship at the Pennsylvania Academy of the Fine Arts, he gave primacy throughout his career to rendering accurately the organic solidity of the human figure and its convincing placement within a setting. But as with the abstraction of light in *Mrs. Mahon*, so his late works often gave up the previous clarities of spatial recession, usually established by meticulous underlying perspective drawings, in favor of undefined dark enclosures. Although the sitter's physical presence remains palpable, even stronger than the objective facts of physiognomy is the light shining on an emotional and psychological interior.

Furthermore, color, texture, and accessories carry their own expressive weight. What color there is here, the soft yellows and reds, gives warmth to the face and life to the eyes. At the same time, Mahon's watery pupils and the red-

Figure 66. Thomas Eakins, *Portrait of Mrs. Edith Mahon*, 1904. Oil on canvas, 20 x 16 in. Smith College Museum of Art, Northampton, Massachusetts, Purchased, Drayton Hillyer Fund, 1931 (1931.2)

dened rims hint of somber feelings within. Likewise, Eakins uses a thick, pasty brushwork for the aging skin of her chest, the swelling tendon in the neck, and puffy cheeks. Yet for all this uncompromising observation, the fundamental intelligence and strength of personality remain firm, and whatever time's erosion of the flesh has been, Eakins recognized the capacity for self-acceptance and an enduring passion of spirit. A couple of other details subtly frame the figure's emergence from the surrounding darkness. At the lower left, floral highlights on her dress and the black bows silhouetted against her bust complement the reflected edges of the scroll carving atop a tall Victorian armchair behind Mrs. Mahon. This chair was one Eakins had used frequently during his career both as a prop and as a visual commentary on his sitters. It made an early

Figure 67. Thomas
Eakins, *The Cello Player
(Portrait of Rudolph
Hennig)*, 1896. Oil on
canvas, 64¼ x 48⅛ in.
The Pennsylvania
Academy of the Fine
Arts, Philadelphia,
Joseph E. Temple Fund

appearance in *Katherine* (1872; Yale University Art Gallery), where its ample forms comfortably surround Eakins's first fiancée and play off the several curved, relaxed shapes of her head and limbs. In his 1878 portrait of *Mrs. John H. Brinton* (private collection) only the back and scrolled top of the chair are visible as they frame the woman's upper torso. A closer viewpoint and cropping of the subject enhance the more concentrated posture of quiet reflection.

Probably the most familiar use of the chair came with the 1891 portrait of *Amelia Van Buren* (Phillips Collection, Washington), where Eakins seemed to exaggerate its scale as if overwhelming the sitter in her pensive reverie. The broad, flat back behind her and the two solid arms projecting forward at each side, along with the fan across her lap, almost imprison Miss Van Buren visually. The contrast between the chair's massive vertical form and the flowing diagonals of her body, as well as its darker browns in contrast to the silvery grays and delicate pinks of her dress and hair, augment her resilience and indepen-dence of mind. Finally, her gaze outside the picture's frame toward the light affirms the sense of release from physical bonds. One late use of the same chair occurred with *The Old-Fashioned Dress* (1908; Philadelphia Museum of Art), a portrait of Helen M. Parker as a young girl posing stiffly in an heirloom dress. She stands beside the chair and rests her hand on its top, of which we see only a narrow vertical rectangle rigidly placed parallel to the picture plane, its wood-en hardness and carved details calling attention to the awkward discomfort of the young woman wearing a fancy gown from another age. These various uses of the chair bring us back to its isolated scroll carving, detached and hovering above Mrs. Mahon's head. It disappears into the darkness behind her, barely a fragment of the solid physical world, certainly separable from the abstracted realm of thought and will Eakins found in the face and eyes of the woman before him.

This balance between individual specificity and universal humanity was one of the triumphs of Eakins's late portraiture. As others have pointed out, he often painted figures as identifiable individuals but also as professional types. Moreover, he was usually at his best in treating people who were creative or accomplished in their disciplines and who thereby stood before him as equals, worthy of comparable self-examination, respect, and sympathy. Ever since his first portraits of Philadelphia physicians alone or in group compositions in the 1870s, he painted professionals in numerous callings, but no more so than the number and variety during the decade around 1900; these included students, writers, artists, surgeons, musicians, actresses, clerics, and teachers. Among the artistic figures were painters, an architect, and a collector; among the musicians a cellist, singer, violinist, oboist, and pianist; and among the scholars were an anthropologist and professors of physics and medicine.[91] The titles of several works indicated his conscious linking of the personal and the generic, such as *The Cello Player: Portrait of Rudolph Hennig* (1896; fig. 67) and *The Actress (Portrait of Suzanne Santje)* (1903; colorplate 15).

After the turn of the century, Eakins was a frequent visitor to the St. Charles Borromeo Seminary in the Philadelphia suburb of Overbrook, where he painted a large number of portraits of Catholic clerics. Like Homer, Eakins was not himself a religious person, but the spiritual aspect of the human condition was of intense interest, and in the hierarchy of this venerable denomination he found deep intelligence and compassion. Nearly a dozen of his most impressive canvases between 1900 and 1906 were the result.[92] Some of these were notable for their unusual format or coloring. *Cardinal Martinelli* (1902; Armand Hammer Collection, Los Angeles), like the portrait of the writer *Frank Jay St. John* (pri-vate collection) two years earlier, were striking profile compositions, appropri-ate in their contrived artifice and near abstraction of design to men of thought.

Similarly, *Very Reverend John S. Fedigan* (1902; St. Charles Borromeo Seminary , Overbrook, Pa.) and *Monsignor James P. Turner* (1906; Nelson-Atkins Museum, Kansas City, Mo.), like the portrait of Suzanne Santje, all depict figures robed in brilliant raspberry red, where color is not merely descriptive but seems to exert a powerful, expressive life of its own. Obviously, the red is suitable for higher orders of the church, symbolic of Christ's passion, but the color also reveals the passions of the flesh. It was one of Eakins's culminating achievements that he could explore equally the interrelated conditions of the physical, even sensual and sexual, and the cerebral, even transcendent. As with Peto in these same years, color and light moved from functioning in an objective realism to newly subjective and conceptual roles.

Three other categories of Eakins's work in this period further clarify these changes in style and interpretation. For the first time since the mid-1880s, when Eakins had painted *Swimming* (Amon Carter Museum, Fort Worth, Texas), he turned for a final look at athletic subjects. Unlike his earlier sporting pictures of rowing, sailing, hunting, and swimming, all set outdoors, this last group in 1898–99 devoted to wrestling and boxing are shown in darkened interiors.[93] Instead of active figures in motion across clearly illuminated and plotted spatial expanses, the late scenes show individuals locked in place or paused during the principal action. The emphasis is more on mental than physical condition. In the culminating work, *Between Rounds* (1899; fig. 68), it is significant that the timekeeper occupies a position of prominence in the foreground, complementing and similar to the seated boxer above. Both are contemplating the passage of time, what has passed in the round before and what is to come in the round to follow. The strongest light falls on the boxer at the corner of the ring, in contrast to the shadowy crowd in the tiered seats beyond, drawing attention to the subtle relationships between the isolated individual and society surrounding him. There is another metaphoric image here, that of the performer in the arena, voyeuristically observed and criticized by others, an analogue in Eakins's mind to the artist at work in both his private and his public worlds. Like the boxer Billy Smith, the painter must consider what he has accomplished and what he is still capable of. The outward pause in action allows reflection, creativity, and determination to become the principal subject, and paralleling Homer and Peto, Eakins unflinchingly probed human psychological depth with fresh originality.

The autobiographical strain in Eakins's later work is especially evident in the numerous family portraits he completed in this same period. There were at least a handful of his father-in-law, William H. MacDowell, painted between 1890 and 1904, a final portrait of his father, one of his wife, and his own *Self-Portrait* in 1902 (fig. 69). Interestingly, the paintings of his wife and himself are close-up frontal views and convey unavoidable images of sad isolation. Such

Figure 68. Thomas Eakins, *Between Rounds*, 1899. Oil on canvas, 50⅛ x 39⅞ in. Philadelphia Museum of Art, Gift of Mrs. Thomas Eakins and Miss Mary Adeline Williams

Figure 69. Thomas Eakins, *Self-Portrait*, 1902. Oil on canvas, 30 x 25 in. National Academy of Design, New York

direct gazes were rare for him and seemed most possible with those family members or colleagues closest to him.[94] One senses that few others could bear the ruthless examination.

One subgroup of Eakins's professional portraits deserves final attention, the isolated full-length figure. Stylistically, these pictures reflect his lifetime admiration for the abstracted tonal portraits of Velázquez, whose work he saw on his youthful trip abroad in the 1860s, and for the precision of technique he learned from Gérôme in Paris. Some of Eakins's most sensitive and penetrating canvases came at the turn of the century: *The Dean's Roll Call* (1899; Museum of Fine Arts, Boston), which is a portrait of Professor James W. Holland, the architect *John J. Borie* (1896–1900; Hood Museum of Art, Dartmouth College, Hanover, N.H.), *Professor Leslie Miller* (1901; Philadelphia Museum of Art), and, most compelling of all, the portrait of his brother-in-law Louis Kenton, *The Thinker* (1900; fig. 70). One argument has suggested that its

Figure 70. Thomas Eakins, *The Thinker: Portrait of Louis Kenton*, 1900. Oil on canvas, 82 x 42 in. The Metropolitan Museum of Art, New York, Kennedy Fund, 1917 (17.172)

title came by association from Rodin's recently famous sculpture, although its characterization of a mood linked to a particular individual was a constant practice for Eakins.[95] In any case, its composition is one of his most reductive and suggestive.

With barely an indication of a slightly receding baseboard, the space is otherwise empty save for the energies of changing brushwork and the subtle shift of tones from floor to wall surface. As a consequence, the eye is able to read this as both a flat and a spatial design, at once isolating the form within its flat silhouette and allowing it a sense of weight, substance, and gravity. Remarkably, the whole figure clothed in black could have seemed lifeless, yet Eakins is able to convey the organic integrity and standing mass convincingly but without any distracting detail. Where detail does become evident, reinforced by the selective intensity of lighting, is in the shadowed wrists and highlighted key chain, and most strongly on the downcast face supported by the bright curve of his collar. For so long in his art Eakins had addressed the crucial interdependence of head and hands as emblems of the respective abilities of mind and body, intelligence and action, deliberation and execution. Here he once again focuses on the inner vision, borne by the head, the face, and the eyes. All else is diffuse and detached. Only the intensity of thought has clarity and substance.

Kenton was married only briefly to Susan Eakins's sister Elizabeth MacDowell, and this portrait's solemnity may reflect some of the difficulties brought about by the separation. But its brooding isolation surely also embodies something of the artist's own situation at the time when he was criticized and rejected repeatedly; the pursuit of all his late art was a lonely enterprise, and all too often in the faces of others he saw his own. Other than Kenton's figure, the canvas contains only one other important detail, Eakins's signature and date in the lower right corner. Always the master of perspective from his early days at the Pennsylvania Academy, and strengthened by the study of drawing with Gérôme, Eakins inscribed his name receding on the plane of the floor rather than that of the canvas surface. This was, of course, a demonstration of technique, but it was also the placement of self in the realm of his subject, whose glance unifies that association by looking downward to that very area. Kenton also literally stands next to the date 1900, as it were, on the threshold of the new century, wondering perhaps what it will hold.

The Self as History and Literature: Henry Adams

TEN YEARS before the century's end Henry Adams turned his attention to the American past in a speculative frame of mind that was as much concerned with his country's present as with its future. Perhaps the most astute and versatile intellect of his time, Adams first explored national and personal history as a sustained effort to confront a period he felt could be framed less in declarations than in questions. Between 1889 and 1891 he published his magisterial nine-volume *History of the United States of America during the Administrations of Thomas Jefferson and James Madison,* among the finest historical writing ever produced by an American, an eloquent achievement in its own right, but also a revealing prelude to Adams's autobiography, *The Education of Henry Adams,* which engaged him a decade later. Historians over time have lavished praise on his history, although in recent years it has come under scrutiny for certain factual and interpretative weaknesses.[96] Certainly, as we have considered here the optimistic worlds of Franklin, Jefferson, and Noah Webster, Adams's outlook also seems unduly pessimistic. One explanation is his disappointment with the state of politics in his own time, which unavoidably hardened his appraisal of the past. Descendant of presidents, he turned a cynical eye from his vantage point on Lafayette Square toward the contemporary occupant of the White House and concluded, "that, two thousand years after Alexander the Great and Julius Caesar, a man like Grant should be called—and should actually and truly be—the highest product of the most advanced evolution, made evolution ludicrous. . . . The progress of evolution from President Washington to President Grant, was alone evidence enough to upset Darwin."[97]

History

In Adams's mind, "The man who in the year 1800 ventured to hope for a new era in the coming century could lay his hand on no statistics that silenced doubt." A little over a decade after writing this he found in "1900, his historical neck broken by the sudden irruption of forces totally new."[98] Despite the uncertainties he felt about his own time, his observations about the federal age were actually a mix of hope and adversity. He saw as daunting challenges the enormity of the wilderness, travel distances, and the ultimate task of national unity: "Nature was rather man's master than his servant. . . . five million Americans struggling with the untamed continent . . . every increase of distance added to the difficulties of the westward journey. . . . Nature has decided that the experiment of a single republican government must meet extreme difficulties. . . . The union of New England with the Carolinas, and of the seacoast with the interior, promised to be a hopeless undertaking. . . . Each group of states had a life apart. . . . a short journey no slight effort. . . . In the Southern States the difficulties and perils of travel were so great as to form a barrier almost insuperable."[99] Adams worried that the physical impediments would also be psychological: "The task of overcoming popular inertia in a democratic society was new, and seemed to offer peculiar difficulties. . . . an impression sober if not sad. A thousand miles of desolate and dreary forest . . . No prudent person dared to act on the certainty that when settled, one government could comprehend the whole. . . . A nation as yet in swaddling-clothes, which had neither literature, arts, sciences, nor history; nor even enough nationality to be sure it was a nation."[100]

At the same time, optimistic insights punctuate the skepticism. In particular, Adams cited the disposition of Americans toward hard work, inventiveness, and native creativity. Of the first he noted that "the true American was active and industrious. . . . every such man in America . . . actually did the work of two such men in Europe. . . . Life was quickening within it as within all mankind—the spirit and vivacity of the coming age could not be wholly shut out. . . . his native energy and ambition already responded to the spur applied to them. Some of his triumphs were famous throughout the world."[101] Regarding American ingenuity, a theme he continued to contemplate subsequently in his *Education,* Adams memorably praised the man who would also be a model for his autobiography: "Franklin's active mind drew the lightning from heaven, and decided the nature of electricity. No one in America had yet carried further his experiments in the field which he made American. . . . An independent people . . . must devise new processes of their own. . . . in order to make the Americans a successful people, they must be roused to feel the necessity of scientific training. . . . The American people were about to risk their future on a new experiment."[102] This last phrase, of course, alluded even more to the fledgling political and social framework under construction.

A third area drawing more optimism than pessimism (as we have seen, Adams elsewhere asserted the young nation had "neither literature, arts, sciences") was in fact the country's cultural independence and promise: "New conditions and hopes could hardly fail to produce a literature and arts more or less original. . . . Young as the nation was, it had already produced an American literature bulky and varied. . . . Benjamin Franklin had raised high the reputation of American printers. . . . What single production of an American pen reached the fame of Thomas Jefferson's Declaration of Independence?"[103] Lastly, Adams admired America's capacity for practicality combined with ambition: "Americans were a race without illusions or enlarged ideas. . . . Of all historical problems, the nature of a national character is the most difficult and the most important. . . . Jefferson aspired beyond the ambition of a nationality, and embraced in his view the whole future of man. . . . He wished to begin a new era."[104] Many of these ideas remained on Adams's mind through the turn of the century.

Indeed, he felt a similar ambivalence about his own time, and the forces of change around 1900 seemed just as bewildering. This was the lens through which he examined the past, but he was also engaged in the craftsmanship of literature, and his thoughtful summary of the state of America at the outset of the nineteenth century (which constituted the first six chapters of his monumental history) has commanded respect for its perfected style of expression over its perceived factual inadequacies. As his phrases reveal, we should also understand his historical writings as essential reflections of his own time and self. Like the artifice of his *Education* that followed, these were detached and disciplined explorations of reflection and memory. In sum, Adams was preoccupied, along with many of the other most interesting minds of his generation, with the self and with American history.

Autobiography has been an American interest since Franklin, flourishing with original energy in the hands of Thoreau and Whitman. By the end of the nineteenth century, the consciousness of self was pervasive, and autobiographical expression met a number of different needs for figures as diverse as Eakins, Peto, Homer, Twain, Sullivan, James, Du Bois, Washington, and Douglass. Perhaps one of its greatest attractions was the freedom of form and of content it allowed its practitioners, who, in Franklin's words, created a second life or wrote a "second edition." Because the form involves memory and imagination, autobiographers have the opportunity to fuse subjective recollection and public history. In an age of turning inward, writers drew on the impulses of dreams and the subconscious, and autobiography was a way of indulging sentimentally in the past and moving beyond it, however difficult the understandings revealed. As a literary form, it permitted the creative blending of fiction and nonfiction, of artifice and facts. The speculative mind could assess personal and national history for ideas about change. Henry Adams, whose autobiography remains one of the great documents in American culture, thought about the past in relation to the present "to triangulate the future." "Past history is only a value of relation to the future."[105]

The Education

Elegant in literary style, Adams's autobiography was also challenging in its thoughts about science, politics, history, and learning and farsighted in articulating what would be central issues for the coming century. He titled it *The Education of Henry Adams* to indicate that its subject and authorship were one. Radically, he wrote in the third person, as if casting himself as a still life to be composed and viewed with detachment. This single, crucial fact allowed him the distance to shape and select recalled events, so that he could account not only for the formal education of his earlier years, but also, more importantly, make his recollections and writing a current, open form of learning. Thus, the education he leaves for us is not a passive, completed experience but an active, dynamic one.

The sequence of chapter titles gives some clues to the book's trajectory. While there is no rigid or even systematic grouping of topics, the beginning half dozen all refer to specific physical places: "Quincy," "Boston," "Washington," "Harvard College," "Berlin," and "Rome." The next dozen titles address thematic ideas or issues rooted in particular chronological events that occurred around the Civil War years—for example, "Treason," "Diplomacy," "Political Morality," "The Perfection of Human Society," "Dilettantism," "Darwinism," and "The Press." The mood changes radically midway with "Chaos" and "Failure." The latter title covered the year 1871, after which Adams omitted the next two decades, apparently overwhelmed by his wife's suicide, to resume with a chapter titled simply "Twenty Years After." The only place mentioned thereafter was the chapter "Chicago," by which Adams meant not the city but the World's Columbian Exposition, which he visited and where he began to formulate his ideas about modern history. Many of the later chapter titles—"Silence," "Indian Summer," "Twilight"—convey a psychological mood of pessimism and elegy. A few hint at his mental process of seeking balances or (one of his favorite words) relations—"The Dynamo and the Virgin," "The Height of Knowledge," and "The Abyss of Ignorance." The final subjects dealing with 1903–4—"The Grammar of Science," "A Dynamic Theory of History," and "A Law of Acceleration"—brought him to the realm of science, which he saw as a modern form of literature and the future form of history.

Adams's text actually begins with an editor's preface, which bears the signature of his friend and former student Henry Cabot Lodge, though Adams wrote it, signaling the imaginative artifice of his project. In setting out his intentions, he even quoted from himself:

> This volume, written in 1905, as a sequel to the same author's "Mont-Saint-Michel and Chartres," was privately printed. . . . "Setting himself to the task, he began a volume which he mentally knew as 'Mont-Saint-Michel and Chartres: A Study of Thirteenth-Century Unity.'" From that point he proposed to fix a position for himself, which he could label: 'The Education of Henry Adams: A Study of Twentieth-Century Multiplicity.' With the help of these two points of relation, he hoped to project his lines forward and backward indefinitely. . . . " His own preface came next, in which he acknowledged the two paradigms of modern autobiography: "American literature offers scarcely one working model for high education. The student must go back, beyond Jean Jacques, to Benjamin Franklin, to find a model even of self-teaching."[106]

This last phrase would form the substance of Adams's education, as his narrative evolved from chronology into ideas.

The principal elements of Adams's style were evident from the opening paragraph of his first chapter:

> Under the shadow of Boston State House, turning its back on the house of John Hancock, the little passage called Hancock Avenue runs, or ran, from Beacon Street, skirting the State House grounds, to Mount Vernon Street, on the summit of Beacon Hill; and there, in the third house below Mount Vernon Place, February 16, 1838, a child was born, and christened later by his uncle, the minister of the First Church after the tenets of Boston Unitarianism, as Henry Brooks Adams.[107]

We thus learn at the outset that this story is a voyage of sorts, first from shadow presumably into light, and by convolutions around and through places of power, to reach finally the authorial identity. The whole paragraph is one long, carefully constructed sentence in two major parts, given rhythm by commas and held together by a semicolon at the center. In its intricate yet clear structuring and its lines of motion, the style subliminally conjures up the imagery of the thirteenth-century architecture Adams so much admired. The two sinuous parts of his long sentence are analogous to the rising and falling arcs of a pointed Gothic arch. Adams's intention to link the past with the present appears in his simple juxtaposition of the verbs *runs* and *ran,* which anticipates his later, charged meanings in such words as *race* and *acceleration.*

Although the family's history was associated with Quincy, Massachusetts, Adams's birthplace was Boston, literally, politically, and intellectually; from there his life would run eventually to the nation's capital and history. The phrase "a child was born" is an obvious allusion to Christ's birth, a signal of the beginning of an unusual life. What follows will be a search for a modern religion and spiritual life.

Before Adams could engage in self-teaching, he needed to account for the sequential stages of his nineteenth-century education, all of which in various degrees failed him. Of his earliest school days he recalled, "If school helped him, it was only by reaction. . . . He thought his mind a good enough machine, if it were given time to act, but it acted wrong if hurried. Schoolmasters never gave time. . . . In any and all its forms, the boy detested school, and the prejudice became deeper with years." Ready to enter Harvard in 1854, he later recalled "the American boy of 1854 stood nearer the year 1 than to the year 1900. The education he had received bore little relation to the education he needed. Speaking as an American of 1900, he had as yet no education at all." Enrollment in America's most venerated university proved no better: "The entire work of the four years could have been easily put into the work of any four months in after life. Harvard College was a negative force, and negative forces have value." He concluded, "Self-possession was the strongest part of Harvard College, which certainly taught men to stand alone. . . . Whether this was, or was not, education, Henry Adams never knew."[108]

With his father posted as minister to London during the Civil War, Adams could absorb the opportunities there and travel to some of the great centers of learning on the Continent. Yet in Berlin, "as his last experience of education he tried the German high school. The experience was hazardous. . . . All State education is a sort of dynamo machine for polarizing the popular mind. . . . The German machine was terribly efficient. Its effect on the children was pathetic." He went on to Rome but "after staying as long as he could and spending all the money he dared, he started with mixed emotion but no education, for home. . . . The ten long years of accidental education had changed nothing for him there. He knew no more in 1868 than in 1858." His views of the English were just as disappointing: "The best educated statesman England ever produced did not know what he was talking about. . . . Knowledge of English human nature had little or no value outside of England. . . . The young American who should adopt English thought was lost."[109] Once back home in the United States, Adams tried teaching at Harvard, but he did not find it satisfying. He turned his eye again to the nation's capital (which he had visited before the Civil War), wondering if he might find intellectual or political leadership there. But, "in the amusement of Washington, education had no part. . . . Proverbially Washington was a poor place for education."[110]

At each juncture Adams came to a similar conclusion: "He had been mistaken at every point of his education. . . . He knew he knew nothing. . . . If he were ever to amount to anything, he must begin a new education, in a new place, with a new purpose. . . . Not that his ignorance troubled him! He knew enough to be ignorant. His course had led him through oceans of ignorance."[111] These rather pessimistic sentences largely appear in the central chapters of the *Education,* and the last quote set the tone for the chapter called "Failure." More important, buried within them was the clarifying awareness that the more we know, the more we realize how much we don't know. Adams had at last come to understand that passive education and received knowledge could yield to active

Figure 71. Augustus Saint-Gaudens, *The Adams Memorial (Grief),* 1886–91. Rock Creek Cemetery, Washington, D.C.

learning and an inquiring imagination.

Compounding the failure of Adams's institutional education was the suicide in 1885 of his wife, Marion Hooper "Clover" Adams, an incident recently blamed by some on Adams himself. Whatever the actual circumstances, he subsequently destroyed all their correspondence and his own diaries of this period, leaving the twenty years surrounding the event a dark void in his book. After Clover's death, Adams and his friend John La Farge traveled to the South Seas. Before he left, Adams asked Augustus Saint-Gaudens to design a memorial for his wife, the figure commonly known as *Grief* (1891; fig. 71) installed within an enclosure of holly trees in Rock Creek Cemetery in northwest Washington. An ambiguous and abstracted figure informed by Western classical precedents fused with oriental forms, the sculpture is one of the most powerful and expressive in the history of American art. Even if it cannot explain an inexplicable death, its haunting silence engages the viewer's contemplation of mortality and life beyond death. Back from the Pacific, Adams immediately went to Rock Creek to see the bronze figure: "He supposed its meaning to be the one commonplace about it—the oldest ideas known to human thought. . . . The interest of the figure was not in its meaning, but in the response of the observer. . . . Like all great artists, St. Gaudens held up the mirror and no more." By now Adams realized he had to find answers by asking questions; his true education was to be self-teaching. When his narrative resumed in 1892, he began to struggle with the new forces emerging in his own life and in America by the last decade of the century.

When Adams visited the Columbian Exposition in Chicago in 1893, he began to contemplate what he perceived to be an image of American unity in the uniform Empire architecture of the White City. He read this endeavor as an effort to make sense of the increasing fragmentation, or multiplicity, of contemporary life. Then and in the years following, his observations revealed concepts that would come to define the modern condition: "The facts were constantly outrunning his thoughts. The instability was greater than he calculated; the speed of acceleration passed bounds. . . . Chicago asked in 1893 for the first time the question whether the American people knew where they were driving."[112] This last word was typically prophetic, as Adams's use of it preceded the widespread use of the automobile by almost a decade, a development that would truly change the speed of acceleration in everyday life.

Learning

In subsequent chapters Adams formulated his new idea of active learning, one that gained strength first by his own work on the Middle Ages and that period's relevance to his own time, and later by his intense interest in the great dynamos he saw on display at the Universal Exposition in Paris in 1900. The latter prompted him to associate learning with movement: "Education must fit the complex conditions of a new society, always accelerating its movement. . . . Ignorance required that these political and social and scientific values of the twelfth and twentieth centuries should be correlated in some relation of movement." At last he had found a language of expression suitable for the momentum of the present: "Adams read and failed to understand; then he asked questions and failed to get answers. . . . Probably this was education. . . . History had no use for multiplicity; it needed unity; it could study only motion, direction, attraction, relation."[113] He took note respectively of the new research on radium, the X ray, and the atom, not certain of their physical nature, but sure of their intellectual impact on history's trajectory: "In these seven years man had translated himself into a new universe which had no common scale of measurement with the old. . . . The sequence of thought was chaos, he turned at last to the sequence of force. . . . He found himself lying in the Gallery of Machines at the Great Exposition of 1900, his historical neck broken by the sudden irruption of forces totally new. . . . History broke in halves."[114]

Gradually, in the forces of contemporary science he sought metaphors to explain: "He knew not what new direction to turn, and sat at his desk, idly pulling out of the tangled skein of science, to see whether or why they aligned themselves. . . . The magnet in its new relation staggered his new education by its evidence of growing complexity, and multiplicity, and even contradiction, in life. . . . All one's life, one had struggled for unity, and unity had always won. . . . Yet the greater the unity and the momentum, the worse became the complexity and the friction." Paradoxically, modern unity could only be in multiplicity, contradiction, relation and motion, rather than in fixed or absolute points. This led him to see the force lines of history as a means of clarifying direction: "Adams sought only instruction—wanted only to chart the international channel for fifty years to come; to . . . fix the acceleration of movement in politics since the year 1200, as he was trying to fix in philosophy and physics; in finance and force." Much as he regarded the magnet to be a revealing image of current science, so did he find the apparently chaotic nature of kinetic gas. This particular discussion concluded with one of the great sentences in the *Education:* "In plain words, Chaos was the law of nature; Order was the dream of man."[115] Here he uses the same syntactical device he employed so effectively in the book's opening paragraph—a semicolon joining in balance the paradox or tension of opposites. Following the introductory phrase, two six-word statements, with their own implicit contradiction of plain words and complex ideas, pivot on either side of the semicolon, each beginning with a strong abstract noun and concluding with the juxtaposed realms of man and nature. This was vintage Adams as thinker and stylist.

In the book's closing chapters Adams urgently explored ways of coming to terms with the changed realities of his time: "The child born in 1900 would, then, be born into a new world which would not be a unity but a multiple. Adams tried to imagine it, and an education that would fit it. . . . Order was an accidental relation obnoxious to nature." Writing just at the moment when Einstein was formulating his new theories, Adams went on in his own terms: "A dynamic law requires that two masses—nature and man—must go on, reacting upon each other, without stop, as the sun and a comet react on each other, and that any appearance of stoppage is illusive." Now nearing the end of his own life and experience of learning, he realized, "for past history, this way of grouping its sequences may answer for a chart of relations. . . . Any law of movement must include, to make a convenience, some mechanical formula of acceleration." Finally, in the penultimate chapter, "A Law of Acceleration," he could admit, "Meanwhile he was getting education. . . . The new forces would educate. . . . he had learned his ignorance. . . . The next great influx of new forces seemed near at hand, and its style of education promised to be violently coercive." A few pages before closing, he spoke with a wise melancholy: "Even in America, the Indian Summer of life should be a little sunny and a little sad, like the season, and infinite in wealth and depth of tone—but never hustled."[116] We encounter that same bittersweet mood in the still-life images of Peto and in the memoirs of Henry James.

Adams not only created his dynamic theory of history, which allowed him to educate himself, and in turn left an active, open education for his readers, but he also foresaw many of the political and cultural concerns that would tighten their grip on the twentieth century. Even if he failed in his relationship with his wife, he projected from his study of the Virgin of Chartres as a symbol of spiritual power in the Middle Ages an analogous importance for women in American life: "She was reproduction—the greatest and most mysterious of all energies. . . . Adams owed more to the American woman than to all the American men he ever heard of. . . . He was studying the laws of motion, and had struck two large questions of vital importance to America—inertia of race and inertia of sex."[117] Certainly no feminist in the modern sense, Adams nonetheless struck a familiar and sensitive nerve in linking the issues of gender and race—issues that have reverberated throughout the century to its very end.

Trajectories Forward

Although he had no explicit foreknowledge of the coming revolutions in mathematics and physics or the upheaval of an international war, Adams wrote that the world in 1901 "showed other infallible marks of coming mental paroxysm. . . .

In 1901 the world had altogether changed. . . . A new avalanche of unknown forces had fallen on it, which required new mental powers to control." He astutely recognized the explosive forces generated in the physical sciences: "The man of science must have been sleepy indeed who did not jump from his chair like a scared dog when, in 1898, Mme Curie threw on his desk the metaphysical bomb she called radium." This was but one example of the "energy of modern science"[118] to be followed by Max Planck's quantum theory of physics and Niels Bohr's theory of atomic structure. For determining the properties of radium and radioactive phenomena, Curie received the Nobel Prize in 1903. Clearly, the grammar of science was a language equally useful to the sciences and to literature.

In the sphere of politics Adams was just as prophetic when he remarked on relations with Russia, Germany, and China, which, like the magnetic forces of gravity, were in constantly dynamic tension, as they would be for much of the twentieth century.[119] "Committed to the task of keeping China 'open,' he saw China about to be shut. . . . In 1903 [John] Hay saw Russia knocking away the last blocks that held back the launch of this huge mass into the China Sea. The vast force of inertia known as China was to be united with the huge bulk of Russia in a single mass which no amount of new force could henceforward deflect."[120] Among European nations, "A mere glance showed him that here was a Germany new to mankind. . . . The next, and far more difficult step, was to bring Germany into the combine. . . . If Germany could be held there, a century of friction could be saved."[121] Nearly a century later, historians still debate this point and the amount of friction it has generated.

In the end, however, we must see Adams's work as less an acute social and political analysis than a creative and transforming autobiography. The examination of one's consciousness was an act that was shared by Homer and Eakins, among others. Adams acknowledged the book's true autobiographical focus in his third chapter, where he wrote, "This was the journey he remembered. The actual journey may have been quite different, but the actual journey has no interest for education. The memory was all that mattered. . . ." Later, as he thought about Darwin and the classification of the sciences, he admitted that "psychology was to him a new study, and a dark corner of education." And in a chapter toward the end he added, "The only absolute truth was the subconscious chaos below, which every one could feel when he sought it. Whether the psychologists admitted it or not, mattered little to the student who, by the law of his profession, was engaged in studying his own mind." If we hold up any late Eakins portrait, say *The Thinker,* in our mind's eye, we can sense the same profound poignance that Henry Adams finally confessed in these sentences: "Of all studies, the one he would rather have avoided was that of his own mind. He knew no tragedy so heartrending as introspection."[122]

The New Century's New Energies

THE SUBCONSCIOUS. Acceleration. Relation. Sequence of force. Mysterious energy. Multiplicity. Out of his search for a modern scientific grammar Henry Adams produced several terms or phrases that dovetail strikingly with some of the most inventive efforts in other fields at the same time. For example, during the same decade, Adams finished the *Education,* Sigmund Freud published his theory of psychoanalysis, Frank Lloyd Wright built the first of his new Prairie-style houses in Illinois, Albert Einstein announced his theory of relativity, the age of the carriage and still photography gave way to the automobile and "moving pictures," and the Wright brothers lifted off the earth for the first time in an airplane. Concurrently, intellects in different spheres were defining the revolutionary realities of the new century, and a decisive transformation occurred in the understanding of the physical and metaphysical world.

Besides noting "the sub-conscious chaos below," as we have seen, Adams also referred to the dark corner of psychology, introspection, and the study of the mind. What the practices of autobiography and psychoanalysis shared was the systematic exploration of memory and retrospection. Just as Freud concentrated on explicating dreams, Adams wrote about "the journey he remembered." Having initially intended to study law, Freud soon turned to medicine in the 1870s, concentrating on physiology and neurology. By the nineties he was a specialist in nervous illness and therapeutic healing. In 1895 he coauthored *Studies of Hysteria* and for the first time analyzed one of his own dreams.[123] This and other studies led to the publication in 1900 of his *Interpretation of Dreams.* He recalled as a particularly traumatic event the death of his father in 1896, a tragedy that had a comparable impact on the careers of Peto and Homer. That same year Freud used the word "psychoanalysis" for the first time, and shortly afterward he began to formulate his notion of the Oedipus

Figure 72. Thomas Eakins, *Portrait of Henry O. Tanner*, 1902. Oil on canvas, 24$^{1}/_{16}$ x 20$^{1}/_{4}$ in. The Hyde Collection Art Museum, Glens Falls, New York

complex. For a more general audience he published *Psychopathology of Everyday Life* in 1904, followed by his books on theories of sexuality and psychoanalysis. Out of all this pioneering research have come such accepted observations as "dreams were simple and undistinguished *wish fulfillments*" and "every dream without any possible exception goes back to an impression of the past few days. . . . analysis invariably brings to light a significant experience."[124] Although they were engaged in the different acts of painting and writing, Thomas Eakins in his late portraits and Henry Adams in his autobiographical self-education offer analogous expressions of discovery at this key juncture. We could also note the dream imagery dominant in the paintings of the 1890s by such disparate artists as Albert Ryder, Ralph A. Blakelock, and Henry O. Tanner (fig. 72).

Frank Lloyd Wright

Perhaps Henry Adams's words *relation* and *multiplicity* make the most interesting correlation with Frank Lloyd Wright's early architecture. If Louis Sullivan had taken buildings in a new upward direction for the twentieth century, then Wright developed modern architecture in another direction, outward into its surrounding environment. Instead of treating a building as a unitary cubic block, where the solid walls separate outside from inside, Wright created a new unity of multiple parts flowing in relation to each other. Space was no longer conceived as an inert contained volume, but as a fluid and active sequence (to recall another Adams concept) tying interior and exterior together. Solid and void, positive and negative, became interchangeable through Wright's use of cantilevered roofs, projecting porches and terraces, and open ranges of windows, which allowed light to dissolve boundaries. Of course, the new technology of reinforced concrete was what allowed both Sullivan and Wright to shape these new formal and spatial relationships, but it was an energetic artis-

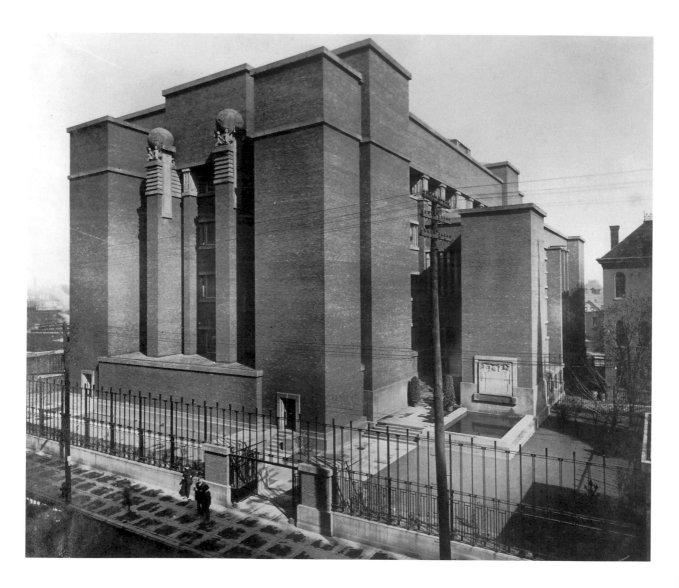

tic vision appropriate to the modern age that created them.

Born in Wisconsin in 1867, Wright moved to Oak Park, Illinois, in 1889, when he married and built his own house and studio there. His next few years in the employ of Adler and Sullivan coincided with the firm's most creative and successful years, and Wright rose from apprentice to the position of head draftsman and worked on many of Sullivan's most important buildings of the early nineties. On his own by 1893, Wright began the most inventive period of his own work, which shaped his early maturity and has been posited by architectural historians as the turning point of his career.[125] Until 1909, when he left for a European sojourn, he developed his signature Prairie Style in a series of houses mostly constructed in the western suburbs of Chicago. Concurrently, he designed his first important nondomestic building of the new century, the Larkin Building (1903–4; fig. 73) in Buffalo, New York. In both efforts Wright broke down the traditional composition of a building into dynamic forms and spaces that were decidedly modern. The Larkin Soap Manufacturing Company needed new quarters for its mail-order business, and Wright sought to design a functional interior within an exterior imagery of industrial form, as he said, "to house the commercial engine of the Larkin Company."[126] Although the impulses to serve functionalism and organic harmony came from Sullivan's example, the stark abstraction and complexity of the exterior massing suggested an even newer spirit. Instead of a cubic block with planar facades, the roofline, wall surfaces, and corners were broken up by interlocking vertical piers, with a resulting effect of dramatic power and energy. Light entered the large interior atrium court from a full skylight above, but the shifting forms and silhouette on the outside also contributed to a sense of dynamic framework.

In the streets around his own house in Oak Park as well as in other nearby neighborhoods, Wright designed a sequence of Prairie-style houses notable for their radically open plans, interpretation of masses and spaces, and projecting rooflines, all used to tie the structure to its setting. One of the finest early examples is the Ward Willetts House (1902–3; figs. 74, 75) in Highland Park.[127] Breaking out of the standard uniform rectangle, its plan is cruciform with wings extending asymmetrically from the central core; in the words of one historian that would have appealed to Henry Adams, "the house is the center of a field of energy."[128] Wright elaborated on his ideas in the Cheney House (1903–4) in Oak Park and brought them to a high point in the well-known Robie House (1908–10) in Chicago. Beyond their formal emulation of the flatness of the midwestern plains, these structures exhibit what Adams called the "sequence of force" or "chance collision of movements." As Adams's theory of history directed, Wright's buildings provide an analogous balancing of opposites, an equilibrium of tension rather than stasis, a triangulation forward and backward, inside

Figure 73. Frank Lloyd Wright, Larkin Company Administration Building, 1903–4. Buffalo, New York

Above: Figure 74. Frank Lloyd Wright, Ward Willetts House, 1902–3. Highland Park, Illinois

Right: Figure 75. Frank Lloyd Wright, Ground-floor plan of the Willetts House, redrawn c. 1940

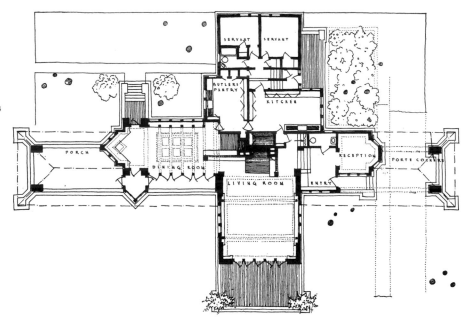

and out, in a moving continuum. Another expression of this process, cited by many historians, was emerging almost simultaneously in France with the Analytic Cubism of Picasso and Braque.

New Scientific Energies

But the flow of space and the interchange of solids and voids were evident not just in the visual arts and not just in Adams's grammar that talked of "the magnet in its new relation," the link between energy and inertia, or "the kinetic theory of gas"; they were at the heart of the new inventions and discoveries of Thomas Edison, Marie Curie, and Albert Einstein, who were revealing and defining the invisible forces of the new century. Curie's discovery of radium and polonium highlighted science's increasing knowledge of the basic elements, while Einstein's theories of relativity introduced the crucial notion of relative motion and its distortion of fixed points in space and time. He showed that space is active and all matter moves, that all bodies in the universe generate gravitational fields and hold them in motion with each other, and that the velocity of a moving object is relative according to the position of the viewer.[129] As Adams had realized that there were no longer fixed absolutes in politics or history, Einstein argued that there was no fixed reality or absolute space. Wright's architecture only gave form to what mathematics and physics were concurrently charting.

Once, when Einstein was ill as a young child, his father gave him a magnetic compass to occupy his time, and the unseen pull on the needle fascinated him thereafter. By the age of sixteen he had become intrigued with the nature and velocity of light waves and continued to pursue electromagnetic theories. Soon after the death of his father, in 1902, he plunged deeper into the challenges of science; the next few years saw him produce his series of famous papers on thermodynamics and electromagnetic phenomena, matched by the equally radical pronouncements of Max Planck in his quantum hypothesis of physics. From this moment came the understandings of the reality of the atom, of light as consisting of particles, and of time as relative according to separate events.[130] Einstein's famous equation of 1905 asserted that energy and mass were equivalent, a postulate that took the rest of the century to analyze and verify.

The Cinema

In America the practical and prolific inventor Thomas A. Edison registered more than a thousand patents during his lifetime for his devices and formulas, most of which involved the new energy of electricity. So taken was he with the possibilities of the telegraph that he gave the nicknames Dash to his son and Dot to his daughter. Probably best known for his development of the phonograph in the 1870s and the lightbulb during the 1880s, he also worked on electric rail transportation and a lighting system for New York City. As he said, "Electricity is not power; electricity is a method of transporting power."[131] Although most identified with the practical applications of this modern force, Edison was fascinated by the concepts of magnetism and the gravitational forces in our planetary system. He also devoted attention to other transformations of motion at this time, helping to develop a motion-picture machine in the late nineties and the idea for an electric storage battery for automobiles. Edison and his company, including his assistant W. K. L. Dickson, played a crucial role in the early stages of creating American film. Already during the 1880s several critical developments provided important catalysts. Edison learned of the experiments in stopped-action serial photography by the French scientist Étienne-Jules Marey and British-born American photographer Eadweard Muybridge. These efforts had made clear the separate moments and parts of motion and led directly to a new visualization of movement. Equally important was the technical breakthrough in 1888 of the creation of celluloid film, which soon led to Dickson's invention of the Kinetoscope, a camera and viewing machine in which images were recorded on a perforated film strip. When the strip was attached between two spools and driven by electric motor, the film's frames were sequentially illuminated for projection as a moving image.[132]

On October 6, 1893, Dickson filed on behalf of Edison the first copyright listing with the Library of Congress for a commercially distributed film. Edison had hoped to, but did not, have ready for display a model of the new invention at the World's Columbian Exhibition that year in Chicago, an event noted for the concurrent triumph of electricity and artificial illumination. But within a year he did open the first peep-show parlor in New York City to instant acclaim. This was but one of a number of new forms of public entertainment that emerged around 1890, especially in cities, including amusement parks such as Coney Island, major-league baseball, and vaudeville. Edison's Kinetoscope peep show was a prelude to the building soon thereafter of ever grander palaces for entertainment.

The proliferation of storefront theaters, along with projection in vaudeville arenas, which could offer varying fare from one-minute travel films to longer stories, led next to the creation of the nickelodeon (named for its five-cent admission), a small projection room at the back of a penny arcade. Another watershed date followed in 1905, when the Pittsburgh entrepreneur Harry Davis opened the first full-scale cinema theater, which he called the Nickelodeon, devoted solely to showing films. In two year's time he had opened a chain of twelve more theaters in other cities, given such suggestive names as the Dreamland, Pictorium, Jewell, Electric, and Bijou Dream. The numbers of establishments and the attendance were comparably impressive: by mid-decade New York boasted more theaters than any other city in the world and by decade's end some 26 million viewers were attending shows each week.[133]

What did audiences see when they went to these darkened spaces? At first, historians tell us, the subjects were carried over from stereographs: scenes of sports, vaudeville, well-known people and places, railroads, parades, expositions, and machines. Usually posed or still, the scenes soon gave way to moving forms such as breaking waves, trains, and fire engines. Not surprisingly, Edison put the New York subway on film soon after its opening.[134] Public and political events also attracted interest, such as the dramatic explosion and sinking of the *Maine* in Havana Harbor in 1898, U.S. naval activities the next year in the Philippines, the Boxer Rebellion in China in 1900, and President McKinley's assassination a year later. Needless to say, some of these images had to be staged, but they forecast future efforts at news journalism and the capturing of unfolding contemporary stories.

The rapid shift from static to moving images was accompanied by another major development for film-making—telling stories. From fixed and centrally framed figures the camera soon began to exploit different points of view, close-ups, and fluid compositional arrangements. Such devices suited themes as different as Passion plays and boxing and wrestling matches. Between 1897 and 1899 Edison filmed a number of prizefights at his New Jersey studio, anticipating their well-known pictorial counterparts painted a decade later by George Bellows. *The Life of an American Fireman*, a film of 1902, also touched a popular nerve with the modern urban public in its excitement and explosive visual drama. Sometimes, during this first period before sound, producers would accompany their screenings with singers, performers, lecturers, or pianists. Since most films were relatively short, programs could be repeated often for changing audiences, and as early as 1903 theaters began to organize formal exchanges of films to maintain a fresh repertory. The low price of admission merely clinched the popularity of moviegoing.[135]

In 1903 one of the film-makers employed by Edison, Edwin S. Porter, who had made several short films, became famous for creating *The Great Train Robbery,* arguably the first important movie. Certainly, it brought the previous experimental stages of the medium to a new level of achievement and forecast its development during the century. Incorporating some twenty different shots and a dozen locations, the film was remarkable for the variety of scenes and the quick action between events. Above all, it made clear in popular form the possibilities of motion and space in the new medium and affirmed Edison's company as one of the most eminent in the industry. One measure of this film's popular appeal was its earning an estimated two million dollars for Edison in its first five years of release.

Soon movie production centered in New York City: Edison moved his company there from Orange, New Jersey, in 1901: two years later the Biograph Studio located nearby in Union Square, at the same time that the first French companies, George Méliès and Pathé, were opening offices in the city.[136] Of course, further dramatic advances and changes would come during the second decade of the century, both in content and in production. D. W. Griffith, for example, would introduce full-scale, complex storytelling, and companies soon began to move their base of activities to Florida and California, where the longer duration of natural sunlight made filming easier and less costly. What cinema introduced, and future film-makers from Griffith on would exploit, was the potential for controlling or adjusting time through editing. This was yet another arena in which linear and fixed chronology was susceptible to expansion, contraction, or interruption, in short, manipulated according to will or imagination. With astonishing swiftness in the few years on either side of 1900, American cinema evolved, as film historian David Robinson has summarized, into the "most universal entertainment form in history."[137] Both technically and imaginatively movies transformed American life.

The Automobile

Edison's contemporaries were also pioneering in the most American forms of new acceleration: the bicycle, automobile, and airplane. By the mid-1890s Henry Ford had produced a motorized buggy frame mounted on four bicycle wheels, powered by gasoline, which he called a "quadricycle." From this came the Ford A and over the next few years the Model T, called by one historian "democracy on wheels." Ford proclaimed, "I will build a car for the great multitude. It will be large enough for the family but small enough for the individual to run and care for. . . . to enjoy with his family the blessing of hours of pleasure in God's great open spaces."[138] Of course, motorized transportation was a long time developing, and steam power existed much earlier in the nineteenth century. There were several exigencies for the development of modern forms of urban travel, perhaps foremost the health problems of tuberculosis and yellow fever, which were thought to result from the dust of drying horse manure. Horses often died from overexertion, and the delay in removing the remains from city streets caused both congestion and pollution: in 1880 it was reported that New York alone had to dispose of some fifteen thousand equine corpses. It was also self-evident that in an age of accelerating industrial production horses could not be marketed, standardized, or mass-produced like machines.[139] The question was how to bring modern propulsion to the existing comforts of horse-drawn conveyances, that is, to produce a "horseless carriage."

By the 1870s a successful compression engine was developed in Germany, and a single-cylinder engine followed in the eighties. The Germans had also developed gas-powered motorcycles and began to pursue their application to four-wheel carriages. By 1891 the first gas-powered tricycle was driven in Ohio, and soon after, three different models were operating in the United

States. Additional comfort and convenience came in 1889 with the introduction of inflated rubber wheels and, a decade later, the steering wheel in lieu of a tiller. Meanwhile, the bicycle craze of the 1890s prompted greater attention to the maintenance of public roads, which proved readily adaptable to the new motorized vehicles.[140] As with the early evolution of motion pictures, the conjunction of several imaginative and technical advances led to the creation and rapid availability of the new invention.

By 1894 German developers were selling vehicles in France, and a year later one of America's first firms, the Duryea Motor Wagon Company of Springfield, Massachusetts, went into business. Charles and Frank Duryea were former bicycle mechanics and typified the natural evolution from work in bicycle-repair shops to early automobile production. Their initial reputation was secured when they won the first automobile race in the country, in which Frank drove a buggy at an average of five miles an hour. By the end of 1896 thirteen of their models were on the road, and American car production was under way.[141] During the following year Francis and Freelan Stanley experimented with steam engines as an alternative to gas-powered motors in their famous Stanley Steamer. American automobile advertising began in 1898, when the Winton Motor Carriage Company of Cleveland, Ohio, placed a small notice for their new vehicle that year in *Scientific American:* it was priced at one thousand dollars, "costs about 1/4 cent a mile" to run, with "speeds from 3 to 20 miles an hour."[142]

However, it would be a young Michigan farmboy with experience in agricultural machinery who emerged as the best-known pioneer of the American automobile at this time. Henry Ford had worked at installing and refitting small steam engines on farm equipment, and he adapted the technology to internal combustion power for his quadricycle, which he drove through the city of Detroit in 1896. Three years later he had become chief engineer and minority stockholder in the Detroit Automobile Company, and in 1903 he was able to form his own Ford Motor Company. That year he brought out his first car, the Ford A, which soon improved to the extraordinarily popular and successful Model T. In just the first decade of the century American car production rose from about 4,000 to 187,000 vehicles annually. Meanwhile, in Cleveland, Ransom Eli Olds sold an estimated 12,000 of his first models between 1901 and 1904.[143] At the same time in Europe some of the industry's most familiar names—Daimler, Mercedes, Rolls-Royce, Fiat, and Renault—also had production of their own brands well in hand.

Other developments at this time facilitated the pace of advances in production, comfort, and sales. In 1901 the first oil gusher at Spindletop on the Texas Gulf Coast, along with other rich fields across the Southwest, signaled the beginning of one of the twentieth century's most important fuel industries.[144] Soon America's first parkways were being paved with asphalt, and by 1905 adaptable financing terms were being created to suit customers' needs. In aiming for practicality, flexibility, and economy, American car manufacturers in particular were able to produce and sell motorized vehicles for all individual tastes and needs. Like the cinema, the automobile rapidly offered universal pleasure, but perhaps more importantly it provided independent mobility and the sense of individual freedom. Finally, here was another instance in which experimentation in the realm of science evolved into one of the most pervasive democratic experiences of modern times.

The Airplane

Of all the new forms of velocity, to borrow Henry Adams's term, the most portentous was airplane flight. Not only was this means of motion faster than that of foot, bicycle, horse and carriage, or horseless carriage—with each one altering our relation to the passing landscape—but the airplane lifted us off the ground and gave us a moving view from above. When Orville Wright rose for about twelve seconds above the beach near Kill Devil Hills at Kitty Hawk, North Carolina, with his brother Wilbur running alongside, the two collaborators had taken man physically and imaginatively in a new spatial direction. This moment marked the breakdown of the perspective system of ordering space, from foreground to background, and instead of a distant horizon there was now either the shifting ground below or unmeasurable space above. In leading to the reality of space travel, the "attraction" (Adams's word again) of the twentieth century, flight above and beyond the earth could no longer use the traditional compass. Once in space, the coordinates of north and south, up and down, left and right, lost their moorings.

The bicycle, which had played a critical role as intermediary between horse and automobile transportation, also provided in its basic technology key precedents for early airplane construction. The Wright brothers and their several siblings were born in the Midwest, where their father rose from preacher to bishop in his evangelical church. The boys grew up with the rapid rise of the bicycle craze, which reached its apogee in the mid-nineties as they were in their twenties. They were familiar with its various technical aspects, such as electrical welding, ball bearings, chain and shaft transmissions, and the production of rubber tires. Moreover, many people at the time drew analogies between bicycles and flying machines in their capacity for speed, escape, and sense of freedom. Indeed, one minister proclaimed the bicycle "a scientific angel," giving mortals the opportunity to fly, a wishful vision the modern film-maker Steven Spielberg gave us in the finale of *E.T.*[145] For the Wright brothers another toy of childhood, a propeller on a stick, further teased their imaginations; by 1896 they were aware of propelled-glider experiments in both Germany and at home in Washington, D.C. To this information they added the new knowledge of lighter and stronger internal combustion engines being developed for automobiles. Finally, they observed birds in flight and learned their control over flight with the crucial turning of their wing tips. The ability to twist was an essential element of propulsion.

Understanding the differing functions of the propeller and wings of an airplane and adapting the transmission systems from bicycle technology, the Wrights first tested gliders and kites and then engine-driven planes, with success coming at the end of 1903. Not only would this achievement transform our experience of motion and space, but it was also to have a profound impact on the conduct of warfare in World War I just a few years later. America and the world would soon realize a new threshold had opened, practically and politically, spatially and intellectually. The Wright brothers' enterprise was a significant step toward the modern reality of spatial flux and relativity as it was then being charted by Einstein. At the same time the idea of penetrating from the exterior to the interior of things was occurring variously through the X ray, Frank Lloyd Wright's organic architecture, psychology and autobiography, and the advent of Analytic Cubism. (A few years later, its principal creators, Pablo Picasso and Georges Braque, nicknamed each other Orville and Wilbur.)

Lastly, in this context we should recall once more the distorted and dislocated spaces of Homer's late seascapes. Besides his obscuring the horizon in oils such as *Kissing the Moon* and *Right and Left,* some of his watercolors after 1900 show fish suspended against an indeterminate watery background: we are uncertain whether the view is through the water or down toward its surface. It is worth noting that at about the same time Claude Monet in Giverny was also turning his angle of view downward onto the waterlily pond, with no horizon line above or stabilizing forms at either edge. Reflected light from the sky further obscures the depth of field and releases us from the observed world. The loss of the horizon, for the first time since the invention of perspective at the beginning of the Renaissance, signaled the breakdown of a fixed and unified system of spatial measurement and coincided directly with the flux and abstraction of modern reality. More than earlier focal periods in American culture, the issues around 1900 were as much international as national. That they were largely the ones to define the twentieth century understandably now brings us to the questions of what will define the twenty-first.

EPILOGUE

Circa 2000

AS HENRY ADAMS felt drawn at the end of the nineteenth century to appraise its beginnings in his *History*, so we are drawn a hundred years later again to look at chronological turning points. And as he attempted also to understand the trajectory of history forward, so modern historians have ruminated about the end of the twentieth century and the turn of a new millennium. During the late 1980s and through the 1990s books have appeared with titles like *The End of Nature*, *The End of Art History*, *The End of History*, *The End of Science*, and even *The End of Time*.

In approaching this new moment of culmination and transition, our world is once more experiencing the transformation of space and time. We may not yet know their full meaning or direction, but it is worth looking back one last time to consider another repeated leitmotif of this history—circularity. The arcs and rotations of the circle, either by defining forms in space or movements through it, provide cumulative images of both America's state of mind and the mind of the state. Recall that federal planning often favored the softer curves of ovals, ellipses, and spirals. Still lifes by the Peales displayed plump fruits encircled by baskets or dishes. Jefferson framed his house at Monticello with his roadway roundabouts and his gardens at the University with serpentine walls. First in his private dome room and then in his public Rotunda he referenced the cosmos, and he likened the new federal government to the planetary system.

The cycle of the seasons and the key hours of the day became central themes for Hudson River landscape painting. Emerson's essay *Nature* not only gave us the seminal image of his becoming "a transparent eyeball," but also enabled us to witness "the currents of the Universal Being circulat[ing] through me." Thoreau found constant meaning in the orbs of the sun and moon and in the circumference of Walden Pond. Whitman joined cosmos and sexuality in allusions to the lunar cycle. In classical revival architecture the sphere and the cylinder were prominent organizing forms for centralized spaces within and the march of columns without.

For his time Henry Adams found significance in the great spinning dynamos he first saw at the Paris fair. The rotation of other machine parts—wheels of automobiles, spools of film, and the propellers of planes—introduced the new dynamics of modern time and space. At the close of the twentieth century scientists cannot be certain whether the universe will continue to contract or will expand. Space is reshaped one way into the microchip and another into the black holes of the universe. It also exists in alternative forms such as so-called virtual reality and cyberspace. Because timekeeping is now digital, recorded by electrical impulses rather than the turning wheels of a clock, the twenty-first century is unlikely to know the directional meaning of the terms *clockwise* and *counterclockwise*. There is also the loss of human connotations in the replacement of mechanisms named after parts of the body, the hands and face of a clock. What may have been most ironic about this millennial date was the fear that computerized clocks literally could not tell time, unable to distinguish between 1900 and 2000! Whatever the defining expressions that come to be associated with this turning point, how appropriate that this tie to the past should accompany our anticipation of the future.

NOTES

Introduction

1. For a brief history of the creation of Standard Time, see Stephen Kern, The Culture of Time and Space, 1880–1918 (Cambridge, Mass., 1983), 11–33.
2. Beyond these, other singular periods or dates have recently been the subject of close study, for example, Kenneth Stampp's America in 1857: A Nation on the Brink (1990), Tom Lutz's American Nervousness, 1903: An Anecdotal History (1991), Stanley Elkins and Eric McKitrick's The Age of Federalism (1993), Margaret C. S. Christman's 1846: Portrait of the Nation (1996).
3. The three sections of this book evolved out of prior essays that initially laid out some of the comparative issues in each period: essays on Rembrandt Peale (1800), George Caleb Bingham and Fitz Hugh Lane (1850), and Augustus Saint-Gaudens, John Frederick Peto, Winslow Homer, and Thomas Eakins (1900). See John Wilmerding, "Rembrandt Peale's Rubens Peale with a Geranium," "George Caleb Bingham's Geometries and the Shape of America," "Luminism and Literature," "Fire and Ice in American Art: Polarities from Luminism to Abstract Expressionism," "Locating Augustus Saint-Gaudens," "John F. Peto and the Idea of Still-Life Painting in America," "Winslow Homer's Maine," "Winslow Homer's Right and Left," "Images of Lincoln in John F. Peto's Late Paintings," and "Thomas Eakins's Late Portraits," all originally published on different occasions, reprinted in American Views: Essays on American Art (Princeton, 1991), 35–48, 69–81, 123–162, 178–194, 223–304. See also John Wilmerding, "The Tensions of Biography and Art in Thomas Eakins," in Thomas Eakins, and the Heart of American Life (exh. cat., National Portrait Gallery, London, 1993), 16–35.
4. Samuel G. Freedman, "Can Tranquil Times Yield Great Works?" New York Times, August 30, 1985, Section 2:1, 18–19. He was writing about the arts during the relatively prosperous and quiet decade of the Reagan eighties.
5. Thomas Jefferson, First Inaugural Address, March 4, 1801, in Writings (New York, 1984), 492; Abraham Lincoln, "Draft of a Speech," December 1857, in Speeches and Writings, 1832–1858 (New York, 1989), 417; and Theodore Roosevelt, quoted in H. W. Brands, T. R.: The Last Romantic (New York, 1997), 387.
6. The terminology has continued through the twentieth century in phrases now almost clichéd, such as the New Deal, New Frontier, New Society, and New World Order.

Prologue

1. See Albert E. Stone, Introduction to J. Hector St. John de Crèvecoeur, Letters from an American Farmer, (New York, 1988), 7; Garry Wills, Explaining America: The Federalist (New York, 1981), xi; and James M. Cox, Recovering Literature's Lost Ground: Essays on American Autobiography (Baton Rouge, 1989), 16.
2. For discussion and biographical information on Crèvecoeur, see Stone, Introduction to Letters, 7–25; and Larzer Ziff, Writing in the New World: Prose, Print, and Politics in the Early United States (New Haven, 1991), 18–33.
3. Crèvecoeur, Letters, 42–43, 68, 81, 91.
4. Ralph Waldo Emerson, Nature, 1836, in The Complete Essays and Other Writings of Ralph Waldo Emerson, (New York, 1950), 5–7.
5. Crèvecoeur, Letters, 67, 68–69.
6. Ibid., 69–70.
7. Ibid., 83; Henry David Thoreau, Thoreau: The Major Essays, Jeffrey L. Duncan, ed. (New York, 1972), 205; and Norman Mailer, Of a Fire on the Moon (New York, 1970), chap. 5.
8. Wills, Explaining America, xii–xiii.
9. See Clinton Rossiter, Introduction to The Federalist Papers (New York, 1961), xi.
10. Wills, Explaining America, 257.
11. Federalist Papers, 36, 367, 384, 452.
12. Ibid., 33.
13. Ibid., 38, 47–48.
14. Ibid., 77, 81. See also Wills, Explaining America, xi.
15. Federalist Papers, 83; and Wills, Explaining America, 257.
16. Federalist Papers, 91, 99.
17. Ibid., 89, 99, 102–3, 249.
18. Ibid., 244, 249, 256, 301, 321, 325.
19. Ibid., 301, 310, 313.
20. Ibid., 321; see also 450, 454.
21. Ibid., 255, 425.
22. Ibid., 104–5; see also 226: "The novelty of the undertaking strikes us."
23. Ibid., 527.
24. For discussion of the chronology of the text and its publication, see Leonard W. Labaree, et al., eds., Introduction to The Autobiography of Benjamin Franklin (New Haven, 1973), 22–37.
25. Cox, Recovering Literature's Lost Ground, 14–16.
26. Franklin, Autobiography, 43.
27. Ibid., 43, 62, 70, 122, 129.
28. Ibid., 148.
29. Ibid., 52–53, 58–59, 64, 79, 106, 130. See also 57, 89.
30. Ibid., 130–31.
31. Ibid., 134, 136.

32. Ibid., 135.
33. Ibid., 148.
34. Ibid., 165, 172, 182, 193, 195–97, 201, 203–4.
35. Ibid., 208–9.
36. Ibid., 257–59.
37. See Herbert Leibowitz, Fabricating Lives: Explorations in American Autobiography (New York, 1989), 51; Cox, Recovering Literature's Lost Ground, 17; and Mark R. Patterson, Authority, Autonomy, and Representation in American Literature, 1776–1865 (Princeton, 1988), 6. All three offer useful insights into Franklin's prose style and content.
38. George Washington, Farewell Address, September 17, 1796; quoted in James D. Richardson, ed., A Compilation of the Messages and Papers of the Presidents, Bureau of National Literature (Washington, 1912), 208, 214.
39. Ibid., 208, 214.
40. Ibid., 207.
41. Ibid., 207.
42. Ibid., 208.
43. Ibid., 209, 211.
44. Ibid., 212.

Part One

1. See Frederick Doveton Nichols and Ralph E. Griswold, Thomas Jefferson: Landscape Architect (Charlottesville, 1978), esp. chap. 3, "The City of Washington," and the discussion comparing the plan of the federal city with that of Versailles, 56–61.
2. See D. W. Meinig, The Shaping of America: A Geographical Perspective on 500 Years of History, vol. 2, Continental America, 1800–1867 (New Haven, 1993), 3–66.
3. See Laurence Urdang, ed.: The Timetables of American History (New York, 1981), 154–58; and Charles Coleman Sellers: Mr. Peale's Museum: Charles Willson Peale and the First Popular Museum of Natural Science and Art (New York, 1980), 160.
4. See Ziff, Writing in the New World, 59–82.
5. See Sellers, Mr. Peale's Museum, 188–89.
6. Joel Barlow, The Columbiad, Books I and VIII, quoted in American Poetry: The Nineteenth Century, vol. 1, Philip Freneau to Walt Whitman (New York, 1993), 18, 22.
7. Jules David Prown, "Style in American Art: 1750–1800," in Charles F. Montgomery and Patricia E. Kane, eds., American Art: 1750–1800, Towards Independence (exh. cat., Yale University Art Gallery, New Haven, 1976), 32.
8. Ibid., 33.
9. See William H. Pierson, Jr., American Buildings and Their Architects: The Colonial and Neo-Classical Styles (New York, 1970), 221–28.
10. On Bulfinch, see ibid., 240–68.
11. Ibid., 350.
12. On Latrobe, see ibid., 335–72.
13. Benjamin Henry Latrobe, "Anniversary Oration, Pronounced Before The Society of Artists of the United States . . . On the Eighth of May, 1811," The Port Folio, vol. 5 (1811), 24; quoted in Linda Bantel, et al., William Rush, American Sculptor (exh. cat., The Pennsylvania Academy of the Fine Arts, Philadelphia, 1982), 22.
14. See ibid., 96–177.
15. See Beatrice B. Garvan, Federal Philadelphia, 1785–1825, The Athens of the Western World, (exh. cat., Philadelphia Museum of Art, Philadelphia, 1987).
16. See William Rush, 128–29; and Frederick Rudolph, ed., Essays on Education in the Early Republic (Cambridge, Mass., 1965), 1–40.
17. See Gordon S. Wood, ed., The Rising Glory of America, 1760–1820, revised ed. (Boston, 1990), 234.
18. Benjamin Rush, "An Inquiry into the Comparative State of Medicine, in Philadelphia, Between the Years 1760 and 1766, and the Year 1805," Medical Inquiries and Observations, 2nd ed. (Philadelphia, 1805), IV: 364–405; quoted in Wood, Rising Glory, 252.
19. See Gordon S. Wood: The Radicalism of the American Revolution (New York, 1992), 125.
20. Wood, American Revolution, 7, 369.
21. See James M. Cox, Recovering Literature's Lost Ground, 36.
22. See Prown, "Style in American Art," 37. On Jefferson in this context, see Cox, Essays, 43.
23. Letter, Charles Thompson to Thomas Jefferson, March 6, 1785, Library of Congress; quoted in Charles A. Miller, Jefferson and Nature: An Interpretation (Baltimore, 1988), 123.
24. Thomas Jefferson, Notes on the State of Virginia, in Merrill D. Peterson, ed., The Portable Thomas Jefferson (New York, 1986), 47.
25. Ibid., 115.
26. Ibid., 203.
27. Ibid., 102–4.
28. See Charles E. Clark, "James Sullivan's History of Maine and the Romance of Statehood," in Clark et al., Maine in the Early Republic (Hanover, N.H., 1988), 184–97.
29. Jefferson, Notes, 211.
30. Merrill D. Peterson, The Political Writings of Thomas Jefferson (Charlottesville, 1993), 120–21, 126, 140.
31. Thomas Jefferson, First Inaugural Address, in Peterson, Political Writings, 139; and Jefferson, Notes, 48–49.
32. Jefferson, Inaugural Address, 140.
33. Jefferson, Inaugural Address, 139; and Peterson, Political Writings, 25, 29, 133–34.
34. Jefferson, Inaugural Address, 141.
35. Peterson, Political Writings, 144.
36. For a useful summary chronology of Jefferson's life and career, see Peterson, Political Writings,

20–21; and for a thorough and sympathetic examination of Monticello's history, environment, and significance, see William Howard Adams, Jefferson's Monticello (New York, 1983), 2–33.

37. For discussion of Monticello in relation to Jefferson's ideas of nature, see Miller, Jefferson and Nature, 220.

38. Quoted in ibid., 114.

39. For sensitive analyses of the architecture and meaning of Monticello, see Pierson, American Buildings, 292–93, 298–316; and Adams, Monticello, 26–109.

40. For discussion of the University of Virginia, see Pierson, American Buildings, 316–34; and Paul Goldberger, "Jefferson's Legacy: Dialogues with the Past," in New York Times, May 20, 1993, Arts and Leisure, 33.

41. Jefferson, Notes, 48; Peterson, Political Writings, 139; and quotation in Adams, Monticello, 44. The latter continues with the well-known exclamation, "How sublime to look down on the workhorse of nature, to see her clouds, hail, snow, rain, thunder, all fabricated at our feet!" See also Adams, Monticello, 232–33.

42. See Meinig, Shaping of America, 3–12; and Alan Brinkley, The Unfinished Nation: A Concise History of the American People (New York, 1993), 186–89.

43. Meriwether Lewis and William Clark, The History of the Lewis and Clark Expedition (Elliott Coues, ed., 3 vols., (New York, nd.), I: xxvi.

44. Ibid., xxvii–xxviii.

45. Ibid., xxxiv, 1, 4, 38.

46. For a useful summary chronology on Peale, see Edgar P. Richardson, et al., Charles Willson Peale and His World (New York, 1982), 17–19.

47. The images of himself include The Peale Family (c. 1770–73 and 1808), Self-Portrait in Uniform (c. 1777–78), Angelica with Her Father and a Portrait of Rachel (c. 1790), self-portraits dated c. 1794, c. 1804, 1821, 1822, 1824, The Exhumation of the Mastodon (1806–8), and The Artist in His Museum (1822). Among notable family portraits are Mrs. Charles Peale and Her Grandchildren (c. 1782), James Peale Painting a Miniature (c. 1790), James Peale Family Group (c. 1791), The Staircase Group (1795), Sophonisba Anguisciola and Charles Linnaeus Peale (c. 1796), Hannah and Elizabeth (c. 1805), Franklin Peale (1808), Hannah Moor Peale (1816), Raphaelle Peale (1817), Charles Linnaeus Peale (1818), Titian Ramsay Peale II (1819), and James Peale (The Lamplight Portrait) (1822). For illustrations of these, see Charles Coleman Sellers, Charles Willson Peale: A Biography (New York, 1969), frontis., 80, 99, 179, 215, 261, 265, 271, 274, 275, 297, 307, 377, 395, 397, 399, 402, 403.

48. See Richardson, Charles Willson Peale, 88; Lillian B. Miller and David C. Ward, New Perspectives on Charles Willson Peale: A 250th Anniversary Celebration (Pittsburgh, 1991), 5; and Sellers, Mr. Peale's Museum, 81–84.

49. See Lillian B. Miller, "Charles Willson Peale as History Painter: The Exhumation of the Mastodon," in Miller and Ward, New Perspectives, 184; and Sidney Hart and David C. Ward, "The Waning of an Enlightenment Ideal: Charles Willson Peale's Philadelphia Museum, 1790–1820," in Miller and Ward, New Perspectives, 219.

50. Quoted in ibid., 222. See also 220–21, 228.

51. Quoted in Sellers, Charles Willson Peale, 102. See also 99, 101.

52. Quoted in ibid., 123; and Miller and Ward, New Perspectives, 149. Good accounts of the entire venture are in Sellers, Charles Willson Peale, 123–131; and Miller and Ward, New Perspectives, 145–152.

53. Quoted in Sellers, Charles Willson Peale, 149. For a chronology of the excavations and museum installation, see ibid., 128–149.

54. Quoted in Miller and Ward, New Perspectives, 145.

55. The most thorough analysis of this painting is in ibid., 145–157.

56. See ibid., 156–57. For a full list of identifiable figures present, see Richardson, Charles Willson Peale, 85.

57. See Miller and Ward, New Perspectives, 151–55. For an illustration of the sketch, now in the American Philosophical Society, Philadelphia, see Sellers, Charles Willson Peale, 132.

58. For a full analysis of this work see John Wilmerding, "America's Young Masters: Raphaelle, Rembrandt, and Rubens," in Nicolai Cikovsky, Jr., et al., Raphaelle Peale Still Lifes (exh. cat., National Gallery of Art, Washington, 1968), 72–93.

59. For summary information about the Bartrams and the association of other natural scientists in Philadelphia, see Richardson, Charles Willson Peale, 110–11, 126–28, 193.

60. Ibid., 111, 128.

61. See ibid., 126; and Ann Shelby Blum, Picturing Nature: American Nineteenth-Century Zoological Illustration (Princeton, 1993), 30.

62. See ibid., xxix, 19–26. Blum has an excellent discussion and analysis of the founding of an independent American science at this time.

63. Quoted in ibid., 46.

64. Quoted in Richard M. Rollins, ed., The Autobiographies of Noah Webster, From the Letters and Essays, Memoir, and Diary (Columbia, S.C., 1989), 5. For biographical information on Webster, see also Ervin C. Shoemaker, Noah Webster: Pioneer of Learning (New York, 1966), 3–30.

65. Quoted in ibid., 64.

66. Quoted in ibid., 52, 55. For discussion of these ideas, see also ibid., 42–50.

67. Quoted in ibid., 69, 247.
68. Walt Whitman, Leaves of Grass, The First (1855) Edition (New York, 1986), 5.
69. Quoted in Adams, Monticello, 21.
70. See Miller, Jefferson and Nature, 112; and Thomas Jefferson, Letter to John Waldo, August 16, 1813; Letter to the Honorable J. Evelyn Denison, M.P., November 9, 1825; and "Report of the Commissioners for the University of Virginia," August 4, 1818, in Jefferson, Writings, 465–66, 1294–1300, 1502–5.
71. Quoted in Wood, Rising Glory, 224–26.
72. Quoted in ibid., 163, 165, 169.
73. Quoted in Shoemaker, Webster, 77. This book contains a full chronology of Webster's publications.
74. Quoted in ibid., 145.
75. Quoted in ibid., 74, 134.
76. Ibid., 96, 129.
77. Ibid., 144, 187–88.
78. Quoted in ibid., 251. See also 218, 222, 233, 284, 306.
79. Quoted in Rollins, Autobiographies of Noah Webster, 319.
80. Shoemaker, Webster, 306.
81. Samuel Harrison Smith, "Remarks on Education, 1798," in Rudolph, Essays, 188, 220–23.

Part Two

1. See Alan Brinkley, The Unfinished Nation: A Concise History of the American People (New York, 1993), 325–30. This chapter is an outgrowth of ideas first proposed in summary form in John Wilmerding, "Bingham's Geometries and the Shape of America," in Michael Edward Shapiro, et al., George Caleb Bingham, (exh. cat., Saint Louis Art Museum, Saint Louis, 1990), 175–81.
2. See Brinkley, The Unfinished Nation, 330–50.
3. See James M. McPherson, Battle Cry of Freedom: The Civil War Era (New York, 1988), chap. 1, "The United States at Midcentury," 6–46.
4. See Samuel Eliot Morison, The Maritime History of Massachusetts (Boston, 1961), 342; and John Wilmerding, American Marine Painting (New York, 1987), 146.
5. Much of his material appears in the modern publication, Horatio Greenough, Form and Function: Remarks on Art, Design, and Architecture (Berkeley and Los Angeles, 1962).
6. Ibid., 22.
7. Ibid., 60–61.
8. Ibid., 9, 118, 120.
9. Ibid., 57.
10. Ibid., 19, 58, 81, 128.
11. Ibid., 62, 71.
12. Quoted in Sylvia E. Crane, White Silence: Greenough, Powers, and Crawford, American Sculptors in Nineteenth-Century Italy (Coral Gables, 1972), 204, 222. See also William H. Gerdts, American Neo-Classical Sculpture: The Marble Resurrection (New York, 1973).
13. For further discussion of mid-century American still life in historical context, see John Wilmerding, "The American Object: Still-Life Paintings," in An American Perspective: Nineteenth-Century Art from the collection of JoAnn & Julian Ganz, Jr. (exh. cat., National Gallery of Art, Washington, 1981), 85–112; and John Wilmerding, Important Information Inside: The Art of John F. Peto and the Idea of Still-Life Painting in Nineteenth-Century America (exh. cat., National Gallery of Art, Washington, 1983), 37–56. For more detailed information on Roesen, see Judith Hansen O'Toole, Severin Roesen (Lewisburg, Pa., 1992), and Lois Goldreich Marcus, Severin Roesen: A Chronology (Lycoming, Pa., 1976).
14. Walt Whitman, Leaves of Grass: The First (1855) Edition (New York, 1959), 14.
15. Ibid., 128; see also 29, 37, 40, 41, 55, 57, 59, 69, 138.
16. See David S. Reynolds, Beneath the American Renaissance: The Subversive Imagination in the Age of Emerson and Melville (New York, 1988), 339, 387.
17. For a provocative and insightful analysis of Spencer's imagery, see David M. Lubin, Picturing a Nation: Art and Social Change in Nineteenth-Century America (New Haven, 1994), 159–204. Also see the chapter, "Lilly Martin Spencer: Images of Women's Work and Working Women, 1840–1870," in Elizabeth L. O'Leary, At Beck and Call: The Representation of Domestic Servants in Nineteenth-Century American Painting (Washington and London, 1996), 66–108.
18. See the thorough monograph on Duncanson by Joseph D. Ketner, The Emergence of the African-American Artist: Robert S. Duncanson, 1821–1872 (Columbia, Mo., 1993), and the thoughtful probing of his work by David M. Lubin in Picturing a Nation, 107–57.
19. See the discussion on Durand's painting included in Bryan Wolf's essay "When Is a Painting Most Like a Whale?: Ishmael, Moby-Dick, and the Sublime," in Richard H. Broadhead, ed., New Essays on Moby-Dick, or, The Whale (New York, 1986), 147–54.
20. Lubin, Picturing a Nation, 116–17.
21. Wolf, "When Is a Painting," 153.
22. For full monographic discussions of Lane, see John Wilmerding, Fitz Hugh Lane (New York, 1971), and John Wilmerding et al.: Paintings by Fitz Hugh Lane (exh. cat., National Gallery of Art, Washington, 1988).
23. Most of these paintings are illustrated in color and discussed in Wilmerding, Paintings by Fitz Hugh Lane, 25–34.

24. For fuller discussion of this period in Lane's life, see Wilmerding, Fitz Hugh Lane, 38–48.

25. Mary B. Cowdrey and Theodore Sizer, American Academy of Fine Arts and American Art-Union Exhibition Record, 1816–1852 (New York, 1953), 221. For discussion see also Wilmerding, Fitz Hugh Lane, 47; Wilmerding, Paintings by Fitz Hugh Lane, 132–36; and John Wilmerding, The Artist's Mount Desert: American Painters on the Maine Coast (Princeton, 1994), 45–67.

26. This series is discussed by Earl A. Powell III and illustrated in color in Wilmerding, Paintings by Fitz Hugh Lane, 46–59.

27. Major examples include Approaching Storm, Owl's Head (1860; private collection), The Western Shore with Norman's Woe (1862; Cape Ann Historical Association), Ipswich Bay (1862; Museum of Fine Arts, Boston), Stage Fort across Gloucester Harbor (1862; The Metropolitan Museum of Art, New York), Lumber Schooners at Evening on Penobscot Bay (1863; National Gallery of Art, Washington), and Brace's Rock (1864; Collection Mr. and Mrs. Harold Bell).

28. On the question of these proposed pendants, see Henry Adams, "A New Interpretation of Bingham's Fur Traders Descending the Missouri," Art Bulletin, 65 (1983), 675–80.

29. Bingham reworked Fur Traders in Trappers' Return (1851; Detroit Institute of Arts), and Raftsmen Playing Cards in a Quandary (also 1851; Huntington Library and Art Collections, San Marino, Cal.). Usually, his second versions of a subject were less successful, often drier in both execution and feeling.

30. See Adams; and Nancy Rash, The Paintings and Politics of George Caleb Bingham (New Haven and London, 1991), 40–54.

31. See Rash, Bingham, 66–93.

32. Also in the collection of Boatman's Bankshares, Inc., St. Louis, is the second version Bingham painted of The County Election (1852). All these are illustrated and discussed in Barbara Groseclose, "The 'Missouri Artist' as Historian," in Michael Edward Shapiro et al., George Caleb Bingham (exh. cat., Saint Louis Art Museum, Saint Louis, 1990), 53–91.

33. Other related paintings are Above the Clouds at Sunrise (1849; The Warner Collection, Tuscaloosa, Ala.), Beacon off Mount Desert Island (1851; private collection), Grand Manan Island, Bay of Fundy (1852; Wadsworth Atheneum, Hartford), Morning (1848; Albany Institute of History and Art), Ira Mountain Vermont (1849–50; Olana State Historic Site, N.Y.), The Wreck (1852; The Parthenon, Nashville), and A Country Home (1854; Seattle Art Museum). For discussion of these in relation to luminism, see John Wilmerding et al., American Light: The Luminist Movement, 1850–1875, 2nd. ed. (Princeton, 1989); in the

context of Church's career see Franklin Kelly et al., Frederic Edwin Church (exh. cat., National Gallery of Art, Washington, 1989); and in the light of his Maine experience, see Wilmerding, The Artist's Mount Desert, 69–103. For a more recent, revisionist view of both Cole and Church, see Angela Miller, The Empire of the Eye: Landscape Representation and American Cultural Politics, 1825–1875 (Ithaca and London, 1993).

34. See also La Magdalena (Scene on the Magdalena) (National Academy of Design, New York) and Tamaca Palms (Corcoran Gallery of Art, Washington), both 1854.

35. F. O. Matthiessen, American Renaissance: Art and Expression in the Age of Emerson and Whitman (New York, 1941). In more recent times the term has also referred to a later period at the end of the nineteenth century, when the arts and architecture more consciously and broadly emulated the forms and values of the Italian Renaissance, to promote the perceived sense then of an American empire. By contrast, Matthiessen admitted that his study was not about a rebirth but rather an instance of national cultural maturity comparable in its defining importance. See vii.

36. Ibid.

37. Matthiessen's original list also included Emerson's Representative Men (1850), Hawthorne's The House of Seven Gables (1851), and Melville's Pierre (1852). He subsequently noted that within just the first two-year period Hawthorne as well published The Blithedale Romance (1852). Other nearly as important works appeared then too: Whittier's Songs of Labor (1850), Longfellow's Hiawatha (1855), and one year before this canonical list, Thoreau's Week on the Concord and Merrimack (1849). Finally, along with Stowe was the emergence of women writers at mid-century, among them Susan Warner, Maria Cummins, Lydia Sigourney, and Emily Dickinson. See Matthiessen, American Renaissance, vii, 188; and Reynolds, Beneath the American Renaissance, 339, 387.

38. Matthiessen, American Renaissance, 140–52, 596–613.

39. Ibid., 599.

40. Ibid., 67.

41. See McPherson, Battle Cry of Freedom, 88; and Joan D. Hedrick, Harriet Beecher Stowe: A Life (New York, 1994), 223.

42. See Hedrick, Stowe, vii; and McPherson, Battle Cry of Freedom, 90.

43. Quoted in Hedrick, Stowe, 206, 208.

44. Quoted in ibid., 208, 218.

45. Both quoted and discussed in Josephine Donovan, "Uncle Tom's Cabin": Evil, Affliction, and Redemptive Love (Boston, 1991), 76, 91.

46. For example, see Broadhead, Introduction, New

Essays on Moby-Dick, 9.

47. Herman Melville, Moby-Dick, or, The Whale (New York, 1988), 3–4.
48. Matthiessen, American Renaissance, 291; see also 286–87.
49. Melville, Moby-Dick, 182. For interpretive commentary on this chapter, see Wolf, "When Is a Painting," 147–54.
50. Melville, Moby-Dick, 169, 253.
51. Ibid., 145–49. See also Bryan Wolf's remarks in New Essays on Moby-Dick, 159–64.
52. Henry D. Thoreau, Walden (Princeton, 1989), 91.
53. Ibid., 3.
54. See Sharon Cameron, Writing Nature: Henry Thoreau's Journal (Chicago, 1985), 5, 25.
55. For example, see H. Daniel Peck, Thoreau's Morning Work: Memory and Perception in "A Week on the Concord and Merrimack Rivers, the Journal, and "Walden" (New Haven, 1990). Also newly accessible in paperback form is A Year in Thoreau's Journal: 1851 (New York, 1993), with an introduction by Peck.
56. Melville, Moby-Dick, 3.
57. January 10, 1851, and after January 10, 1851, in Journal: 1851, 5, 7.
58. February 27, July 2, August 21, and December 31, 1851, in Journal: 1851, 24, 91, 170, 328.
59. November 12, July 18, August 21, and December 20, 1851, in Journal: 1851, 290, 112, 312.
60. August 19, September 4, August 23, and November 12, 1851, in Journal: 1851, 164, 196, 175, 289.
61. See Peck, Morning Work, 25, 57.
62. February 12, May 19, June 11, and October 12, 1851, in Journal: 1851, 16, 44–45, 65, 264.
63. June 22 and December 12, 1851, in Journal: 1851, 83, 305.
64. February 9, February 12, February 27, May 1, May 25, August 23, and September 12, 1851, in Journal: 1851, 13, 16, 24, 34, 53, 221.
65. January 10, June 15, July 10, August 31, September 1, September 7, September 11, December 24, and December 25, 1851, in Journal: 1851, 5, 82, 100, 184, 186, 208, 217, 318–19.
66. July 11, July 23, September 5, and September 21, 1851, in Journal: 1851, 102, 126, 201, 229.
67. August 5 and October 6, 1851, in Journal: 1851, 146, 254.
68. February 13, August 21, October 9, and December 14, 1851, in Journal: 1851, 17, 172, 260, 308.
69. December 20, December 21, and December 27, 1851, in Journal: 1851, 311, 312, 315, 321.
70. Thoreau, Walden, 319.
71. Ibid., 3, 4, 19, 21.
72. Ibid., 84, 205; see also 45, 59.
73. Ibid., 7, 92, 329.
74. Ibid., 101, 108, 140–41, 240.
75. Ibid., 86, 87, 89–90, 138.
76. Ibid., 98, 175, 176, 189, 225.
77. Ibid., 84, 112, 301, 323.
78. Ibid., 131, 138, 299, 313, 314, 318.
79. Ibid., 115, 287, 186, 176, 289, 174, 185.
80. Ibid., 191, 302, 183, 130, 298, 320.
81. Ibid., 328, 333.
82. One recent biography, Walt Whitman's America: A Cultural Biography, by David S. Reynolds (New York, 1995), has an especially useful chapter on the writing of Leaves of Grass in the context of contemporary visual arts, including discussion of Mount, Greenough, Church, and others: chap. 9, "Toward a Popular Aesthetic: The Visual Arts," 279–305.
83. Quoted in Reynolds, Whitman's America, 341.
84. Whitman, Leaves of Grass, 5–6.
85. Ibid., 7.
86. Ibid., 21, 22, 24. For discussion of the first edition and its critical reception, see Reynolds, Whitman's America, 306–82.
87. On this point, see Cox, Recovering Literature's Lost Ground, 23.
88. Whitman, Leaves of Grass, 43, 85, 88, 91.
89. Ibid., 26, 28–29, 31.
90. Ibid., 34.
91. Ibid., 44, 45, 49, 56, 78.
92. Ibid., 87, 105, 109, 116–17.
93. Ibid., 26, 44, 47, 87, 144.
94. See Matthiessen, American Renaissance, 528; see also Betsy Erkkila, Whitman: The Political Poet (New York, 1989), 82.
95. Whitman, Leaves of Grass, 36, 51, 55, 69, 75, 80, 83, 94, 105, 106, 113. For further discussion of his grammatical innovations, see Erkkila, Whitman, 5.
96. Whitman, Leaves of Grass, 37, 41, 40, 55, 57, 69.
97. Ibid., 46, 55, 58–59, 60, 130.
98. See Barbara Novak, Nature and Culture, American Landscape and Painting, 1825–1875 (New York, 1980), 18–33.
99. See Pierson, American Buildings, esp. chap. 10, "American Neoclassicism, The National Phase: The Greek Revival," 395–460.
100. For discussion of Mills's early career, see Pierson, American Buildings, 373–94.
101. For discussion of Mills's work in Washington, D.C., see Rhodri Windsor Liscombe, Altogether American: Robert Mills, Architect and Engineer (New York, 1994), 155–226.
102. For more detailed discussion of this monument, see Pamela Scott, "Robert Mills and American Monuments," in John M. Bryan, ed., Robert Mills, Architect (Washington, 1989), 146–54; and Liscombe, Altogether American, 63–73.
103. See ibid., 170–201.
104. See Bryan, Robert Mills, Architect, 164.
105. A full chronology and analysis may be found in ibid., 157–71.
106. Quoted in Liscombe, Altogether American, 277.

Part Three

1. On the development of the wireless, see Kern, The Culture of Time and Space, 9–11, 68. For the history of the New York subway, see Clifton Hood, 722 Miles: The Building of the Subways and How They Transformed New York (New York, 1994); and more specifically Michael W. Brooks, Subway City: Riding the Trains, Reading New York (New Brunswick, N.J., 1997), 7, 46–47, 53, 106.
2. Adams, The Education, 380.
3. See Shearer West, Fin de Siècle: Art and Society in an Age of Uncertainty (Woodstock, N.Y., 1993), 1–2, 11, 15–16, 50.
4. Adams, The Education, 461.
5. Quoted by Robert L. Shurter in his Introduction to Edward Bellamy, Looking Backward (New York, 1951), x, where he makes a brief, telling comparison between Howells and Bellamy.
6. See Kern, Time and Space, 58, 332; also Kenneth M. Roemer, The Obsolete Necessity: American Utopian Writings, 1888–1900 (Kent, Ohio, 1976); Lewis Mumford, The Story of Utopias (New York, 1922); and Vernon L. Parrington, Jr., American Dreams: A Study of American Utopias (Providence, 1947).
7. Bellamy, Looking Backward, 276.
8. Henry James, The American Scene (Bloomington, Ind., 1969), 469.
9. For example, ibid., 54, 57, 92, 107, 175, 312, 323, 377, 407.
10. Ibid., 342–43; see also ix, 479–82.
11. Ibid., 275, 277.
12. Ibid., 369, 371, 374, 386.
13. Ibid., 335, 339, 341, 355.
14. Ibid., 15, 17.
15. Ibid., 149–51, 261.
16. Ibid., 185, 209–10, 212–13, 216, 223.
17. Ibid., 295, 309, 332–33.
18. Ibid., 408, 419, 449, 451.
19. Ibid., 53, 55, 57, 229, 243.
20. Ibid., 1, 5, 72, 103, 158.
21. Ibid., 159, 191.
22. Ibid., 64, 74–75.
23. Ibid., 80, 114, 192, 237.
24. Ibid., 110, 112–13, 130.
25. Ibid., 76–78, 81–83, 87–88.
26. Ibid., 90–91.
27. Ibid., 139–40.
28. Ibid., 92, 95–96, 134.
29. Ibid., 99, 101, 105, 117, 134, 176.
30. See Kern, Time and Space, 242.
31. Louis Sullivan, "The Tall Building Artistically Considered," quoted in Wim de Wit, ed., Louis Sullivan: The Function of Ornament (exh. cat., Chicago Historical Society and The Saint Louis Art Museum, Chicago, 1986), 74.
32. Quoted in William H. Jordy, "The Tall Buildings," in Wit, Sullivan, 126.
33. Quoted in Wit, Sullivan, 168.
34. See J. Peter Burkholder, All Made of Tunes: Charles Ives and the Uses of Musical Borrowing (New Haven, 1995), 1–4.
35. See ibid., 20, 36, 75.
36. See ibid., 89–120.
37. Ibid., 133–36.
38. See Edward A. Berlin, King of Ragtime: Scott Joplin and His Era (New York, 1994), 3, 11, 47, 61.
39. Quoted in ibid., 106.
40. See ibid., 124, 153, 168.
41. For discussion of these points, see Louis R. Harlan, Booker T. Washington: The Making of a Black Leader, 1856–1901 (New York, 1972), and Booker T. Washington: The Wizard of Tuskegee, 1901–1915 (New York, 1983), 4–33; and James M. Cox, "Autobiography and Washington," in Recovering Literature's Lost Ground, 130–34.
42. For discussion of these points, see the insights of Cox, "Autobiography and Washington," 124, 135.
43. See Arnold Rampersad, Introduction to W.E.B. Du Bois, The Souls of Black Folk, (New York, 1983), xxiii–xxvi.
44. James, American Scene, 418.
45. Du Bois, Souls, 5, 16.
46. Ibid., 44–45.
47. Ibid., 141, 150–51.
48. See Shamoon Zamir, Dark Voices: W.E.B. Du Bois and American Thought, 1888–1903 (Chicago, 1995), 4–8, 28–30, 216.
49. See James M. Cox, Mark Twain: The Fate of Humor (Princeton, 1976), 267; and Charles Neider, ed., The Autobiography of Mark Twain (New York, 1959), x–xi.
50. Quoted in ibid., xi–xiii.
51. Ibid., 1–3.
52. Ibid., 12–16.
53. Ibid., 25, 290–91.
54. Ibid., 322–72. See also Cox, Twain, 268.
55. Ibid., 375, 379.
56. Ibid., 103, 109, 213, 282, 284–85.
57. Ibid., 286, 288–89, 348–49.
58. For discussion and illustrations in color of many of these painters, see May Brawley Hill, Grandmother's Garden: The Old-Fashioned American Garden, 1865–1915 (New York, 1995).
59. See Paula Blanchard, Sarah Orne Jewett: Her World and Her Work (Reading, Mass., 1994), 17, 57, 98, 197.
60. Sarah Orne Jewett, The Country of the Pointed Firs (New York, 1994), 1, 2, 5, 8, 19.
61. Ibid., 30.
62. Ibid., 32, 39, 63.
63. Ibid., 88.
64. Ibid., 3–4, 7, 11, 34–35, 78.
65. Ibid., 6, 9, 33, 51, 54–55.
66. Ibid., 22, 25, 31, 48, 86–87.
67. Kate Chopin, The Awakening (New York, 1994), 14.
68. Ibid., 103; see also Emily Toth, "A New

Biographical Approach," in Kate Chopin, The Awakening, 114–19.

69. Chopin, The Awakening, 31, 44, 67, 80.

70. Ibid., 108–9.

71. For discussion of the Sherman's evolution, creation, and installation, see John H. Dryfhout, The Work of Augustus Saint-Gaudens (Hanover, N.H., 1982), cat. no. 184; Kathryn Greenthal, Augustus Saint-Gaudens: Master Sculptor (exh. cat., The Metropolitan Museum of Art, New York, 1985), 156–64; Burke Wilkinson, Uncommon Clay: The Life and Works of Augustus Saint-Gaudens (New York, 1985), 299–328; Louise Hall Tharp, Saint-Gaudens and the Gilded Era (Boston, 1969), 320–34; and John Wilmerding, "Locating Augustus Saint-Gaudens," in American Views: Essays on American Art (Princeton, 1991), 264–76.

72. James, American Scene, 172.

73. In recent years extensive monographic study has gone to The Artist's Studio in an Afternoon Fog (1894; Memorial Art Gallery, University of Rochester, N.Y.), The Gulf Stream (1899; The Metropolitan Museum of Art, New York), Searchlight, Harbor Entrance, Santiago de Cuba (1901; The Metropolitan Museum of Art), Right and Left (1909; National Gallery of Art, Washington), and Driftwood (1909; Museum of Fine Arts, Boston). See Patricia Junker, "Expressions of Art and Life in The Artist's Studio in an Afternoon Fog," and John Wilmerding, "Winslow Homer's Maine," both in Winslow Homer in the 1880s: Prout's Neck Observed (exh. cat., Memorial Art Gallery, University of Rochester, N.Y., 1990), 34–65, 86–96; Nicolai Cikovsky, Jr., "Homer Around 1900," in Winslow Homer: A Symposium, Studies in the History of Art, 26 (National Gallery of Art, Washington, 1990), 133–54; John Wilmerding, "Winslow Homer's Right and Left," in Studies in the History of Art, 9 (National Gallery of Art, Washington, 1980), 59–85; and Theodore E. Stebbins, Jr., "Driftwood, Winslow Homer's final painting," The Magazine Antiques, 150, no. 1 (July 1996), 70–79.

74. William Howe Downes, The Life and Works of Winslow Homer (Boston, 1911), 223.

75. See Albert Ten Eyck Gardner, Winslow Homer, American Artist: His World and His Work (New York, 1961), 209–11.

76. Philip C. Beam, Winslow Homer at Prout's Neck (Boston, 1966), 232–33.

77. James Thomas Flexner, The World of Winslow Homer, 1836–1910 (New York, 1967), 112.

78. See Bruce Robertson, Reckoning with Winslow Homer: His Late Paintings and Their Influence (exh. cat., Cleveland Museum of Art, Cleveland, 1990), 37–38.

79. Nicolai Cikovsky, Jr., Winslow Homer (New York, 1990), 138–40.

80. Driftwood is not quite a perfect square—it measures 24½ by 28½ inches—but we perceive it as such. For the definitive discussion of this topic, see William H. Gerdts, "The Square Format and Proto-Modernism in American Painting," Arts Magazine, 50 (June 1976), 70–75.

81. See Beam, Homer at Prout's Neck, 74–75. Examples of Homer's photographs with this camera are in the collection of the Bowdoin College Museum of Art, Brunswick, Maine.

82. Examples include Two Men in a Canoe (Portland Museum of Art, Maine) and Three Men in a Canoe (private collection), both 1895. For discussion of these see Helen A. Cooper, Winslow Homer Watercolors (exh. cat., National Gallery of Art, Washington, 1986), 200–203.

83. For a full discussion of Chevreul's ideas and their application in this painting by Homer, see Junker in Winslow Homer in the 1890s, 57–59.

84. Variants are in the Museum of Fine Arts, Boston, the Cleveland Museum of Art, Portland Museum of Art, Maine, and the Brooklyn Museum of Art. For illustrations in color and discussion of these, see Nicolai Cikovsky, Jr. and Franklin Kelly, Winslow Homer (exh. cat., National Gallery of Art, Washington, 1996), 266–68.

85. The deer series includes Solitude (1889, private collection), A Good Shot (National Gallery of Art, Washington), Deer Drinking (Yale University Art Gallery, New Haven), and The Fallen Deer (Museum of Fine Arts, Boston), all 1892. The Caribbean fishermen appear in The Coral Divers (1885; private collection), The Sponge Diver (1889; Museum of Fine Arts, Boston), The Turtle Pond (The Brooklyn Museum of Art), and Rum Cay (Worcester Art Museum). The fishing series begins with Nassau and Sloop, Nassau (both 1899, both The Metropolitan Museum of Art, New York), and continues with Fishing Boats, Key West (The Metropolitan Museum of Art), Key West, Hauling Anchor (National Gallery of Art, Washington), Key West (Harvard University Art Museums), and Stowing the Sail (Art Institute of Chicago), all 1903. Most of these are illustrated in color and discussed in the Homer monographs by Cooper and by Cikovsky and Kelly.

86. See Cikovsky and Kelly, Homer, 369–71, 382–83; and Albert Boime, "Blacks in Shark-Infested Waters: Visual Encodings of Racism in Copley and Homer," Smithsonian Studies in American Art, 3 (Winter 1989), 19–47.

87. See Cikovsky, Homer, 135–36.

88. For a comprehensive discussion of Peto's biography and art, see John Wilmerding, Important Information Inside: The Art of John F. Peto and the Idea of Still-Life Painting in Nineteenth-Century America (New York, 1983).

89. For discussion of militarism in later nineteenth-

century culture, see T. J. Jackson Lears, No Place of Grace: Antimodernism and the Transformation of American Culture, 1880–1920 (New York, 1981).

90. For illustrations and detailed discussion of the works, see Wilmerding, Peto, 183–231.

91. A sampling of some major examples painted just between 1895 and 1905 include the anthropologist Frank Hamilton Cushing (c. 1895; Gilcrease Institute, Tulsa), critic Riter Fitzgerald (1895; Art Institute of Chicago), painters Charles Linford (1895; former IBM collection) and William Merritt Chase (1899; Hirshhorn Museum, Washington), collector of musical instruments Mrs. William D. Frishmuth (1900; Philadelphia Museum of Art), actress Signora Gomez d'Arza (1902; The Metropolitan Museum of Art, New York), The Oboe Player: Portrait of Dr. Benjamin Sharp (1903; Philadelphia Museum of Art), violinist Hedda van den Beemt in Music (1904; Albright-Knox Art Gallery, Buffalo), painter Henry O. Tanner (1900; Hyde Collection, Glens Falls, N. Y.), and physics professor Henry A. Rowland (1897; Addison Gallery, Andover, Mass.).

92. Besides those noted in the text, in this sequence were Monsignor James P. Turner (c. 1900), Monsignor Patrick Garvey (1902), The Translator (Monsignor Hugh Henry, 1902), and Monsignor James F. Loughlin (1902; all St. Charles Borromeo Seminary, Overbrook, Pa.), Right Reverend Denis J. Dougherty (1903; private collection), Archbishop William Henry Elder (1903; Cincinnati Art Museum), Archbishop Diomede Falconio (1905; National Gallery of Art, Washington), and Reverend Philip R. McDevitt (1901; Notre Dame University). For illustrations and discussion of this group see Sylvan Schendler, Eakins (Boston, 1967), 197–215.

93. The best-known examples are Wrestlers (1899; Columbus Museum of Art), Taking the Count (1898; Yale University Art Gallery, New Haven), Salutat (1898; Addison Gallery, Andover, Mass.), and Between Rounds (1899; Philadelphia Museum of Art).

94. For further discussion of poses and gazes, see John Wilmerding, "Thomas Eakins's Late Portraits," in American Views: Essays on American Art (Princeton, 1991), 244–63.

95. For analysis of this picture, see Schendler, Eakins, 192; Lloyd Goodrich, Thomas Eakins (Cambridge, Mass., 1982), 2: 179–82; Natalie Spassky et al., American Paintings in the Metropolitan Museum of Art (New York, 1985), 2: 622–26; H. Barbara Weinberg, "The Thinker: Portrait of Louis N. Kenton," in John Wilmerding, ed., Thomas Eakins and the Heart of American Life (exh. cat., National Portrait Gallery, London, 1993), 148–49; and H. Barbara Weinberg, "Thomas Eakins and The

Metropolitan Museum of Art," The Metropolitan Museum of Art Bulletin (Winter 1994/95), 35–37.

96. "The finest piece of historical writing in our literature" (Henry Steele Commager); "probably the greatest American history written by an American" (Ruth Lassow Barolsky); "most impressive work" (William Dusinberre); "one of the most brilliant surveys of any period of American history" (Douglas T. Miller); "a masterpiece of analytic discourse" (J. C. Levenson); "this magisterial work" (C. Vann Woodward); "the finest historical writing ever done by an American" (Paul C. Nagel); all quoted in Nobel E. Cunningham, Jr., The United States in 1800: Henry Adams Revisited (Charlottesville, Va., 1988), 2–4. Cunningham effectively reevaluates these views by pointing out Adams's missestimation of national growth and capacity for change; his relative neglect of the west; overemphasis on a backward, stagnant economy, lack of capital resources, and economic development; and missing a real sense of the young country's political maturity. See Cunningham, United States in 1800, 3–7, 19, 26, 46.

97. Henry Adams, The Education of Henry Adams (Boston, 1961), 266. See also Cunningham, United States in 1800, 9, 41, 49.

98. Henry Adams, The United States in 1800 (Ithaca, N.Y., 1971), 12; and Adams, The Education, 382.

99. Adams, 1800, 4–10.

100. Ibid., 52, 112–13.

101. Ibid., 40–41, 55, 130.

102. Ibid., 43, 52, 116.

103. Ibid., 53, 96, 130.

104. Ibid., 105, 123, 126.

105. Adams, The Education, 423, 488. Much of this section was published as "Essential Reading," in American Art, 11: 2 (Summer 1997), 28–35.

106. Adams, The Education, xxi, xxiii.

107. Ibid., 3. For further brief discussion of his writing style, see Herbert Leibowitz, Fabricating Lives: Explorations in American Biography (New York, 1989), 4; and for analysis of the autobiography see Cox, "Learning Through Ignorance: The Education of Henry Adams" in Recovering Literature's Lost Ground, 144–67.

108. Adams, The Education, 37, 53, 60, 69.

109. Ibid., 77–78, 97, 155, 180, 193, 236.

110. Ibid., 255, 266.

111. Ibid., 120, 215, 223, 300.

112. Ibid., 329, 339, 343.

113. Ibid., 347, 376, 377.

114. Ibid., 381–83, 392.

115. Ibid., 396–98, 423, 451.

116. Ibid., 457, 478, 488, 497–98, 502.

117. Ibid., 384, 442, 444, 458.

118. Ibid., 391, 404, 452, 461, 479.

119. See ibid., 409–10, 412–15, 438–39.

120. Ibid., 436, 439–40.

121. Ibid., 414, 423, 438.

122. Ibid., 43, 231, 432–34.

123. For pertinent factual information and comment, see Peter Gay, "Freud: A Brief Life," in Sigmund Freud, On Dreams (New York, 1989), x–xiv.

124. Freud, Dreams, 21, 35–36. Note also the parallel dream imagery in the paintings of the 1890s by Paul Gauguin and Odilon Redon in France and the publication of Bram Stoker's Dracula in 1897. See West, Fin de Siècle, 104.

125. See Neil Levine, The Architecture of Frank Lloyd Wright (Princeton, 1996), xv, 1–3.

126. Quoted in Levine, Wright, 37.

127. Other early examples of Prairie-style houses include the Bradley House (1900; Kankakee, Ill.); Fricke House (1901; Oak Park); Dana-Thomas House (1902; Springfield); Heurtley House (Oak Park); Coonley House (1907; Riverside); and the May House (1906; Grand Rapids, Mich.). For fuller discussion of this group, see Levine, Wright, 1–57; James F. O'Gorman, Three American Architects: Richardson, Sullivan, and Wright, 1865–1915 (Chicago, 1991), 113–54; and William H. Jordy, American Buildings and Their Architects, vol. 3, Progressive and Academic Ideals at the Turn of the Twentieth Century (New York, 1972), 180–216.

128. Levine, Wright, 37.

129. See Kern, Time and Space, 18–19, 81, 135–36, 154, 185.

130. For relevant biographical information and a help-ful summary of Einstein's principal achievements, see Banesh Hoffman, Albert Einstein: Creator and Rebel (New York, 1972), 3–82.

131. Quoted in Neil Baldwin, Edison: Inventing the Century (New York, 1995), 138.

132. See Kern, Time and Space, 21; Baldwin, Edison, 209–15, 273; and David Robinson, From Peep Show to Palace: The Birth of American Film (New York, 1966), 19–39.

133. See Robert Sklar, Movie-Made America: A Cultural History of American Movies (New York, 1994), 4–24; and Robinson, From Peep Show to Palace, ix, 39, 62–63, 89–90.

134. Information principally from ibid., 71–73. See also Brooks, Subway City, 69; Sklar, Movie-Made America, 27–34; and Kern, Time and Space, 30, 88.

135. For fuller discussion of these various cinematic subjects, see Robinson, From Peep Show to Palace, 73, 80–85.

136. Ibid., 81, 113, 134.

137. Ibid., 176.

138. Quoted in Baldwin, Edison, 301; see also 303–4.

139. See Eric Dregni and Karl Hagstrom Miller, Ads That Put America on Wheels (Osceloa, Wisc., 1996), 16–17; and Christopher Finch: Highways to Heaven: The AUTO Biography of America (New York, 1992), 25.

140. For a fuller discussion of the early history and significance of the automobile, see Finch, Highways to Heaven, 25–64.

141. Ibid., 24, 37–40.

142. Dregni and Miller, Ads, 16.

143. This historical information is from Finch, Highways to Heaven, 42–67.

144. R. W. Apple, Jr., "A City of Surprises, Not All Big," New York Times, February 20, 1988, Section E, 33; and Finch, Highways to Heaven, 72.

145. This summary of the Wright brothers' achieve-ment is fully discussed and analyzed in Tom Crouch, The Bishop's Boys: A Life of Wilbur and Orville Wright (New York, 1989), 106–243. See also Robert Wohl, A Passion for Wings: Aviation and the Western Imagination, 1908–1918 (New Haven, 1994), 1–66.

INDEX

PHOTOGRAPHIC CREDITS